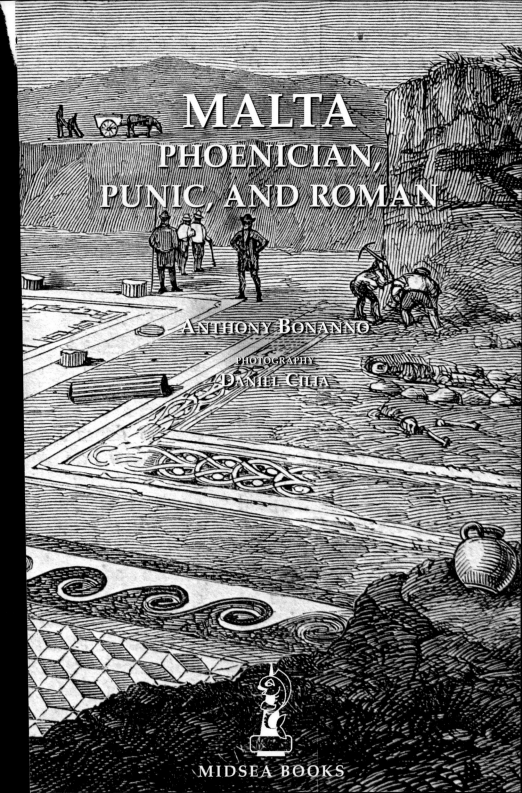

MALTA
PHOENICIAN, PUNIC, AND ROMAN

Anthony Bonanno

photography
Daniel Cilia

MIDSEA BOOKS

The Cover Image:
This is a composite image of items from the
National Museum of Archaeology inspired
by an illustration in Jean Houel's Voyage
Pittoresque des Iles de Sicile, Malte et
Lipari.
Not all items in the original illustration
are present in the picture. Furthermore,
two sides of the same sculptured base
of dubious antiquity (one showing the
Trinacria, the other a man pouring water)
are illustrated in both images.

Images on previous pages:
Page 1: A terracotta mask from Rabat
(Malta)
Pages 2-3: An etching of the 1881
excavation of the Roman domus in Rabat
(Malta), from a contemporary magazine.

Images on the Time Chart on pages 8-9
(from left to right).
Top: Baħrija bowl; Gilt Phoenician
arm band; Żurrieq Punic building;
Roman glass rhyton; Head of Emperor
Antoninus Pius; Early Christian lamp.
Bottom: She-wolf suckling twins: Rome;
Grimacing terracotta mask: Cagliari,
Sardinia; Marble sarcophagus: Palermo,
Sicily; Basalt portrait of Caesar: Rome;
Trajan's column: Rome; Byzantine
mosaic: Ravenna

CONTENTS

Marble slab, found in Rabat before 1934, representing the Greek heroes Odysseus and Diomedes ambushing the Trojan Dolon.

History vs. Prehistory

The prehistoric part of the story of the Maltese islands has been most admirably narrated by David Trump in the first volume of this series. My task is to take up the narrative where he leaves off.

History starts where prehistory ends. Had I been writing about prehistory I would have logically stated that prehistory ends when history starts, and I would have ended my account with the start of the latter. But as my remit is to deal with Malta in ancient history, I have to turn the statement on its head.

Prehistory is normally made to end (and history to start) with the appearance of writing. With this statement, I do not wish to deny Malta of a 'history' before the introduction of the alphabet. Not at all! I am only allowing myself the use of conventional terminology to better define my terms of reference in this volume. In Malta, the first written documents known so far, consist-

ing of two Phoenician inscriptions found in the vicinity of Rabat, used to be dated to the sixth century BC; now most textbooks and scholars of repute seem to prefer a seventh century BC date [see p. 42 Chapter 2]. Strictly speaking, therefore, if we had to take this maxim literally, we would have to make Malta's ancient history start only from that point in whichever century they were engraved. We have, however, ample evidence that the Phoenicians, at least a consistent group of them, had established themselves permanently on the islands as far back as 700 BC, at the latest. Furthermore, more and more claims are being made for an increasingly earlier presence of this literate people, even if it were not necessarily of a permanent nature. For my part, I would rather wait for more cogent archaeological evidence for any activity of these intrepid sailors on the islands earlier than the eighth century, given that similar evidence is absent also in other, traditionally earlier established colonies in the western Mediterranean, such as Lixus, Gadir, and Utica, and in eastern Sicily. In the light of the present state of our knowledge, therefore, it would be more justifiable, and safer, to make Malta's ancient history, and the archaeology of this period, to start with the seventh century BC.

Proto-history

Having said that, it may come as a surprise to many to learn that, like many other areas of the Mediterranean, Malta also had a proto-history, that is a period during which the islands were not quite here nor there. The islands are referred to in writings originating in other geographical areas, even though life in them is shown by the archaeological record to be still clearly of a prehistoric nature. In previous writings I have already tried to put forward a handful of objects retrieved during Temi Zammit's excavations at Tarxien (which, I have reason to believe, came from the *Tarxien Cemetery* horizon) as evidence of a closer connection between the prehistoric cultures of the Maltese Bronze Age (2500-700 BC) and the proto-literate cultures of the Aegean, namely, the Minoan and Mycenaean civilizations. Moreover, we find allusions in Classical writers, such as Lycophron, Callimachus, and Ovid, which can be interpreted as distant recollections of these contacts between the Aegean world and the contemporary inhabitants of these islands.

The Hellenistic poet Lycophron (*Alexandra*, 1027-1033), for example, makes the Trojan prophetess Cassandra relate how, at one point during their wanderings around the Mediterranean, a group of Greek warriors were to settle in Malta, as they were hampered by the gods from reaching their homelands after their long siege and eventual destruction of Troy. Callimachus (frag. 470), another Hellenistic writer, identified Gozo, the second largest island of the Maltese archipelago, with the Homeric Ogygia, the island of Calypso, on which the Greek hero Odysseus was shipwrecked and spent seven of his ten-year-long *nostos*, or home-bound return journey. The Latin poet Ovid (*Fasti*, iii. 547), on the other hand, connects the legendary reign of a king of Malta, Battus by name, with Anna, the refugee sister of Dido, queen of Carthage. The latter, according to another legend, gave hospitality to another Homeric hero, Aeneas the mythical Trojan ancestor of the Romans.

According to the literary tradition, the Phoenician princess Elissa, the Latin Dido, was forced by her brother Pygmalion (or Pumayyaton), king of Tyre, to flee her motherland to the west where she founded Carthage in the year 814/813 BC. After her death, her sister Anna found refuge in the court of Battus, king of Malta, until the latter gave in to fears of reprisals from Pygmalion and persuaded her to leave Malta and settle near Rome, where she committed suicide by throwing herself into the river Numicius, and became a nymph.

Although the Latin poet Virgil immortalized Dido by making her contemporary with Aeneas, thus making her active in the early twelfth century BC, Dido's and Anna's adventures in the western Mediterranean more probably reflect political and social tensions in Phoenicia in the late ninth century, resulting in the Phoenician colonizing expansion in this part of the Mediterranean. This time may very well correspond with the earliest contacts made by Phoenician traders with the prehistoric inhabitants of the Maltese islands, a time that can justifiably be termed 'proto-historic'.

This time-chart illustrates a succession, this time of foreign dominations resulting from the gradual colonization of Malta by the first literate people, the Phoenicians, and from the eventual integration within the Roman empire and finally within the Byzantine empire. This is a period of turbulent centuries

1000BC	800 BC	600BC	400BC	200BC

BORĠ IN-NADUR
AND BAHRIJA

ROMAN REPUBL

PRE-COLONIZATION   PHOENICIAN   PUNIC

1000 BC	600 BC	200BC

CARTHAGE FOUNDED

ROME FOUNDED

PHOENICIAN AND
  GREEK COLONIZATION

WARS BETWEEN CARTHAGE
  AND SICILIAN GREEK CITIES

PERSIAN INVASIONS OF
  GREECE

PARTHENON BUILT

ALEXANDER THE GREAT

FIRST PUNIC WAR

SECOND PUNIC

SLAVE REVOLT

CIVIL WAR

ASSASSINATIO

END OF REPUB

CONSTITUTIC

characterized by frequent wars between commercial powers contending initially for the commercial rights and later for outright political domination of increasingly greater segments of the land bordering the Mediterranean Sea. Malta found itself at the very centre of these contentions.

1 AD	200 AD	400 AD	600 AD	800 AD

...AN	ROMAN IMPERIAL	BYZANTINE

ARABS

	200 AD	600 AD

...AR

...F CAESAR

...AN

OCTAVIAN FIRST EMPEROR

FURTHER EXPANSION OF EMPIRE

SACK OF JERUSALEM

CONSTANTINOPLE FOUNDED

SPREAD OF CHRISTIANITY

'BYZANTINE' ROME

RAVENNA

ARAB CONQUEST OF NORTH AFRICA, SPAIN, & SICILY

*Gradually the Maltese islands assume
a strategic role resulting from their
central position in the Mediterranean.
To understand why, we have to look first
at the origins of the Phoenicians and the
motivations of this first historical people
to colonize it. The Phoenician colonization
of the islands is intricately connected
with that of Sicily by the Greeks and with
the Phoenician interests in the western
Mediterranean.*

CHAPTER 1

A PHOENICIAN COLONY
IN THE MAKING

An account of this chapter of Malta's ancient
history cannot but start with the celebrated passage from Diodorus Siculus' *Historical Library*
(*Bibliothekè Historikè*). This is how it goes:

> "For to the south of Sicily three islands lie
> out in the sea, and each of them possesses
> a city and harbours which can offer safety
> to ships in rough weather.
> The first one is called Melite, which
> lies about 800 stadia from Syracuse and
> possesses many harbours which offer
> exceptional advantages, and its inhabitants
> are blest in their possessions; for it has
> artisans skilled in every manner of craft,
> the most important being those who weave
> linen, which is remarkably sheer and soft.
> The dwellings on the island are worthy
> of note, being ambitiously constructed
> with cornices and finished in stucco with
> unusual workmanship.

An udjat *eye amulet. A faience (glass paste) pendant
worn for magico-religious purposes, such as to ward
off evil. Whitish paste with light turquoise glaze;
brown pupil. From Tal-Ħorob, Gozo.*

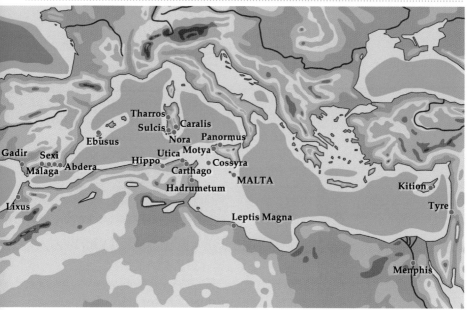

Map showing the location of Tyre, in the motherland, and some of the Phoenician colonies in the central and western Mediterranean.

This island is a colony planted by the Phoenicians, who, as they extended their trade to the western ocean, found in it a place of safe retreat, since it was well supplied with harbours and lay out in the open sea; and this is the reason why the inhabitants of this island, since they received assistance in many aspects through the sea-merchants, shot up quickly in their manner of living and increased in renown.

After this island there is a second one which bears the name of Gaulos, lying out in the open sea and adorned with well-situated harbours, a Phoenician colony."

(Diod. Sic. V, 12)

In this passage of his work, known also as the *Universal History,* the Sicilian Greek historian, Diodorus, writing in the first century BC (between *c.*60 and 30 BC), described Malta and Gozo as 'Phoenician colonies', using the present tense. As the Maltese islands had become a Roman possession more than a century-and-a-half before, Diodorus was certainly referring, in so far as the Phoenician identity of the islands is concerned, to a past age, to a historical reality that had started to come about by the beginning of the seventh century BC at the latest. Diodorus does not specify from which Phoenician city the colonizers originated, but since most of the early Phoenician colonies in the west were of Tyrian foundation, it is very likely that it was the same with Malta. Five centuries later, the dedication to Tyrian Melqart in the bilingual inscriptions on the Maltese marble candelabra seems to point in the same direction, even though we should not ignore this enormous difference in time before we rush to categorical conclusions. For this last reason, it is difficult to accept a recently proposed view that close similarities linking the iconography of the Maltese coinage of the second-first century BC with contemporary coins from Byblos might indicate a pre-colonial Phoenician presence from that city rather than from Tyre.

Diodorus further tells us that the Phoenicians set up a colony in Malta as they extended their trade to the western Mediterranean basin precisely because they found in it good harbours that offered safe shelter and because it was situated out in the open sea, that is, away from the bases of their Greek rivals and on the direct sea route that connected Phoenicia with its western colonies. We are also told that through their contact with the Phoenicians, the Maltese inhabitants strengthened their economy, particularly by textile production, raised sensibly their standard of living, as well as established a good reputation for themselves.

The Phoenicians

But who were the Phoenicians? Who were these intrepid and daring seafarers that have captured the imagination of so many writers and so many more readers?

To put it as simply as possible, as we know them today the Phoenicians were the inhabitants of a string of cities of various size and importance dotting the northern stretch of the eastern coast of the Mediterranean, the heartland of Phoenicia coinciding with today's Lebanon. The northernmost city was Arwad, the ancient Aradus, while the promontory of Mount Carmel marked the southern frontier. The Lebanon Mountains, which run parallel to the coast, formed the eastern frontier, providing protection from the east. The two cities that left

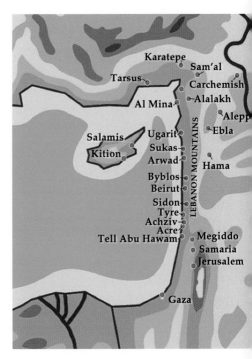

The geopolitical map of the Levant with some of the most important archaeological sites, and cities mentioned in the ancient texts. Arwad is the northernmost Phoenician city, Achziv is the southernmost one.

their strongest mark on the history of the Mediterranean were Tyre and Sidon, but Byblos was much older. The other more important cities were Aradus, Berytus, and Sarepta. Together they formed Phoenicia, the land of the Phoenicians, a people without a proper state and without political unity.

Perhaps the strangest thing about this people is that they did not call themselves by this name. *Phoinikes* is the name by which the Phoenicians were known to the Greeks and to the Hellenized

The Phoenicians are credited with having diffused the alphabet, a system of writing with one sign standing for one sound, to the rest of the Mediterranean world. The same alphabet was later adopted by the Greeks and, eventually, by the Romans.

peoples, including the Romans. The fact that they are still known by this name is part of our Greek legacy. In the Greek language one of the meanings of this word is 'red', referring either to the red colour of the skin of these seasoned seafarers, or to the purple colour of the fine draperies that the Phoenicians are known to have manufactured and traded intensively, as early as the time of Homer and Hesiod (eighth century BC). According to another view, they derived this name from their eponymous hero Phoinix, the mythical inventor of the purple dye or the father of the Phoenicians. The first time that we read about them in literature by that name is in Homer who also calls them 'Sidones' or 'Sidonioi', that is, those who hail from Sidon, one of the two most powerful Phoenician cities.

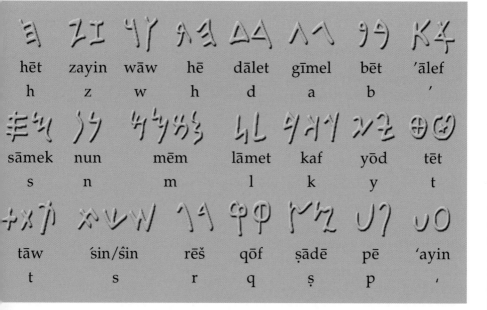

hēt	zayin	wāw	hē	dālet	gīmel	bēt	'ālef
h	z	w	h	d	a	b	'

sāmek	nun	mēm	lāmet	kaf	yōd	tēt
s	n	m	l	k	y	t

tāw	śin/ŝin	rēš	qōf	ṣādē	pē	'ayin
t	s	r	q	ṣ	p	,

A typical Nuzi tablet with Akkadian cuneiform writing datable to the second half of the 15th century. Nuzi was an ancient city situated about ten miles south-west of Kirkuk in what is now north-eastern Iraq. At the time the city was dominated by the Hurrians. The Nuzi tablets are an important source of knowledge for the cultural situation of early biblical history.

In reality, the Phoenicians called themselves 'Canaanites' (*k'an'ani*). In the biblical texts their land, Canaan, corresponded to the coastal plain north of, and in part overlapping, Israel. In the biblical and Assyrian texts the Phoenicians were often called Tyrians, Sidonians, and Giblites, from the name of their city of origin. Reference to Canaan is found as early as the fifteenth century BC. In the Akkadian texts found at Nuzi, datable to the fifteenth-fourteenth century, the word '*kinahhu*' alludes both to Canaan as a country and to its most important export, the red-coloured wool. This duality of meaning anticipates that of the Greek '*phoinix*', which thus appears to be a translation of the same word. This finds a confirmation of sorts in Hecataeus of Miletus,

the sixth century BC historian who remembered that 'Phoenicia' was the transcription into Greek of the Semitic 'Chanaan'. So the original name of the Phoenicians was Canaanites and that is how they called themselves and how their Egyptian and Asian neighbours knew them.

Even as late as in Roman times they were still called and they still called themselves by that name, at least in some areas. In the gospel of St Matthew the woman whose daughter is cured of diabolic possession by Jesus was a Canaanite. In very late Antiquity, St Augustine (AD 354-430) informs us that down to his own times some North Africans, undoubtedly descended from the western Phoenicians, called themselves '*chanani*'.

So how is it that we still prefer to call them by the Greek name? Since the modern world of learning, from the Renaissance onwards, has built up its knowledge about this Semitic people on the foundations of the Classical tradition, a decision to call them otherwise would require a consensus among scholars which, experience has taught us, is next to impossible to achieve. The present consensus seems to be to call 'Canaanites' those people who lived on the coast of Syria-Palestine described above, and who spoke a north-west Semitic dialect, from at least the beginning of the second millennium, and to call 'Phoenicians' the population of roughly the same area from the year 1200 BC onwards. The latter date coincides with a whole set of upheavals, resulting from the arrival and activity in the area of the Israelites and the 'Sea Peoples', which brought about radical changes in the geopolitical set-up of the eastern Mediterranean. It also provides a convenient, albeit arbitrary, line of separation between the Bronze Age and the Iron Age. The Phoenician world falls squarely within the last age, with which the present narrative is concerned.

There was never such a thing as a 'Phoenician nation' although there was a period in which Tyre's extended territory, incorporating that of Sidon, could perhaps be said to form a 'state' of sorts. The geography of Phoenicia, a coastal plain segmented by mountain spurs and river valleys, gave rise to independent city-states. Virtually

Aerial view of Tyre, the Phoenician city that was in the lead in the colonization of the central and western Mediterranean. Originally a small offshore island, it was later linked to the mainland by means of a causeway.

all the Phoenician cities were situated on, or close to the coast. The preferred location was on small promontories dominating a sheltered bay or a small natural inlet that provided protection for their ships from storms. Byblos, Berytus, Sidon, Sarepta, Achziv, and Akko had such a location. Tyre and Arwad occupied small islands close to the coast. Tyre was privileged in having two operating harbours, one to the north facing Sidon, and the second to the south, facing Egypt. This format remained the preferred one even for the establishment of new colonies in the west where coastal promontories and small islands were preferred, Cadiz being the closest parallel to Tyre.

For their food provisions, the Phoenician cities depended for the most part on the fertile agricultural land between the coast and the Lebanon Mountains. The land was irrigated by water courses originating from the same mountains, which also provided a wealth of cedars, cypresses, and pines. These provided the raw materials for the ships of the Phoenicians, as did the rich lignite and iron mines. The sea provided them with fish, part of which was salted, and the mollusc murex for dyeing draperies.

Aerial view of Manoel island. Like Tyre and several other Phoenician colonies in the west, Manoel island occupies an ideal location inside an already sheltered harbour. It is surprising, therefore, that no Phoenician remains have ever been recorded on it.

QUINTINUS AND MALTA

The Frenchman Jean Quintin (1500-1561) resided in Malta between the years 1530 and 1536 when he served the Order of the knights of St John as chaplain of the French knights and auditor of the grand master. He

is better known by the Latinized version of his name, Quintinus, owing to the fact that his description of Malta, the first reasonably long and comprehensive one, was written in Latin. Quintinus was a consummate Latin scholar and was very familiar with the Classical writers. In his Insulae Melitae Descriptio, *published in Lyons in 1536, he dealt with most of the ancient references to Malta. In so doing he gave origin to a number of unfounded or misleading traditions some of which still survive in ancient*

Maltese historiography. He identified two groups of apparently prehistoric remains with the temples of Juno and Hercules mentioned by the ancient writers Cicero and Ptolemy; he located the first on the Birgu peninsula and the second in the area of Marsaxlokk. He also accepted as genuine three of several apocryphal letters relating to an alleged friendship between the Maltese and Phalaris, the tyrant of Agrigento (570-555 BC); he accepted as historically valid the existence of a king of Malta called Battus.

THE PHOENICIAN COLONIES OF THE CENTRAL MEDITERRANEAN

Phoenician Colonization

The Phoenician colonization movement was as much the product of the geomorphology of the land of the Phoenicians as it was of the political and social pressures and the restless, adventurous nature of the people. Squeezed as they were between the Lebanon Mountains and the Mediterranean, with the larger powers pressing from the south and from the north, their only possible route for expansion, if not for survival, was the sea. These were essentially the motivations behind the original long-distance commercial ventures which in time developed into a colonial process with the establishment of settlements in the western basin of the Mediterranean, as far west as the Iberian peninsula and the North African

coast to the south of it. I shall refrain from discussing these motivations as this falls outside the scope of this work.

It was Tyre that took the lead in the commercial policies of all the Phoenician cities to expand westwards in the face of political pressures from neighbouring powers and internal social and economic factors. Tyre emerged as the most important of the Phoenician cities only from the reign of King Hiram I (969-936 BC), from which time onwards the history of Phoenicia becomes one with that of Tyre.

The date of the first colonization of Malta is tied with that of the chronology of the first Phoenician foundations in the west. For the latter, the problem arises from the wide divergence between the dates attributed by the classical authors

BATTUS AND MALTA

Perhaps one of the least exploited traditions originated by Jean Quintin connected with Malta's ancient history is that based on the legendary story recounted by the Latin poet Ovid (Fasti 3. 567-578). It concerns a certain Battus, king of Malta, who was reputed to have been linked by ties of friendship with Dido, the legendary founder and queen of Carthage, and later offered hospitality to her sister Anna. The real Battus was the leader of the Greeks from Thera who founded the colony of Cyrene in North Africa in 631 BC. His real name was Aristoteles and he started to be called 'Battus' after becoming king of this newly-founded colony. According to Herodotus (IV, 145-148) 'Battus' was the local, North African word for 'king'. Indeed, several successors of Aristoteles as kings of Cyrene were in turn called 'Battus'. Elsewhere in ancient legendary accounts, Battus of Cyrene was the one who gave shelter to Anna in her flight from Carthage after her sister's death (Sil. Ital. 8. 50-68, 157-159). How a seventh-century king came to be connected with a twelfth-century mythical figure is hard to explain. Much more so is the transfer of this connection to the island of Malta, unless we should follow up on Herodotus' interpretation of the name Battus and postulate the reign of an African (i.e. Carthaginian) king of Malta sometime before its conquest by the Romans.

to the founding of the western colonies of Lixus, Gadir (Cadiz), and Utica (around 1100 BC) on the one hand, and the earliest archaeological record in these and other centres in the west (not earlier than the eighth century BC) on the other. One possibility that has been postulated to explain this divergence is that of a pre-colonial 'silent' trading activity of the Phoenicians in the west, an activity that might not have left any archaeological traces. Here we have to be very careful lest the argument that 'the absence of evidence does not mean evidence of absence' be extended so far as to actually mean 'evidence of presence'. The debate on the earliest date of a Phoenician presence on Malta has not been spared this line of argument, even though for Malta we do not have the literary tradition to support it.

Of course, one has to distinguish between total absence of evidence, on one hand, and textual tradition unsupported by archaeology, on the other. In the second situation, for the period prior to the second half of the eighth century BC, the most we can do is to consider the Maltese case in the same light as eastern Sicily before the arrival of the Greek colonizers. While Thucydides states that the Phoenicians were firmly established here before they were replaced by the Greeks, no evidence for Phoenician presence has been encountered anywhere in this part of Sicily in archaeological deposits earlier than that date. Although the possibility of such an encounter cannot be ruled out a priori, until it is substantiated we cannot go about pleading for their presence in Malta, as in eastern Sicily, without other supporting evidence.

The Phoenicians enter the Maltese Stage

A look at the location and pattern of distribution of the main Phoenician settlements in the Mediterranean gives us an idea of the significance of the Maltese archipelago for the Phoenicians in their expansion movement to the western Mediterranean. It is here that Diodorus comes to our aid and explains exactly this significance. These are his exact words: 'For to the south of Sicily three islands lie out in the sea, and each of them possesses a city and harbours which can offer

Map of the western Mediterranean basin showing the mainly anti-clockwise sea currents. These are thought to have remained unchanged since Phoenician times and they must have influenced the prevalent sea-routes in those times.

safety to ships in rough weather.' It is precisely because Malta and Gozo, along with Pantelleria, were at a safe distance from Sicily, which by the second half of the eighth century BC had passed under the effective control of another emerging sea power, that of the western Greeks. While they were 'out in the open sea', which did not constitute a problem at all to the consummate Semitic navigators, they had good harbours which provided their ships with a safe port of call on their more direct sea-route between their homeland, Phoenicia, and their colonies in the west. Malta was ideally located half-way on a south, coast-hugging route from Phoenicia that veered north-west at the eastern tip of the Syrtic Gulf on an open-sea, more challenging but time-saving, route directly towards Motya and Carthage. The same can be said for

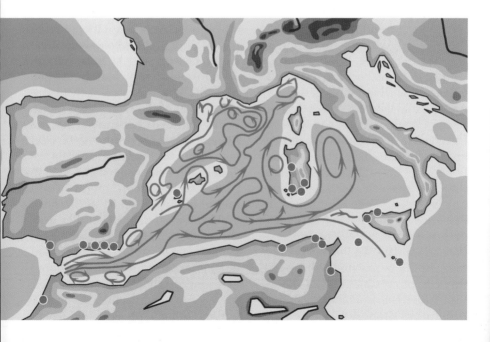

Terracotta architectural plaque representing a Gorgon.
From the temple of Athena, Syracuse (570-550 BC).
Syracuse, Museo Archeologico Regionale.

an even more direct, totally open-sea, navigation departing from Phoenicia with staging posts in Cyprus and southern Crete.

As if to drive this point home, Diodorus gives the same reasons in his fuller treatment of Malta: 'This island is a colony planted by the Phoenicians, who, as they extended their trade to the western ocean, found in it a place of safe retreat, since it was well supplied with harbours and lay out in the open sea.'

There is general agreement that in antiquity open sea faring was limited to the safe months, practically from April to September. Ancient sea routes were strongly influenced, or even determined by the prevailing winds and currents. Although winds did change direction, with cer-

tain ones prevailing under certain weather conditions in certain parts of the Mediterranean, the present sea currents of the Mediterranean do not seem to have changed for the last 3,000 years. The latter are characterized by their anti-clockwise movement along the coasts of this internal sea. This suggests that, following such currents, the sea-route between Phoenicia and its western colonies, such as Motya, Carthage, and beyond, would have followed the north coast, albeit at some distance. From Tyre, ships probably skirted, or called at Cyprus and at Crete, and from there crossed to south-east Sicily and skirted its south coast to reach Motya and beyond. On the way back the favourable west-east current encouraged a south sea route, along

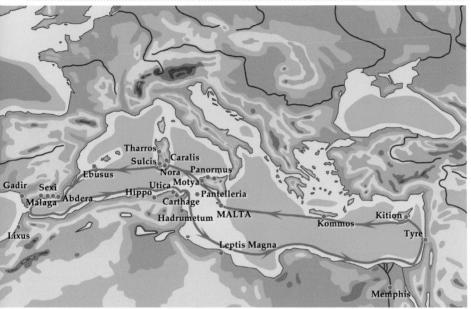

Two possible Phoenician sea routes across the Mediterranean: a north one from Phoenicia to Cyprus, southern Crete, Malta, Carthage, or Motya; a south route hugging the African coast.

the North African coast, avoiding the dangers of the Great Syrtis and the absence of visible landmarks there by cutting across it.

This would have meant that Malta was more likely to receive trading goods hailing from the east than from the west. The archaeological record seems to confirm this, at least for the Phoenician period, that is, for the first two or three centuries of their presence here. It shows that Malta had much more intensive links with the east, including Cyprus, than with Carthage and the west. According to some writers, however, the latter route makes it relatively easy for ships to take a second option, that is, to sail from Cap Bon to Pantelleria and Malta, and from there to cut straight to the eastern end of the Syrtic Gulf, instead of following the Libyan coast.

It is sometime in the eighth century BC, at a point that, as yet, has not been determined with any precision, that the Phoenicians moved into the Maltese landscape. As their main settlement they seem to have selected from the very start an inland site already occupied by the local Bronze Age population, the Mdina promontory. But to venerate their foremost female goddess, Ashtart, the divine protectress of mariners, they chose a small, but prominent hill overlooking Marsaxlokk harbour, their most frequented haven. On top of the Tas-Silġ hill they found the striking remains of an abandoned megalithic temple which they converted into one suited for their own needs. This must have taken place already by the end of the eighth century BC.

Away from the Tas-Silġ sanctuary, the earliest securely datable evidence of their presence on the Maltese islands goes back to the beginning of the seventh century BC and consists of a rock-cut tomb found at Għajn Qajjet about one kilometre west of Rabat. It contained a range of shapes of typically early Phoenician pottery, known as Red-slipped Ware, and two items of datable luxury Greek pottery, namely a Proto-Corinthian kotyle datable to the first half of the seventh century BC and an Eastern Greek 'bird-bowl' datable to the mid-seventh century. Another tomb found at Is-Sandar on the side of Mtarfa hill, about 700m north-west of Mdina-Rabat, contained another piece of Archaic Greek pottery, a Proto-Corinthian skyphos datable to the early seventh century BC. In a recently -published monumental

work on Punic Malta, Claudia Sagona has claimed that there are quite a few earlier tombs than the Għajn Qajjet and Is-Sandar ones. A few examples are: two at Buskett Gardens, one at Għar Barka, another at Għajn Klieb, one in Marsa, one at Mtarfa, and as many as four at Qallilija, besides others in other localities. She dates these to the eighth century, if not earlier (her 'Archaic Phase 1'). In the absence of closely datable Greek pottery and of other datable imported artefacts, she bases her dates on the non-Greek pottery and comparative material outside Malta.

All these tombs are located within very short distances from the Mdina promontory and their location is indicative of the emerging settlement there. Only recently, claims have also been made of discoveries of 'Phoenician ceramics' during rescue operations in Mdina, but these have only been accorded

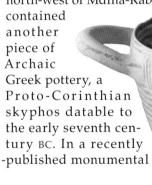

Very fine Proto-Corinthian skyphos (stemless drinking cup) with red painted decoration on pale yellow background. H. 8.75 cm. From Is-Sandar, on the north side of Mtarfa Hill. Date: c.700-650 BC

a preliminary publication. Illustrated examples have been dated to the seventh century BC but the three metres of 'Phoenician strata' from which they were retrieved have been proposed as evidence for a large Phoenician settlement inside Mdina as early as the eighth century.

If there was a precolonization presence of Phoenician traders in Malta before the seventh century, as has been postulated for other western Phoenician colonies, is a matter of educated guessing. It could well be that when Thucydides (VI,2,6) referred to Phoenician settlements in Sicily 'and the adjacent islands' prior to the arrival of the Greeks there in 734 BC, this is precisely what he really meant, that is, a pre-colonization presence. But we can only be sure when securely datable evidence is unearthed by archaeology. For Malta the strongest archaeological argument made in favour of such an early presence is that based on the material found in a typical Bronze Age 'silo-pit' at Mtarfa in which an early Phoenician oil lamp was found mixed with Late Bronze Age pottery fragments. To my mind, however, the archaeological context of the Mtarfa and the Mdina findings are not sufficiently clear to allow us to push the Phoenician settlement to the eighth century BC, let alone the ninth.

The same passage by Thucydides raises another important question: if Malta was one of the 'adjacent islands' of Sicily, how is it that it was not taken over by the Greeks, as the whole of eastern Sicily was by the mid-seventh century BC? This particular passage of Thucydides has already been discredited with respect to his assertion of a Phoenician occupation in eastern Sicily before the arrival of the Greeks. The inclusion of Malta among Sicily's islands that were colonized by the Greeks from the second half of the eighth century onwards is even more questionable. In the first place, it is subject to a correct interpretation of the historian's geography. Did Thucydides really mean to include the Maltese archipelago among these islands? Whether he did or not, the archaeological record does not bear out such a Greek occupation of the Maltese islands, in the same way that archaeology fails to confirm his claim of a Phoenician presence before the Greeks' arrival in eastern Sicily. This, in spite of what many early Maltese historiographers, in particular Dr Annetto Caruana, asserted.

What could be the reasons that kept the Greeks from gaining a foothold on Malta?

Whether they even tried to do so we are not in a position to tell. None of the sources, besides Thucydides, in any way suggest that they did. One possibility is that Malta did not offer sufficient fertile plains for the extensive cultivation of cereals as the typical settlements of Sicily and south Italy did. The most logical reason, however, seems to be quite simply that they were precluded from doing so by the Phoenicians

THE GREEKS NEVER COLONIZED MALTA

The 'bird-bowl'

Up to the end of the nineteenth century there was a deep-rooted tradition in the historiography of ancient Malta which believed that, after an early Phoenician occupation of the islands, which was responsible for the building of the prehistoric megalithic temples, Malta was colonized by the Greeks. This tradition, probably started by the German scholar Philip Cluver in 1619, was mainly based on a (probably mistaken) interpretation of a passage by the otherwise very authorative Greek historian Thucydides. This passage affirms that Sicily and its islands had been occupied by the Phoenicians until they were colonized by the Greeks who relegated the Phoenicians to the western corner of Sicily. Malta was thus considered to have been one of the Sicilian islands to be colonized by the Greeks. Foremost among the historians who were convinced of this were Onorato Bres (1816) and Annetto Caruana (1899). They also believed that this Greek interlude was followed by a Carthaginian domination. The presumed material evidence for a Greek colonization was a number of archaeological objects of obvious Greek identity, including inscriptions and coins. Bres, for example, was convinced that coins inscribed with the legends MELITAION and GAULITON belonged to the Greek colonies existing on these islands between the eighth and sixth centuries BC. These were later found to have been coined after 218 BC, during the Roman rule. Even the Greek inscription on a bronze tablet and the marble candelabra with bilingual inscriptions are now dated to the third century BC or later.

The presence of authentic Greek products in Malta, even the more ancient ones, can be explained in two ways. Some of them were direct imports from Greek sources, like the Proto-Corinthian kotyle and the Eastern Greek 'bird bowl' from the Għajn Qajjet tomb. The western Phoenicians, and later their Punic successors, did trade quite intensively in objects of Greek craftsmanship. From the fourth century onwards, then, Malta was exposed to, and receptive of, Hellenistic influence from the surrounding Greeks in general, and from Sicily in particular. This Greek influence, particularly the infiltration of the Greek language, increased in intensity after Malta's incorporation with the Roman province of Sicily. At this time we even find Maltese characters with Greek personal names, such as Diodorus (Melitensis) and Aristoteles (Melitensis), both close friends of the Roman orator and politician Cicero (70-43 BC).

In conclusion, there is no longer any place for the perpetuation of this myth in Maltese historiography, from whatever quarter. Even if the presence of a group of Greek individuals, of any size, whether of Sicilian origin or from elsewhere, is not to be excluded, either in the early Phoenician stage, or in the later Punic one, this should not be construed to represent a fully-fledged 'colony'.

who had already somehow affirmed their presence there. Whatever the reasons, with the colonization of the greater part of Sicily by the Greeks in the second half of the eighth century and the first half of the seventh century BC, Malta assumed for the first time a strategic importance in the contest between these two commercial, as well as military, power blocks for the control of the sea trade routes and of the trade itself with the native inhabitants of the lands bordering the Mediterranean.

Imperceptible Penetration
We are not in a position to say exactly how the Phoenician traders made their first contacts with the Maltese

Sicily with some of its major Greek colonies.

Two alabastra (perfume bottles) of glass paste originally formed around sand cores. The feather-like decoration in brown, yellow, and green was added on at a second stage. H. of left one: 10.8 cm.

islands and their prehistoric inhabitants. We have the attractive story by the Greek fifth-century historian Herodotus (4: 196) describing the process of barter by trial-and-error adopted by them whenever they wanted to start a trading relationship with primitive - the adjective 'savage' seems to be implied - populations on the Atlantic coasts of Africa. They beached their boat, laid down their attractive wares on the shore, and withdrew on their boat waiting for the natives to inspect the wares and to place their own exchangeable objects, namely gold, nearby. It was then the turn of the natives to withdraw and watch from a safe distance. The visiting traders would then row back to the shore, check

The Mycenaean fragment found during excavations inside the Bronze Age fortified village at Borġ in-Nadur. It was part of a typical Mycenaean cup datable to the Late Helladic IIIb (c.1350 BC)

whether the barter was to their liking. If it was liked, they would collect the locals' offer and sail away to return shortly with more goods. If not, they would show their dissatisfaction by leaving everything on shore and return to their boat for another attempt. Herodotus' account smacks of old wives' tales but, as usual in such tales, it probably contains a kernel of truth and reflects the pioneering trading techniques of the Phoenicians and their tactics to start a more lasting relationship with native inhabitants of new lands.

It is well known that in these parts of the world, that is in the western Mediterranean and beyond the Pillars of Hercules, the Phoenicians were mostly interested in obtaining raw materials, especially metals,

Typically western Phoenician pottery, mostly red-slipped, found in association with two Greek painted pots which help to date it to the seventh century BC. Note the two two-wicked lamps on the centre-left.

preferably precious ones. In exchange they bartered crafted goods which they themselves produced or which they obtained from more advanced and sophisticated peoples of the Near East and, even more so, from the Egyptians. Thus they acted as middlemen and played an important and pioneering role in this supply-and-demand economic system. 'Pioneering' yes, but to a certain extent because, we should not forget, they had been preceded in this quest for raw materials by another eastern Mediterranean people of trading mariners, the Mycenaeans. Perhaps not as far as the British Isles, as prehistoric archaeology of the first half of the twentieth century used to attribute to them, before the arrival of scientific dating techniques; but Mycenaean pottery has been turning up not only on the western coast of

The main gate, called the 'Lions Gate', and part of the formidable fortifications of Mycenae, the major Greek city of the Late Bronze Age.

Italy, where a fully-fledged settlement has been explored on the tiny island of Vivara, in the Bay of Naples, but also further west in Sardinia and eastern Spain.

Now, homing back to the Maltese islands, the question arises immediately: 'in the scenario described above what could the Maltese "natives" offer in exchange for the Phoenicians' goods?' I can hardly think of any commodity that was exclusively manufactured in Malta and that would particularly excite the visiting traders' interest. We know all too well that the islands have no minerals except for excellent building stone, and this could hardly be described as an exchangeable material. The Maltese islands were inhabited at this time – for convenience's sake, let us say all this was happening around the ninth and eighth centuries BC – by a scatter of small communities characterized by a Bronze Age culture, most aptly described in the first volume of this series. Pottery of the *Borġ in-Nadur* style, of the Middle Bronze Age, is also found in large quantities in settlements on the eastern coast of Sicily. We do not know as yet whether this is the result of exchange or wholesale movement of people. In any case, the even more refined *Baħrija* style has so far not been encountered outside the islands. Apart from this, there seems to be nothing that is likely to have attracted the attention of the Semitic traders.

This is precisely where Diodorus' remarks come back to mind. It might not be too daring to suggest that the Phoenician mariners started to see at this very early stage the strategic potential of the islands as a convenient station and shelter in their long voyages from their homeland to the great west. In which case, very much on the lines narrated by Diodorus, the natives would have been all too ready to offer even

the minimal degree of hospitality to these sailors. If anything, these exchanges were bound to add a little bit of colour to their otherwise unexciting insular existence. It was thus that the first nucleus of Phoenician settlers would have started to sink their roots on Maltese soil and to lead their peaceful coexistence with the local population.

Such a scenario of peaceful coexistence between the Bronze Age natives and the new Phoenician settlers has long been invoked as a characterizing feature of this early Phoenician period in Malta, mostly in literature concerning the archaeological exploration of the Tas-Silġ sanctuary (see pages 284-9). Here the excavators found several layers containing pottery of both cultures mixed together and this has been

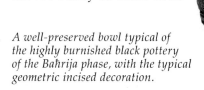

A well-preserved bowl typical of the highly burnished black pottery of the Baħrija phase, with the typical geometric incised decoration.

interpreted as clear evidence of such co-existence. An accurate analysis of the various archaeological contexts of this nature has revealed that none of them had the right type of close association between Late Bronze Age pottery and early Phoenician pottery; therefore, these contexts could not be considered as reliable evidence for this purpose. In most of the examined contexts the prehistoric pottery sherds (not only Bronze Age, it should be noted, but Temple Period as well) were residual, removed from their original context through some rebuilding activity and mixed with later material. Our recent excavation

Some of the surviving rock-cut silo-pits (originally more than 25) at St George's Bay, Birżebbuġa. Some of the pits are now submerged by the sea.

Typical stratification in a Maltese archaeological context taken from the University of Malta excavations at Tas-Silġ (1996-2004). Layers are most frequently stony leaving very little distinction between one and another.

experience on the same site seems to confirm these recently-raised doubts; so that we have to look somewhere else for proof of such coexistence.

The ideal place to look for such evidence is a pure Late Bronze Age context with an obvious Phoenician import; no such thing has as yet been encountered. The early Phoenician oil lamp found in a typical Bronze Age silo-pit at Mtarfa in 1939 is the closest we have been able to get, but not close enough, given the rather insecure context and associated material. John Ward Perkins in his reports admits that the silo-pit must have been disturbed in antiquity. It was, as stated by both David Trump and John Evans, originally a typical *Borġ*

Two of the many silo-pits rediscovered during a clearance operation for the Mtarfa building scheme in 1991 . Most of the silo-pits have now been destroyed or built over. One of them may be the silo-pit excavated in 1939.

in-Nadur silo-pit. Some whole Late Bronze Age pots must have found their way inside them in that period but, at some stage in the Phoenician period, the original deposits were disturbed and the pottery broken when a typically early Phoenician, double-spouted lamp got mixed up with the earlier material. The absence of human bones excludes the use of the pit as a tomb. I wonder whether the presence of just this item of the Phoenician period could be interpreted in a very different way, that is, as an early example of treasure hunting.

A second bottle-shaped silo-pit found in the same place in 1939 contained only Phoenician-Punic material. The Egyptian amulet figures found in it suggested 'an early date, in the seventh or sixth century BC'. Human bones of at least

THE COMBINATION RING

A very intriguing piece of jewellery of the Phoenician-Punic period is a ring of pure gold formed of two individual pieces that could be worn separately but, when worn in combination the serrated edges of its bezel fit perfectly together. The resulting almond-shaped bezel shows an image of a sleek boat with six oars on the viewer's side, the longest oar on the front side, the others getting progressively shorter towards the back. A square-shaped feature behind the mast on the prow could represent either a cabin or a square sail.

According to Themistocles Zammit, who published a short account of it in The Antiquaries Journal *of 1925, the ring could have served as a guarantee for the overseas exchange of confidential despatches. One half of the ring could be sent with a trusted bearer as proof of the genuineness of a message or request.*

It is most unfortunate that the donor of the ring refused to give to Temi Zammit more detailed information on the provenance of the ring. All we know is that it had been found in a rock-tomb in Malta. Today no one seems to know its whereabouts.

twenty individuals were found and the re-use of the pit in later times was clearly for burial.

The second place to look for would be an early Phoenician context with securely identifiable Bronze Age material. Even here we fail to get what we want. However, we do find a few early Phoenician tombs that contain pots which, although they cannot be labelled as genuinely Bronze Age, seem to be derived from such a pedigree. In which case, however, rather than trying to push the date of the former upwards to

Two small Egyptian amulets in glass paste found in one of the silo-pits explored in 1939 to the west of the Married Officers' Quarters, Military Hospital at Mtarfa. 7th-6th century BC. The Bronze Age pit was re-used as a tomb in early Phoenician times.

fit a Late Bronze Age date, we have to bring down the survival of such prehistoric forms to the age of the more securely and reliably dated material.

The best example of this situation is the Għajn Qajjet tomb, already mentioned as the earliest properly sealed archaeological context of the Phoenician period. The Proto-Corinthian kotyle is securely datable to the first half of the seventh century BC and an Eastern Greek 'bird-bowl' is equally securely datable to the mid-seventh century. The two items together date the earliest use of the tomb to the mid-seventh century BC. In the same way they date the associated, typically early Phoenician pottery, known as Red-slipped Ware, to roughly the same age, even though, in theory, it could be of earlier date.

A Proto-Corinthian kotyle (drinking cup) found among the grave goods of the tomb discovered and explored under the Għajn Qajjet (alias Qajjied) Road in 1950. Dated to the first half of the 7th century BC.

What is conspicuously absent among the objects that made up the furniture of the Għajn Qajjet tomb, as well as all the other tombs datable from the early seventh century onwards, including one from Mtarfa, is the native element which before the arrival of the Phoenicians, and possibly for a couple of centuries afterwards, constituted the prehistoric population of the *Borġ in-Nadur* and *Baħrija* cultures. Is it because the tombs that have left an archaeological record belonged exclusively to members of the newly-established Phoenician community who found little or nothing in the material culture of the indigenous population worth including in their funerary furniture? Or was the native population so overwhelmed by the

new culture as to abandon almost completely, and within a very short period of time, their own artisanal production?

One interpretation of this situation sees a cultural decline of the Bronze Age inhabitants with a possible depopulation of the island prior to the arrival of the Phoenicians. But rather than in a scenario of total abandonment of the islands, the answer is probably to be sought in van Dommelen's model of a hybridization of cultures, applied successfully to a study of colonization in Punic Sardinia. In which case we have to keep our eyes open to all the elements in the archaeological record of at least the first two centuries of the Phoenician presence in Malta that might reveal the input of the local

An incense burner in Red-slipped Ware. The lower pan was probably intended to hold the burning charcoal which heated the upper pan in which the incense was placed. Reputedly from a tomb in the vicinity of Rabat, possibly Għajn Klieb.

inhabitants in this hybridization process. *Prima facie,* evidence of such a hybridization of some sort between the prehistoric native population and the literate newcomers was already encountered in a burial cairn in Rabat, Gozo. In this connection we should not forget that we have next to nothing in terms of material remains connected with burial ritual of the Late Bronze Age people of Malta. Antonia Ciasca has even suggested that the early Red-slip Ware characterizing the archaic phase of the Phoenician occupation was locally produced and that it developed from an indigenous tradition. Studies already completed and others currently undertaken by Claudia Sagona are pointing in the same direction.

The evidence for a joint, concurrent use of the sanctuary at Tas-Silġ, where *Borġ in-Nadur* and *Baħrija* pottery was identified in stratigraphic association with the earliest layers of Phoenician occupation has, on the other hand, already been dealt with above, with apparent negative results (above p.13). The picture remains thus very hazy, but we entertain high hopes that the heavy mist will lighten up with many and diverse research projects under way both in Malta and outside as a result of a growing interest in the study of this period. Possible answers to this quandary may well be forthcoming from unexpected quarters, such as palaeo-environmental studies of the materials being excavated by the Department of Classics and Archaeology of the University of Malta on the same site of Tas-Silġ, where pure Bronze Age levels have been encountered, followed by later mixed ones.

The Names of the Islands

In antiquity it was as necessary as it is today to identify geographical bodies by their names. This was particularly desirable with respect to geographical entities, like prominent, albeit small but strategically located islands, which provided useful navigational facilities. There is no doubt that even in prehistory the Maltese islands had their own names by which both the native inhabitants and visiting mariners knew them. Unfortunately, the prehistoric names of the islands have never been registered in any text that has reached us. The controversial identification of proto-historic Malta, (more precisely, Gozo) with the Homeric Ogygia, the island of Calypso, has already been

discussed; in any case, if it were really the right one, that name would have been the one by which the proto-Greeks, not necessarily the rest of the world, knew the island. Later on, the Greeks knew the two major islands by totally different names.

It is very likely that the earliest historical settlers on the island, the Phoenicians, had a name for at least the major of the two islands, if not for both. This could very well be the name that appears on Maltese coins struck after the beginning of Roman domination in 218 BC, i.e. *'nn*; but a distance of at least five centuries between these coin legends and the earliest colonizers is too great to afford us any degree of certainty. It cannot be excluded, on the other hand,

Detail of a Punic inscription on marble found in Gozo. The word for Gozo is the three-letter word with the consonants GWL presumably standing for GAWL. The Greeks knew Gozo by their own version of the name, Gaulos.

that they used the same name, or names, used by their rivals, the Greeks: *Melite* for Malta and *Gaulos*, or *Gaudos* for Gozo.

The earliest written mention of the name *Melite* occurs in Xenophanes of Colophon, in Ionia, the pre-Socratic philosopher who wrote in the sixth century BC. I am, in this context, ignoring the apocryphal letters supposedly addressed to the Maltese by Phalaris, the legendary tyrant of Akragas in Sicily. *Melite* deserved a special mention in Xenophanes' work for the existence of special marine fossils (*plákas sympántōn tōn thalassiōn*) in its geological formation. After that, the next mention is found in the fourth century BC writer Pseudo-Skylax, with a faithful description of Malta's position in relation to Cap Bon in Tunisia. Subsequently, the Greek sources continued to refer to it in exactly the same way until late antiquity. It is beyond the scope of this work to discuss the meaning or the etymology of the name. Suffice it to say that it was later transliterated faithfully into Latin script, with the last letter eventually changing to 'a' (Melita) and, later still, taking its modern form (Malta) through syncopation.

The ancient name for Gozo presents a slightly more complicated story. Its earliest occurrence is in one of a few surviving fragments of a periegetic work by Hecataeus, a Greek *logographos* who lived between the late sixth and early fifth century BC (560-480). Hecataeus refers to the island as *Gaulos* and connects the island with Carthage. So did Pseudo-Skylax in the fourth century BC. After that, the name appears in either the *Gaulos* or in the *Gaudos* form, and it was thus transliterated in the Latin script. Again, I will refrain from discussing the meaning and the etymology of the two names. Of note is the absence of a different Phoenician name for Gozo. Given the late date (third or second century BC) of the Gozo inscription where it occurs, the Punic form *Gwl* for Gaulos appears as an exception that confirms the rule. It is probably no more than a Punic version of the Greek name, even though the word '*gaulos*' itself is the Greek version of the Punic word for a 'round ship'. On the other hand, in Byzantine times *Gaudos* became the first element in a composite name for the two islands, *Gaudomelete*.

Thus, we have valid reasons to believe that the present names of the two islands are derived, through a very simple phonetic process of change, from their Greek forms.

Top: Reverse of a coin minted for Gozo in the 1st century BC, showing an armed soldier holding a shield and hurling a spear, bearing the Greek legend ΓΑΥΛΙΤΩΝ.
Middle: Reverse of a Maltese coin of the 2nd century bc, showing three Egyptian divinities (Isis, Osiris, and Nephthys) and the Punic legend 'nn.
Bottom: Obverse of a Maltese coin of the 2nd century BC showing a female head (probably Ashtart/Isis) and the Greek legend ΜΕΛΙΤΑΙΩΝ.

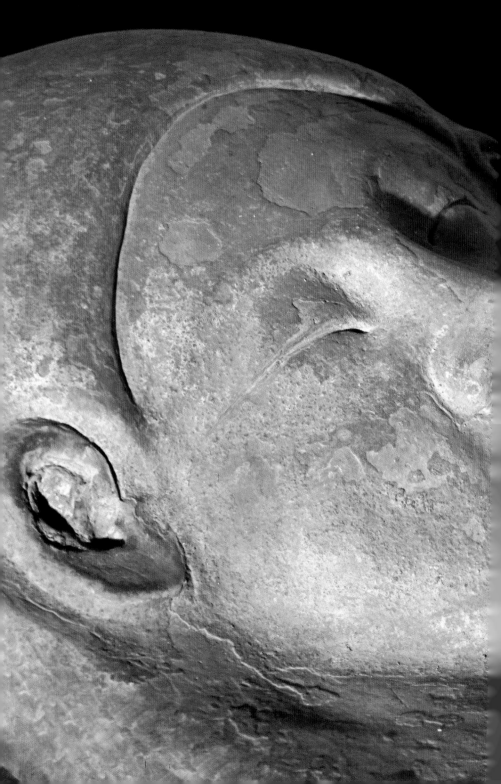

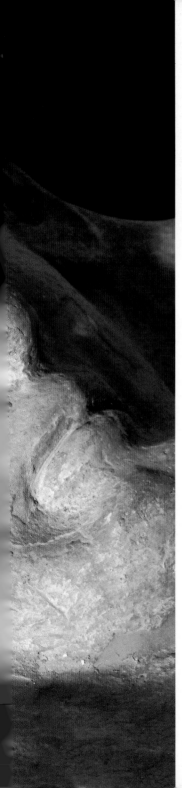

The Phoenician presence on the island becomes increasingly more evident. A concentration of tombs around Mdina, and some recent archaeological finds inside Mdina itself, suggest that the latter was chosen as their main settlement already at this stage. The sanctuary of Ashtart at Tas-Silġ, meanwhile, started to emerge as an important extra-mural religious shrine with an international maritime vocation.

CHAPTER 2

THE EARLY PHOENICIAN PERIOD
(700-500 BC)

Whatever method was used by the early Phoenician traders to ingratiate themselves with the native population and secure a foothold on the islands, their initial makeshift residences must have gradually developed into modest settlements of trading agents, possibly accompanied by their families. In time, this limited settlement grew into a fully-fledged colony, so that by the end of the sixth century BC they very probably came to occupy great part of the Maltese landscape, at least the cultural one, and apparently eclipsing that of their prehistoric predecessors. This hypothetical development is corroborated mostly by the distribution of underground rock-cut tombs over the two islands. Of significance is the fact that the earliest tombs occur in the vicinity of the Mdina-Rabat promontory (Għajn Qajjet, Mtarfa, Għajn Klieb, Qallilija, Buskett, and others) and of Rabat, Gozo (albeit only one, in Racecourse

Detail of the face of the terracotta sarcophagus discovered inside a rock-cut tomb at Ħal Barka, one of the Phoenician burial areas of the ancient city at Mdina/Rabat. Stylistically the head seems to show close links with the art of eastern Greece, mainly the island of Rhodes.

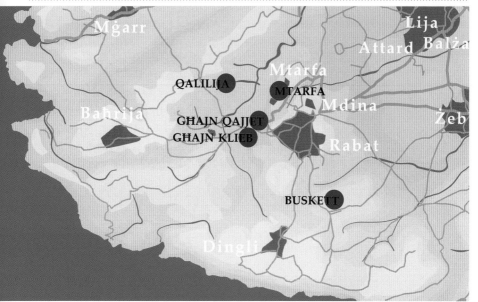

Street), while later ones are found scattered all over the islands with additional major concentrations near the harbours.

In the literature dealing with the ancient history of the central and western Mediterranean it is quite normal to distinguish between an early ('Phoenician') period and a later ('Punic') one. The separating line between the two tends to be somewhat arbitrary and varies from one geographical area to another. Considering various geo-political, historical, and cultural factors, it seems that the year 500 BC is a convenient, dividing point for Maltese archaeology, probably more than the usually used one (550 BC). The period preceding that date saw Malta emerging as an important outpost and eventually a fully-fledged colony of the Phoenicians, maintaining strong physical and cultural ties

The distribution of tombs of the early Phoenician period, such as at Mtarfa, Għajn Klieb, Għajn Qajjet, Qallilija, and Buskett, clearly point to the Mdina-Rabat promontory as the earliest urban centre of Malta.

with the motherland in the east, while in the three centuries after it Malta became inevitably involved in international politics and in the escalating hostilities between the western Phoenician colonies, under the hegemony of Carthage, and the western Greek colonies, mostly over interests in Sicily.

This chapter purports to discuss the various facets of the early period of Phoenician presence on Malta, a period in which, by the looks of it, the Maltese islands were identified even internationally, and to virtually all intents and purposes also internally, with these 'red-skinned' oriental traders.

The Sources

Our sources of information for the early Phoenician period are limited to the extreme. They consist from now on of three types: literary sources, that is, information gleaned from relevant references to Malta in ancient works of literature, be they historical or geographical texts, poetry, published political or legal speeches, and even private letters; epigraphic sources, that is, inscriptions engraved more or less contemporaneously to the commemorated events; and material, or archaeological, evidence. All these need varying degrees of interpretation and we cannot always be sure we are right in our interpretations.

Literary Sources

We can safely say that the literary sources for this period are limited to two: Diodorus Siculus and Stephen of Byzantium. In the previous chapter we have already dealt at length with Diodorus, the Greek Sicilian historian who wrote what to him was a universal history. As he lived and wrote in the first century BC, he was separated from the period under consideration by at least five centuries; it is, therefore, quite obvious that he himself depended on other historical sources. It is known that his major source for the early history of the western Greeks was a history of Sicily by Timaeus of Tauromenion (356-260 BC).

The second reference is found in Stephen of Byzantium's *Ethnika* which is a sort of encyclopaedic work. Acholla, a Phoenician settlement located in Tunisia, which later came under the political hegemony of Carthage, is here described as 'a colony of the Maltese' (Stephen of Byzantium, 152). The German scholar Albert Mayr uses this reference to assert that by the early seventh century BC the Phoenician settlement in Malta must have been large enough to permit the Phoenician settlers to plant their own colonies elsewhere. Given that Stephen of Byzantium wrote in the sixth century AD

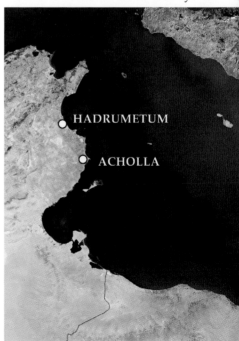

Map of the western coast of Tunisia showing the location of Acholla, reputedly colonized by the Phoenicians of Malta. Archaeological excavations on the site have so far not confirmed this attribution. From its harbour the defeated general Hannibal left for the island of Cercina on his flight to the east. It sided with the Romans in the Third Punic War, thus earning the status of a free (libera) city.

(i.e. more than one thousand years later than the alleged event) and since we have no mention of the colony before that, it is unwise to give too much weight to this late allusion. Acholla was identified in 1947 with an abandoned site on the seashore some 45 km north of Sfax. Though the identification is based on an inscription found there, so far the large-scale excavations of the site have revealed only Roman remains. Of the pre-Roman era only a sanctuary is known, presumably a tophet, but so far the connection

The two cippi with inscriptions commemorating offerings of sacrifices to Baal found on land belonging to the Dominican Order on the south-eastern edge of Rabat. The inscription on the left survives in the collection of the National Museum of Archaeology; the one on the right is known from a drawing in the Archives of the Cathedral Museum in Mdina.

with a Maltese foundation has not materialized. One looks forward to the future exploration of the archaeological site of Acholla in search of elements that would link it to Phoenician Malta.

Inscriptions

The inscriptions that date to this phase are limited to two, a pair, in fact (*CIS* 1, 123 and 123 bis). The two texts are dedications of offerings to the supreme god of the Phoenician pantheon, Baal Hammon. They are inscribed on two small stone rectangular pillars commonly known as *cippi*; the surviving one is supported by a slightly wider base while the other, of which we have only a drawing, had a much narrower base. They are contemporary and dated to the sixth century BC, lately even to the seventh century BC and as early

Two of a large number of stelae in the tophet of Carthage. The tophet was an open-air sacred area where pots containing burnt remains of children and animals were deposited. According to the Bible and to Classical writers, the Phoenicians sacrificed their own children to their gods. Some scholars believe that the human bones were of children who died prematurely rather than sacrificed ones.

as 'around 700 BC'. One mentions an offer of a *molk*, which is generally understood to mean a 'child sacrifice', and the other mentions a *molk omor*, which is thought to refer to a sacrifice of a lamb in lieu of the child. They both refer to a sinister ritual involving the immolation of children, which the ancient sources (particularly Diodorus Siculus) attributed to this Semitic people. This ritual seems to be documented by a specific sacred area, called 'tophet' in which the remains of the young victims of this ritual were deposited in special urns.

Such tophets have been identified in several of the Phoenician colonies of the western Mediterranean, the most notorious one being that of Carthage. Others have been uncovered in Sardinia and one on Motya, a small island near Trapani in Sicily. These inscriptions have been taken to suggest the possibility that such a tophet existed also in Malta. At one stage it was suspected there was one inside the Tas-Silġ sanctuary on the basis of some short inscriptions found there. But this possibility was soon ruled out after a revision of the reading of the relative inscriptions. However, a find of a large number of pots containing bones of animals and birds (one version states 'of children and small animals'), made inside a cavity in the vicinity of Mdina in 1819, seems to have resuscitated the possibility of the existence of a tophet in this area, which was the same from which the inscriptions derive.

Several inscriptions, mostly with the name of the goddess Ashtart have been retrieved during the excavations of Tas-Silġ, both those of the 1960s and the current ones. For some unexplained reason, none of these can be securely dated to before 500 BC, so I prefer to leave the treatment of these to the section dedicated to inscriptions in the following chapter.

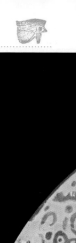

Left: A Corinthian skyphos (cup somewhat deeper than kotyle) from a rock-cut tomb discovered at Mtarfa in 1924 (c.610 BC).

Right: A lid of a large Corinthian pyxis (round jewel or powder box) restored and integrated from four original fragments. Of unknown provenance, but Mayr (1905) lists it among the finds from Phoenician tombs (c.650 BC).

The Material Remains

The archaeological evidence for this phase consists mostly of underground, rock-cut, chamber tombs. Besides these, there are the barely perceptible structural remains, as well as some early pottery deposits and a few objects of material culture that are datable to it, found inside Mdina and the Tas-Silġ sanctuary.

A strange burial, quite unique for the Maltese islands, was found in Racecourse (now Republic) Street in Rabat, Gozo. It is one of the few sites which could show direct contact between the Bronze Age native culture and the Phoenician newcomers.

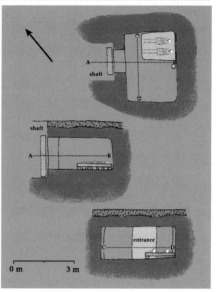

A hypothetical reconstruction of the plan of the burial discovered in 1923 near Villa Rundle in Racecourse Street, Rabat, Gozo. No other tomb of this shape has ever been recorded in Maltese contexts.

Tomb discovered at Għajn Qajjet in 1950. Top: plan showing the position of the raised stone platform on which two skeletons lay. Middle: section from the side. Bottom: section facing the entrance.

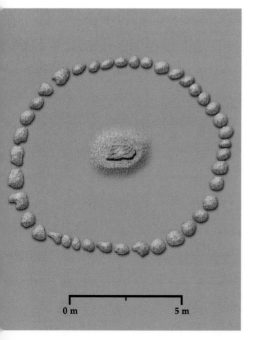

It consisted of a small mound (*tumulus*) covering a capping stone at the centre of a large circle of unworked field stones, some 9 m in diameter. The burial was beneath the capping stone. Tumuli of this type, one with a stone ring, have been recorded at Andalous on the North African coast of Oran. Unfortunately, the Gozo find was badly recorded, but the hybrid nature of the burial would be of great consequence if it could be reinforced with further documentation.

The Għajn Qajjet and the Mtarfa tombs are followed by other tombs of the same type datable to the seventh and sixth centuries, mostly concentrated around Rabat, Malta. This concentration tends to suggest that the area now occupied by

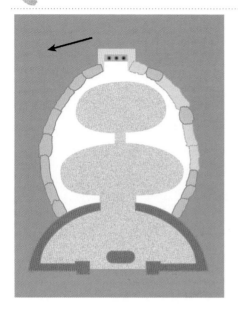

A hypothetical reconstruction of the plan of the earliest Phoenician temple at Tas-Silġ based on surviving foundation remains. The temple incorporated a pre-existing megalithic temple.

Mdina/Rabat was already by then taking shape as the main urban settlement of the largest island. Only a couple of tombs are documented for Gozo for the period 600-450 BC, both in the vicinity of Rabat/Victoria. This seems to indicate that Gozo's main settlement lagged behind in becoming a properly-organized urban centre, which happened more probably in the following period. Having said that, we have to keep in mind that a thin stratum, reputedly containing Phoenician Red-slipped sherds but no structures, was encountered in a long trench cut along the main square of Rabat; that could possibly indicate an occupation as early as the seventh century BC.

Recent archaeological investigations conducted inside Mdina have brought to light remarkable

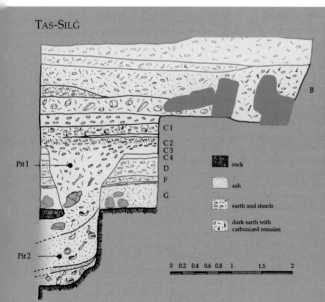

TAS-SILĠ

Section of a stratigraphic trench dug by the archaeologists of the Italian Missione *during their last campaign (1970) in the north area. Besides some large stones in level B, the section shows the sequence of deposits and pits from the earlier ones (bottom) to the later ones (top).*

evidence for this phase. We are informed that 'layer upon layer datable to between the eighth and the sixth century BC were uncovered' under Xara Palace and Mesquita Square. Under the former, as much as three metres of Phoenician layers were cut into by the recent excavation. These are attributed to a sequence of three major construction phases comprising traces of a rectangular structure with rubble foundations and of mortar floors and hearths. Although no structural remains were encountered at Mesquita Square, carbonized impressions in the soil layers have been read to suggest the probable existence of timber structures. Phoenician pottery sherds were also identified in a deep trench in Villegaignon Street in front of the Carmelite convent.

Aerial view of the Phoenician temple at Tas-Silġ showing the foundation remains reproduced in plan on previous page.

Fifteen kilometres away from Rabat, Malta, on the other hand, the standing ruins of a prehistoric megalithic temple had already been converted into a Phoenician temple. This temple, situated on the top of the Tas-Silġ hill, commanding the strategic Marsaxlokk harbour, was dedicated to Ashtart, the Phoenician goddess equivalent to the Greek Hera and the Roman Juno. Very little construction, however, can be securely dated to the Phoenician phase. According to the Italian archaeologists that excavated the site in the 1960s, an extension was added to the outer wall of the prehistoric megalithic temple to produce a building that was very atypical of the temple plan this Semitic people was used to in its land of origin. Nor does it look like any other temple building in the western colonies. The curved façade of the prehistoric temple was enclosed by two straight walls each ending in a square pillar to form a wide entrance. On the other hand, the double cavetto cornice capital that is thought to have crowned one of these pillars has exact parallels in the porticoed temple known as the *Ma'abed* at Amrith (ancient Marathus), in Syria. At the centre in front of the entrance, a large rectangular stone block was laid horizontally in the hollowed-out bedrock. This served to hold three vertical stone elements, called 'betyls', probably representing three divinities. The large rectangular block recalls a similar one set up at Kition, Cyprus (datable to *c*.850-450 BC), while a similar three-betyl altar was found at Kommos in southern Crete.

Material Culture

The richest array of objects of material culture for this period comes from the excavations of the Tas-Silġ sanctuary. These include various items of carved ivory, the most striking of which is a piece of exquisite open-work carving showing the right half of a proto-Aeolic type of capital with a hanging palmette.

Among those items with an artistic aspiration is a fragmentary limestone statuette. It is headless and belongs to a male figure draped in a plain dress with short sleeves. It shows probable Cypriote influence both in the posture and in its construction. From comparisons with Cypriote stone and terracotta

A hypothetical reconstruction of the altar with three holes probably intended to support three 'betyls', or vertical stone elements. The composition has parallels in Cyprus and Crete.

statuary of the Archaic age, Antonia Ciasca has dated the torso to the years straddling the end of the sixth and the beginning of the fifth century BC. The same scholar found close similarities in another torso which had been discovered in a modern field wall in the area of Tas-Silġ in 1963; for it she identified parallels in male ex-voto figures from Umm el-Amed, Amrith, and Ayia Trini.

On the other end of the spectrum, we have so far no indication in Malta of metal-working, especially of iron, as we have for other western Phoenician centres, like Carthage and Motya, in spite of the fact that they are, like Malta, quite distant from the sources of extraction of these metals. The same applies for the manufacture of glass and related jewellery. All the items of these materials are imported.

In tombs, whose number rises progressively as one approaches the end of the sixth century, there is very little in terms of precious objects. Among the most significant exceptions are the three gilt-silver plaques of an *armilla* (dated to the late-eighth/early-seventh century BC) retrieved from one of the tombs of Għajn Klieb, one of which ended up in the Ashmolean Museum at Oxford. Another remarkable exception is the Egyptian gold amulet (seventh-sixth century BC) discovered in 1906 in another tomb in the same area, depicting the Egyptian gods Horus (falcon-headed) and Anubis (jackal-headed) standing back to back (see p. 64-65). Another tomb that stands out in this respect is the one found at Ġnien iż-Żgħir, Rabat in 1909. Its contents included two silver

A magnificent piece of open-work in ivory discovered at Tas-Silġ (now missing). It showed the right half of an Oriental (Aeolic type) capital with hanging palmette. It still preserved traces of gilding.

Two of three gilt-silver plaques which formed part of an armlet (armilla) found in one of the rock-cut tombs at Ghajn Klieb in 1890. Each plaque shows a composition of two winged griffins in heraldic stance flanking a stylized tree, under a winged solar disc.

armlets, fragments of two bronze rings, and a gold medallion found hidden under a cup. Other gold items deriving from other tombs, such as gold beads, rings, and bracelets, are housed in the National Museum of Archaeology.

Among the objects of personal ornament found mostly in funerary contexts, the figurative amulets of faience (glass paste) of different colours, or of steatite, studied extensively by Günther Hölbl, are of great interest. A few of them are of genuine Egyptian origin; the majority are, however, of Egyptianizing style, probably manufactured in some Phoenician centre, or centres. Most of them date to this period, some even quite early (one as early as the eighth century and another around 900 BC); others, admittedly, belong to the following period. To the same category, date, and context belong the various scarabs in steatite and other semi-precious materials found in similar funerary contexts. One such scarab, with an Egyptian scene engraved underneath, was discovered during the recent University excavations at Tas-Silġ.

Pottery

The study of the ceramic repertoire is normally the best method to gauge the existence or otherwise of any continuity between cultures or the superposition of one culture over another. If a continuity or superposition is identified, a study of the evolution of shapes, fabrics, and decoration styles, supplemented by statistical analyses is likely to reveal the degree of such continuity or coexistence of two successive cultures. Unfortunately, this type of study has still not produced satisfactory results. The arguments brought forward to prove that some items of the early, locally-produced Phoenician ware derive from the Bronze Age ceramic repertoire are not entirely convincing.

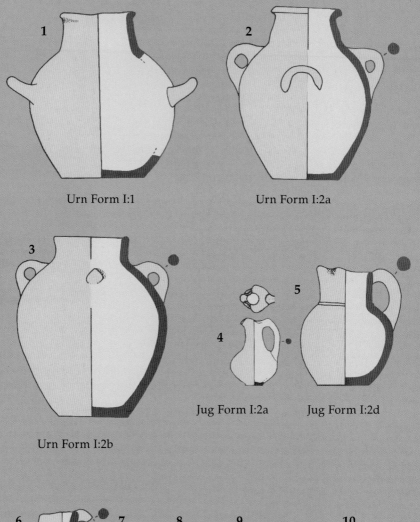

Urn Form I:1

Urn Form I:2a

Urn Form I:2b

Jug Form I:2a

Jug Form I:2d

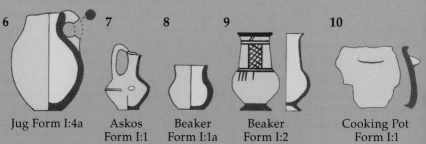

Jug Form I:4a

Askos
Form I:1

Beaker
Form I:1a

Beaker
Form I:2

Cooking Pot
Form I:1

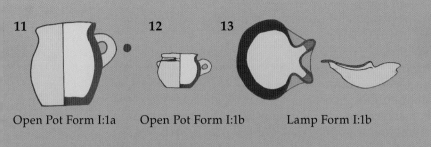

11 **12** **13**

Open Pot Form I:1a   Open Pot Form I:1b   Lamp Form I:1b

14 **15** **16** **17**

Bowl Form I:2   Bowl Form I:6a   Bowl Form I:7a   Bowl Form I:8a

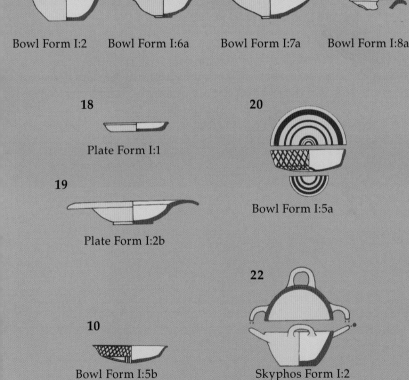

18

Plate Form I:1

19

Plate Form I:2b

20

Bowl Form I:5a

10

Bowl Form I:5b

22

Skyphos Form I:2

Some of the pottery shapes in use in the Early Phoenician phase. A form which is only typical of this early phase is the 'thistle beaker' (9) while the cooking pot (10) next to it remains in use for many centuries, down into the Roman period. Not to scale. (After Sagona 2002)

The presence of one single ceramic item (a Phoenician oil lamp) among Late Bronze Age coarse pottery fragments in one of the Mtarfa silo-pits does not constitute a watertight proof, given the possible taphonomic processes at work in such a context, and there is a certain amount of circular arguments in the reasoning. Besides, the evidence for coexistence between the Bronze Age inhabitants and the Phoenician newcomers at Tas-Silġ has been seriously questioned by one scholar.

Three ceramic jars found in tombs of different phases. In such funerary contexts they were used to contain cremated human remains.

There is next to nothing suggesting a gradual merging of the two styles. There is the sudden appearance of a range of wheel-made pottery with antecedents in the Levant and with parallels in other western Phoenician colonies, namely the notorious 'Red-slip Ware', some shapes of which have been tentatively made to derive from local *Borġ in-Nadur* ware. Most importantly, the coarse, hand-made bowls have shapes that are reminiscent of both *Tarxien Cemetery* and *Borġ in-Nadur* shapes and fabrics. However, the same coarse fabric (also referred to as *impasto*) that characterizes the hand-made cooking ware, which appeared at this stage and was to survive throughout the Punic

Egyptian or Egyptianizing amulets worn as pendants to ward off evil or to invoke protection from the gods. The first one in steatite represents an ibis; from Ta' l-Ibraġġ, Gozo.
The second one in greenish glass paste represents Bes wearing a feather crown; from Tal-Ħorob, Gozo.

period, is not restricted to the Maltese islands, but finds close parallels elsewhere in the central and western Mediterranean. What I find seriously missing in the early Phoenician ceramic repertoire is any influence from, or link with, the pottery style of the very last phase of the Maltese Bronze Age, the *Baħrija* style. The latter is only conspicuous by its total absence, except for the odd residual sherd in the later levels at Tas-Silġ.

It is in the light of the above that judgements on the acculturation processes by which the Phoenician visiting traders eventually 'colonized' the islands and made them theirs have to remain to a certain degree in suspension.

Political Status and the Emergence of an Urban Colony

The systematic political control of the archipelago by the Semitic newcomers probably did not take place before the late-sixth century when, as a result of the loss of political autonomy of the Phoenician fatherland in the east, the western Phoenician colonies rallied under the protectorate of Carthage, the most powerful and prosperous of them, to face the threat of the common enemy, the western Greeks.

Malta, like the other central Mediterranean islands colonized by the Phoenicians, had an identity of its own and enjoyed relative autonomy in both commercial and economic matters; in fact, it is well

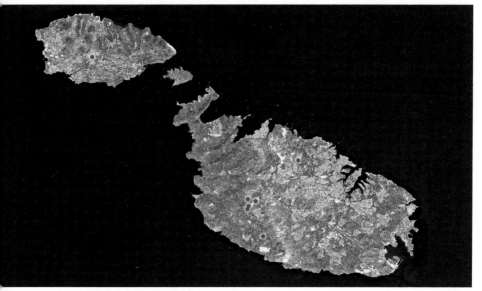

known that up to sixth century the material culture of Phoenician Malta had very strong links with the eastern Mediterranean and the Phoenician motherland and little in common with the western colonies. But, after the sixth century BC, it became, together with the other western Phoenician colonies, an integral part of the Carthaginian economico-political sphere. That happened when Carthage burst forth as a Mediterranean political and military power, first in reaction to the advance of the Greek, mainly Phocaean, trade and, later, the rising power of Syracuse, Agrigento, and Gela in Sicily.

Distribution of Phoenician tombs in Malta and Gozo during the early Phoenician phase.

The coalescence into a proper 'colony' probably did not take place before this stage (late-sixth century BC). The available tomb evidence points to a concentration of Phoenician inhabitants in the Mdina-Rabat area but it is not sufficient to affirm the existence of a large settlement, let alone a proper town. There is, for instance, no single necropolis of any scale. No structures within Mdina-Rabat had ever been assigned to this phase before the recent archaeological investigations provoked by property development and by trenching in the streets of Mdina.

It has been noted by Maria Eugenia Aubet that 'the Phoenician "colony" of Malta, a stopover and port of call for ships in the ancient period, is closer to the western model than to the group of Phoenician colonies in the central Mediterranean', like Sulcis, Motya, and Carthage. There is, admittedly, a certain provisional or transitory aspect in the original

Phoenician settlement, similar to that of the early Phoenician settlements to the west of the Carthage-Sardinia axis. There is no proper necropolis anywhere; only individual tombs scattered here and there, albeit with a degree of concentration around Rabat. Only the sanctuary of Tas-Silġ has a semblance of a permanent establishment, involving considerable investment in the adaptation of an existing prehistoric structure to suit the mariners' religious needs.

Commercial Contacts

The material culture encountered in the tombs of this early Phoenician phase, as well as in the respective levels and structural remains in the sanctuary of Tas-Silġ, reveals intensive commercial contacts with the eastern Mediterranean. This is one of the elements that suggest the key position of Malta in the sea route used by the Phoenicians from east to west, rather than on their return journey from west to east. The gilt ivory palmette, together with other carved ivory objects found at Tas-Silġ, are a clear indicator of these contacts with the Syro-Palestinian region. And so do the various elements of stone religious furniture found at Tas-Silġ and in various tombs, such as the incense-burners (*thymiateria*) with crowns of hanging leaves which derive from an Asiatic Phoenician tradition.

Though a similar item was found in the tomb of Tabnit in Sidon, on the Phoenician homeland, the bronze torch-holder, introduced inside the Għajn Qajjet tomb with its first interment, on the other hand, points more strongly towards Cyprus; so does the male torso in limestone found at Tas-Silġ during the 1960s excavations, as well as a small male head found there in the recent ones. Conversely, the significant number of jewellery items of silver accompanying the two corpses of the Għajn Qajjet tomb (five bracelets and four rings) has induced other scholars to suspect a link with Spain and, consequently, that Malta was a port of call on the return sea-route from Spain. These jewellery items and the fine pottery pieces, all prestige objects, also suggest the emergence of a social elite in this early Phoenician settlement.

The bronze upper part of a torch holder found with the grave goods belonging to the first burial of the Għajn Qajjet tomb discovered in 1950.

Even stronger appear to be the commercial and cultural ties, indirect though they might be, with Egypt. Several items of jewellery of original Egyptian workmanship (including gold ones) must have been worn by the Phoenician settlers during their daily life before being buried with their owners inside the rock-cut tomb chambers. Egyptian amulets of faience and steatite were imports from Egypt, others were copied by the able Phoenician craftsmen. These too found their way in several early tombs (such as those from a silo-tomb at Mtarfa and from the site of Tal-Ħorob, Gozo).

A reconstructed necklace of faience (or glass paste) 'eye' beads. The 'eye' motif in each bead suggests that they had some magico-religious purpose, probably intended to ward off evil.

Small head carved in local limestone showing a man of oriental origin, found during the recent University of Malta excavations at Tas-Silġ. Both the iconography and the style of the carving betray oriental craftsmanship.

It may come as a surprise to some, but the Phoenicians did not shun art and craft products of their Greek rivals and several items of fine painted pottery produced in various Greek centres occur frequently in tombs, as well as in the earlier levels of Phoenician occupation at Tas-Silġ. The best known of the former are the two pieces from the Għajn Qajjet tomb: a Proto-Corinthian kotyle and an eastern Greek 'bird bowl', probably of Rhodian production; but others were found in tombs, such as a Corinthian aryballos at Qallilija and the Proto-Corinthian kotylai at Mtarfa and Buskett Gardens.

An aerial view of Marsaxlokk harbour. Before the construction of stone and concrete quays in the 20th century both arms of this harbour had more extensive sandy beaches.

Ports

There is no doubt that the harbours played a very significant role in making commercial activity possible. In spite of the fact that it was somewhat more open and less sheltered from the south-eastern winds, it looks as if Marsaxlokk harbour was, in Phoenician and Punic times, preferred for the two narrower and deeper harbours on the north coast. One reason could be that it conveniently faced the more frequented route of these ancient mariners. The other reason could be because it offered more extensive beaching facilities.

The technique of laying heavy foundations and building walls under water was discovered after the fourth century BC. For this reason it is probably futile to look for proper harbour constructions and wharves before

THE TORCH HOLDER

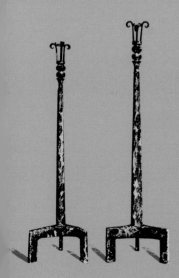

On the right is the head of a torch holder from the Għajn Qajjet tomb, and a reconstruction of a torch holder based on similar ones from Tabnit.

The Tabnit examples are illustrated, on the left, to show how the torch-holder was originally.

The three leaves forming the torch basket in the Maltese example are more rigid while the ones from Tabnit curve in to form volutes.

A wooden rod held together the basket, the underlying lotus flower, and the stem of the torch holder.

the Hellenistic age, both here and elsewhere. In the absence of rock-cut moles for mooring right up against the rocky jetty, and of quays for berthing, ships were normally run up on the beach.

As rightly observed by Claudia Sagona, Manoel island in the Marsamxett harbour, offered the ideal topographical features preferred by the Phoenicians in their choice of sites for planting their settlements. It is a small island, practically attached to the mainland, with small sheltered bays on either side. So far, however, no ancient remains have ever been

Aerial view of Manoel island in the Marsamxett harbour with a very similar setting to that of the city of Tyre. The Phoenicians preferred small islands like this, only a short distance from the mainland, to set up their settlements.

reported on the island, almost half of which is occupied by the Fort Manoel built in the mid-eighteenth century. Promontories jutting out into the Grand Harbour, like Birgu and Senglea, are similarly good candidates for early Phoenician settlements, and it is very surprising that, in the case of Malta, the Phoenicians departed from their norm and decided in favour of the inland ridge head now occupied by Mdina.

Although both the north harbours and the south-eastern ones provided sufficient shelter from winds and currents from opposite directions, only the latter had extensive beaches, such as those existing in the areas of Pretty Bay and Qajjenża on the Birżebbuġa side and Il-Prajjiet and L-Inginier on the Marsaxlokk side, just underneath the Tas-Silġ sanctuary. This might explain why no harbour

Aerial view of the inner harbour of Marsaxlokk. This is the side of the harbour closest to the Tas-Silġ sanctuary which occupies a small hill that has a commanding view over it. Here the ancient Phoenician and other mariners berthed or beached their boats before climbing up the hill to pay their respects to Ashtart, to thank her for a safe voyage, and to pray for the next one.

structures have ever been found anywhere preceding the Roman ones in the Grand Harbour. It also explains why the great extra-urban sanctuary to Ashtart was located inside Marsaxlokk harbour rather than anywhere near the Valletta harbours, as held by the early modern antiquarian tradition.

As for Gozo, the only beaching facilities with some reasonable shelter from the prevailing winds and rough seas were the sandy beaches of Ramla l-Ħamra and, to a limited extent, Xlendi, Mġarr, and Marsalforn. All these are badly affected by strong winds, especially by northwesterly ones. Dwejra Bay offered no beaching facility and the Inland Sea at Qawra could only be used by very small boats, if at all.

Religious Beliefs

Thus the culture of the inhabitants of Malta in the early Phoenician period appears strongly orientalizing in nature, with the Levantine and Egyptian factors predominating. This is even more obvious in the surviving manifestations of their religious beliefs.

The religious rites and beliefs that were introduced in Malta by the Phoenicians can best be gleaned from inscriptions found in various localities. The earliest two inscriptions, datable to the seventh-sixth century, reveal the worship of Baal Hammon, the highest male divinity in the Phoenician pantheon, to whom, according to ancient Greek writers, human child sacrifice (*molk*) was regularly offered. This was

later substituted by the sacrifice of animals (*molk omor*). Together with these inscriptions scores of urns are reported to have been found 'containing bones of children and small animals'.

Another Phoenician text, datable to the same age, this time written on a tiny fragment of papyrus enclosed in a hollow bronze amulet, contains an imprecation against the evil spirits that beset the soul of the dead on its journey to the world beyond. The text probably reproduces the words uttered by the goddess Isis whose image accompanies the text. Not only are the pendant and the depicted divinity Egyptian, but even the content of the inscription and the formula itself referring to the soul's journey over the waters, are essentially Egyptian in concept.

Hollow bronze amulet with the head of Horus, which was discovered in a rock-tomb at Tal-Virtù, outside Rabat. It contained a tiny papyrus scroll with a written text and a drawing of the Egyptian goddess Isis standing in profile to the right.

This item introduces us to the realm of the dead, to the belief system of the early Phoenician colonizers connected with the netherworld. The inscription on papyrus described in the previous paragraph is perhaps the most outspoken document on their beliefs regarding life beyond death. Another inscription, engraved in a tomb at Benghisa datable to the fourth-third century BC (*CIS* 1, 124), speaks of the tomb as the 'eternal home' (or 'house of eternity') of the dead, a concept met with also in funerary contexts back in the Phoenician motherland and in the Bible. The date of the inscription, which strictly speaking, places it in the following phase, shows the permanence of certain beliefs during this earlier phase and into the next. The frequent occurrence of Egyptian amulets with a magico-religious meaning in tombs also points to the perceived need of such protective powers in the next life. The classic case is that of the gold double amulet, datable to the sixth century BC, found in a tomb at Għajn Klieb in 1906. It consists of two figures representing Horus and Anubis joined together back to back.

A remarkable feature connected with the mortuary ritual of the early Phoenician settlers is the re-introduction of burial in rock-cut underground chambers, a type of ritual that had been constantly in use throughout the 1,500 years of the prehistoric Temple culture in Malta, and had disappeared in the intervening two millennia of Bronze Age cultures. Again, we should refrain from rushing into seeing another element of continuity. The disposal of the dead in underground, rock-cut tombs is widely diffused among the contemporary cultures in the Syro-Palestinian area, and the Phoenicians must have brought this tradition with them from their homeland. Besides, it is also found in other Phoenician centres in the west, like Ibiza.

Perhaps the most important difference between the old prehistoric tradition and the new one is the individual inhumation practised by the Phoenicians, as opposed to the collective interments of the *Tarxien* phase. As in the case of the latter's remote antecedents in the *Żebbuġ* phase, burials were made inside sub-circular or oval chambers purposely hewn in the living rock with access from the surface via a vertical shaft. The corpse, however, was laid on its back in an extended position. It was accompanied by a range of pottery items and the occasional personal ornaments or jewellery items. Very rarely, it was placed in a specially-constructed

Close-up view of the head of the Anubis figurine, one of two forming a gold double amulet which is illustrated in the following page.

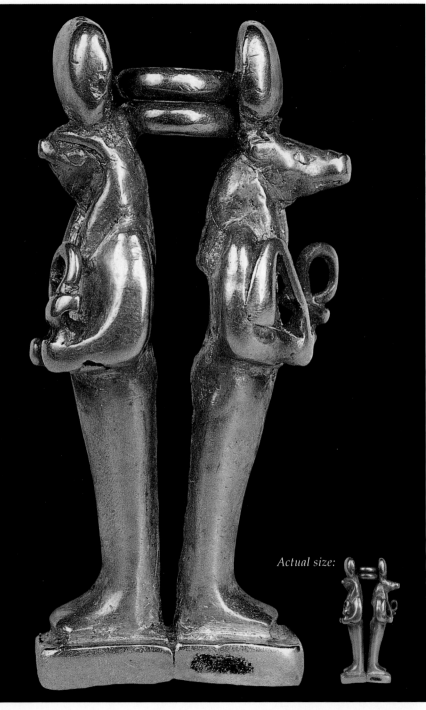

Actual size:

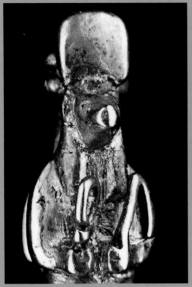 

THE GĦAJN KLIEB AMULET:
The solid gold double amulet from one of the tombs at Għajn Klieb. It consists of two miniature figurines of standing gods, Horus and Anubis, soldered together back-to back. Above are close-up details of the two divinities while below is the inside of the Għajn

Klieb tomb today. The right and back walls have three rows of hollow niches of unknown purpose. The entance and shaft are also visible.
Part of the roof and back wall have been damaged by road trenching some years ago.

stone sarcophagus. Terracotta sarcophagi are also documented. One of these, an anthropoid sarcophagus, was recovered from a rock-cut tomb at Għar Barka, outside Rabat. It is, however, normally dated to the sixth century. It is housed in the National Museum of Archaeology in Valletta, together with another terracotta sarcophagus in the shape of a simple coffin supported on four legs. Other documented sarcophagi, one forming part of Gian Francesco Abela's collection in 1647, seem to have gone lost.

Other types of underground tombs are not lacking. At Mtarfa

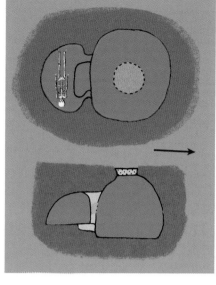

Plan and section of a tomb discovered at Mtarfa in 1923. Originally a typical Bronze Age bottle-shaped silo-pit, a lateral burial chamber was added to it in Phoenician times.

Front view of the face of the anthropoid sarcophagus found at Għar Barka.

use was made of readily available bottle-shaped pits, better known as 'silo pits' characteristic of the Middle and Late Bronze Age cultures. Rare specimens are also recorded of burials inside simple pits in the ground.

One should not forget, however, that the Phoenicians practised another burial rite, that is, cremation. In this rite, the corpse was burned on a pyre and the burnt remains placed inside special pottery urns which were normally deposited inside already existing tombs, probably family tombs. It appears that cremation was practised alongside inhumation throughout the seventh century BC, after which it was virtually

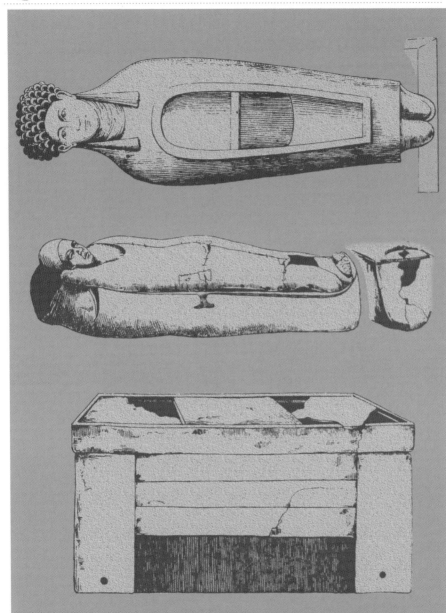

Two anthropoid sarcophagi, one formerly in Gian Francesco Abela's collection, now lost, the other found inside a rock-cut tomb at Ghar Barka in 1797. The third sarcophagus is also in terracotta and seems to reproduce a wooden coffin on four legs.

A cinerary urn, like those illustrated on pages 52-53, containing cremated human bones. Found in Rabat, Malta.

abandoned to be resumed with even greater intensity in the fourth century BC. A thick ashy deposit covering an area of some 23.2m, discovered in 1950 close to the Tac-Ċagħqi tombs in Rabat, has been identified as a possible cremation site.

Although it is not easy to separate any of the hundreds of inscriptions on pottery found at the site of Tas-Silġ and assign them to this early phase, it is quite obvious that the Phoenician divinity worshipped in this sanctuary after its re-instatement as a place of religious cult was Ashtart, the consort of Baal, whose cult was widespread among the Phoenicians. The cult of Ashtart, however, tended to be supplanted by that of Tanit in the western colonies; but not at Tas-Silġ. The

dedication of this temple to Ash-tart, a female divinity connected with fertility, does not necessarily imply a continuity of the cult of an indigenous prehistoric female divinity, as frequently alleged. There is as yet no indication that the initial Neolithic sanctuary retained the same use through the almost two millennia covered by the Bronze Age, even though it was occupied for some, as yet undefined, purpose by the different peoples that succeeded each other during those 1,800 years.

Soon after they set foot on Malta the Phoenicians chose the Tas-Silġ hill as the site for the temple they wanted to set up to serve their own needs and those of the community of sailors and mariners that found shelter in the south-eastern harbour. There

they must have found the standing remains of an impressive building, a well-designed structure built of impressively large and well-dressed standing blocks. I would imagine that, at best, they found it very much in the same state as we see Ħaġar Qim and Mnajdra today. The aura around the structure must have inspired them to adopt it for the worship of their protective goddess and to adapt its layout to their needs, with very little additions. This is precisely what the excavators concluded from their archaeological investigations of the 1960s.

A full-length view of the Għar Barka anthropoid sarcophagus. Note the various repairs, especially of the upper lid and one of the four cramps for the insertion of dowels.

THE EGYPTIAN STELAE FOUND AT BIGHI

Four Egyptian stelae were reported to have been found in December 1829, during excavation work for the foundations of the Naval Hospital at Bighi. A photograph in the archive of the National Museum of Archaeology reproduces all four stelae. The stelae were in 1836 donated by Mr J. B. Collings to the British Museum, where they are now kept in the reserve collection. The same Mr Collings appears as the Clerk of Works for the Bighi project in the Government Gazette of 24 March 1830.

Strangely enough, Margaret M. Murray published them in an article entitled 'Egyptian objects found in Malta' in the journal Ancient Egypt *of 1928, without giving their provenance. This alleged find is surrounded by an aura of uncertainty compounded by the fact that while three stelae (nos. 299, 223, and 218) belong to the XII dynasty (1991-1786 BC), the fourth (no. 287) is dated to the XVIII dynasty (1567-1320 BC). The probability is that these objects were imported from Egypt in historical or modern times. They are certainly Egyptian imports since their material has been established to be Egyptian limestone.*

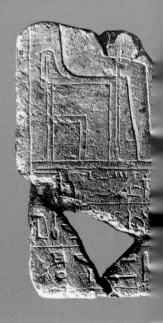

The Punic period is to a great extent a continuation of the Phoenician one. In it, however, the Maltese islands found themselves, like all the other Phoenician colonies of the west Mediterranean, gravitating around the powerful city of Carthage, probably even subjected to her. The Hellenizing influence affecting the rest of the Mediterranean world is also felt here, with increasing intensity in the second half of this period.

CHAPTER 3

THE PUNIC PERIOD (500-218 BC)

It should be noted at this stage that whenever the term 'Phoenician' is used from this point onwards, it refers to the western Phoenician world in the late period, that is, after 500 BC, for which we may, perhaps we should, preferably apply the term 'Punic', an adjective by which the Romans designated their Semitic rivals. But, as the situation is further complicated by the leading role of Carthage in the western Phoenician world in this phase, and by the extensive use of the term 'Carthaginian' to denote the same, I prefer to leave the seemingly futile debate about this matter to the experts in the field.

Life on the Maltese islands from the beginning of the fifth century to 218 BC must have been profoundly influenced, possibly determined, by the commercial, political, and military hostilities that raged around the central Mediterranean at the time, even though Malta's involvement

The two identical marble candelabra, each carrying a bilingual inscription, which formed part of the collection of antiquities of the Maltese antiquarian Gian Francesco Abela before his death in 1655. The inscriptions played a major role in the decipherment of the Phoenician script in the eighteenth century. Notice the slight differences between the two candelabra in the layout of both inscriptions.

in these vicissitudes is nowhere recorded in written texts. War after war was waged between the prosperous Greek cities of Sicily on one side and Carthage on the other; battle after battle was fought on land on that fertile island and in the sea around it.

Another naval power, that of the Etruscans, was also involved in contesting the trading spaces in this part of the world, especially in the Thyrrenian sea. Just before the close of the sixth century, in 535 BC, the combined fleets of the Etruscans and Phoenicians had successfully prevented the Greek Phocaeans from establishing permanent trading posts in Corsica and Sardinia. But the Etruscans' power started to wane after they suffered a disastrous defeat by a joint force of Cumaeans and Syracusans at Cumae in 474 BC. Their influence and involvement in international affairs was already seriously crippled by the Romans' overthrow of the last Etruscan king in 509 BC and by the Romans' encroaching territorial expansion on peninsular Italy thereafter. The whole of Etruria came under the rule of Rome in 309 BC.

By 524 BC the whole of the Phoenician homeland was subjected to Persia. It is no wonder, therefore, that in the conflict between Greece and Persia in 480 BC a large part of the Persian fleet was supplied by the Phoenicians. At the same time, in the west, the struggle was raging around Sicily for the control of the western and central Mediterranean. Phoenicia's loss of independence

to Persia resulted in the western Phoenician colonies seeking their own destiny and rallying under the hegemony of Carthage, the strongest and most powerful of them all. It is perhaps not a coincidence that in the same year of the defeat of the combined forces of the Persians and Phoenicians at Salamis (480 BC), the Carthaginians suffered a major defeat at the hands of the Greeks of Sicily at Himera. After that, it was a continuous series of wars and battles alternately won and lost by either of the two sides. The main base from which Carthage effected her Sicilian war campaigns was Motya, a small circular island situated in a shallow lagoon sheltered from the open sea by another long and narrow island near Marsala, on the western tip of Sicily.

Sicily suffered another serious war trauma, this time originating neither from the Semites of the west, nor from internecine hostilities between the Greek cities for supremacy over the island, but from their Greek cousins in the east. In 416 BC, Segesta, the almost totally Hellenized Elymian city which had been on previous occasions the cause of war between Greeks and Carthaginians, sought assistance from Athens against her Dorian neighbour Selinunte. In 415 Athens sent a large fleet with thousands of armoured troops, including 5,000 Athenians, across the Ionian Sea for Sicily. The target, however, was not Selinunte, but Syracuse, the head of all the Dorian colonies in Sicily. The siege of Syracuse lasted several years and ended with a

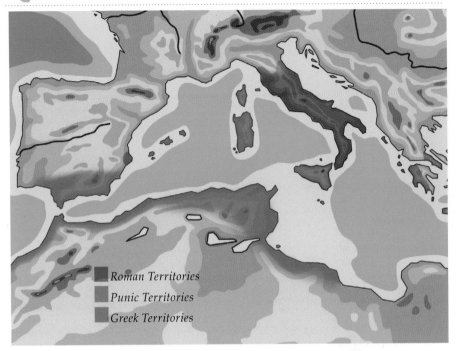

Map of the central and western Mediterranean showing the Roman, Punic, and Greek controlled territory in 264 BC.

humiliating defeat of the Athenians and their allies. Taking place a mere 150 km away, the long siege of Syracuse could not have left the Maltese islands unaffected; these effects are still to be sought and identified in the archaeological record.

Later still, in the last third of the fourth century BC, a brilliant military leader emerged whose exploits were to change the geopolitical face of the world, the half-Greek, Macedonian Alexander. In a whirlwind expedition, he marched and won over the whole eastern Mediterranean and all the lands that had formed part of the Persian empire. What is surprising is that he did not attempt to do the same in the opposite direction, to the west. He might well have conceived the idea, but his untimely death prevented him from even starting to prepare for it. The realization of this dream was attempted half a century later by Pyrrhus, king of Epirus, a descendant of one of Alexander's generals who had inherited and parcelled out his huge empire among themselves.

But Pyrrhus' adventure in Italy against Rome (280-272 BC) only helped to confirm the strong position of the emerging power of Rome, a land power at first, but soon to embark on maritime warfare in the First Punic War (264-241 BC), the first of three successive major conflicts

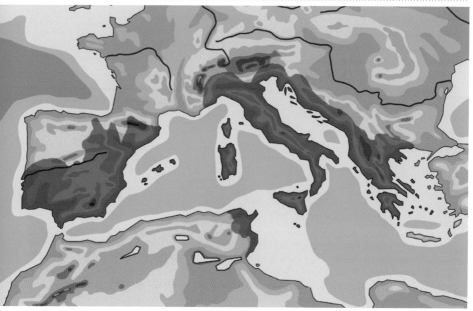

with Carthage (264-146 BC). This war was to bring Malta momentarily in contact with the Romans, when the Roman navy, on the return journey from an expedition to Africa, stopped in Malta and plundered whatever they could carry away, setting fire to the rest. But they did not realize the strategic importance of the island until the beginning of the Second Punic War (218-202 BC). The latter event, however, will take us into the following chapter of our story.

The very silence of the written historical sources for almost the whole of this period implies that the Maltese islands were never directly involved in the wars between the Carthaginians and the Sicilian Greeks. Had there been a serious battle on or around Malta, it is most likely that it would have

Map of the Mediterranean showing the Roman territorial expansion by 146 BC.

been recorded, as was the relatively minor event of the plundering *razzia* of the Roman fleet just mentioned.

The above, and the regular, apparently uncontrolled, presence of pirates on Malta recorded by the Roman orator Cicero (*Verr.*, 2.4.104; 4.46.103), could well mean that, although they fell within the political and military sphere of Carthage, the islands enjoyed a fair amount of autonomy in commercial and economic matters. In fact, the archaeological record reveals that, while the umbilical cord with the Phoenician homeland was, to most intents and purposes, severed, commercial exchanges with the Greek neighbours in Sicily and southern Italy were more than frequent (see section on commerce).

We cannot tell whether Carthage ever required military service from the Maltese inhabitants. About its Sicilian subjects the sources contradict each other. While Timaeus (Diodorus, XIV, 54, 6) asserts that 30,000 troops were recruited from Sicily for the war against Dionysius of Syracuse in 396 BC, Ephoros (Diodorus, XIV, 54, 5) claims that all the Carthaginian forces for the same war were recruited from Africa and Spain. On the other hand, it is known that the majority of Carthaginian troops serving in Sicily during the First Punic War were formed of mercenaries (Polybius I, 65 f.; Diodorus, XXV, 2). The garrison stationed on Malta at the outset of the Second Punic War appears to have been of foreign extraction (Livy, XXI, 51, 1-2).

The Sources:

Literary Sources

As we have already stated, the written sources are almost totally silent with respect to the first 250 years of the period under study in this chapter, a period which was dominated by the hostilities between the Sicilian Greeks and Carthaginians. They make important statements, on the other hand, on events that took place in the last fifty years of the period, when the Romans had replaced the Greeks in the Sicilian war theatre and in the contest for the central and western Mediterranean.

Gozo's association with Carthage seems to be the most important element emphasized in a surviving fragment of the history of Greece by Hecataeus: 'Gozo: an island close to Carthage' (frg. 341). Hecataeus died in c.476 BC, so he is the first to associate Gozo, the second largest island of the Maltese archipelago, with Carthage. It is strange that he does not include a similar entry on Malta, but such an entry could have gone lost. As noted by Albert Mayr, Hecataeus probably means that the

A detail of one of the plates illustrating the monumental work by Jean Houel, the Voyage Pittoresque des Iles de Sicile, Malte et Lipari *of 1787, showing a group of painted Greek pots which must have been imported into Malta in antiquity from Athens or from southern Italy.*

island was dynamically verging on Carthage rather than dominated by her. His work, a 'Guide' (*Periegesis*) written to illustrate his map of the world, survives in loose fragments in quotations. The above fragment is quoted by Stephen of Byzantium.

Apart from the passage of Diodorus Siculus reproduced above which referred to historical and cultural developments of the Maltese islands in this period, the next most important allusion to Malta is by Skylax of Carianda, better known as Pseudo-Skylax, who wrote, also in Greek, in the mid-fourth century BC. Malta and Gozo are mentioned in the last section of his work, the section dedicated to Libya (i.e. North Africa), precisely under the subsection dedicated to Carthage. He gives the geographical position of the two small islands, 'to the east of the Cape of Hermes' (Cap Bon), and refers to the existence of one main urban centre for each of the two islands, Melite and Gaulos (Skylax, 111). He adds that the Maltese islands, together with Lampedusa, were under the political control of Carthage. It is of interest that he assigns a 'harbour' to Malta, but not to Gozo. This probably reflects a better assessment of the geographical realities than that of Diodorus Siculus who attributes Gozo with equally well-placed harbours as he does Malta.

In the introductory paragraphs of this chapter we mentioned the episode of the 'raid' on Malta by the Roman navy during the First Punic War. This is recorded in just two lines from an epic poem, entitled *The Punic War*, by the second known Latin poet, Gnaeus Naevius, who wrote in the second half of the third century BC. All he states is, textually: 'The Roman (army) crosses over to Malta, plunders and devastates by fire the (as yet) unimpaired island and stows away the (plundered) possessions of the enemy' (*Bell. Pun.* IV, 37). There is a variety of opinions as to the date of this episode, but on the basis of information supplemented by a much later writer, Paulus Orosius (fifth century AD), the most plausible date has been fixed to 255 BC.

A satellite view of the central Mediterranean showing clearly Malta's position in relation to that of Cap Bon and the smaller island of Lampedusa.

CAP BON

Malta & Gozo

Lampedusa

Orosius states that 'the Consul Atilius (Regulus) reached out to Lipara and Melita, the better known (or, more important) islands of Sicily, and ravaged them'. There is no doubt that the Atilius referred to is M. Atilius Regulus, the famous Roman consul who conducted the war campaign in North Africa in 256-255 BC. It is difficult to tell whether the epithet *'nobiles'* ('famous', or 'important') for Malta and Lipari reflects the general perception of the two archipelagos at the time of the event (third century BC) or at the time of the writer (fifth century AD).

One question that has never been asked and needs an answer is: what effect did this raid of the Roman army have on the Maltese inhabitants? No mention of the population is made, whereas in other circumstances we know that a proportion of it was sold in slavery.

Has the impact of the event, the devastation by fire it declares, ever been detected in the archaeological record, as it has been in Lipari where burials dated to immediately after the Roman attack of 252/1 BC have been found to be strikingly poor, by comparison with the wealth of those of the previous hundred years? As far as I know, it never has, not even in the excavations of the Tas-Silġ sanctuary. It is likely to prove difficult to detect it in the old excavations of the various villa sites published so far, but a statistical analysis of the number and contents of the burials following the episode might give some indication. I strongly believe that, if the episode is a real one and

not a figment of the imagination of the poet, it could very well be reflected in the archaeological register, and archaeologists should keep their eyes open during excavations of deposits that cover this period.

Probably straddling this phase and the following one is the situation of the Maltese islands referred to by Cicero when he states that the sanctuary of Juno survived intact 'not only those Punic wars that, involving many warships, unfolded themselves almost right in these places, but also the multitude of pirates' (Cic. *Verr.* 2.4. 103-4). This is so because, as we said, the First Punic War falls under the period discussed in this chapter, while the second and third introduce the period dealt with in the next chapter, Malta having become a Roman possession at the beginning of the Second Punic War. Further on in the same passage Cicero adds that 'the navy of the enemy frequently visited this place (that is, where the temple of Juno was situated) and the pirates used to winter there almost every year.'

Inscriptions

An important inscription on a small marble slab is said to have been found in Gozo. It records the construction and restoration of temples or shrines to various Phoenician divinities (*CIS*, I, 132; see box). This inscription sheds important light on the religious belief system as well as on the political organization and social setup in Gozo, by extension presumably also in Malta, in this period. Besides the shrines to various divinities,

CIS I, 132

A small polished marble slab carrying eight lines of elegantly inscribed Punic text has been known at least since 1855, when it was brought to the cabinet of antiquities of the National Library in Malta. (The National Museum, as the official state depository of Maltese antiquities was only set up in 1902). As the text refers twice to 'the people of Gozo', it must have originated from Gozo, whether or not its modern provenance is from Gozo. It is the only known Punic inscription from Gozo.

The dating of the inscription has been determined mostly on grounds of script style. One dating is quite broad, covering a span of three centuries, fourth-second century BC. However, while one scholar advances it to the second century BC, way into the Roman period, another one places it at the

end of the third century. As the last published study seems to imply a late third century BC date also on historical grounds, we take this to be the right dating for this inscription, even though the proxeny decree to which it is compared has been dated by recent research to the first century BC.

A last comment relating to the dating of the decree, it would, of course, make a lot of difference whether the decree was made before, or after, the eventful year of 218 BC, when Malta changed hands from the Carthaginian to the Roman masters. The political set-up described in the inscription makes more sense in a Punic (Carthaginian) context rather than in a Roman one, just after Malta's annexation with the Roman territorial possessions overseas.

including Ashtart, the inscription mentions various eponymous magistrates and an inspector of the quarry. Since all these are of a purely Punic nature, it makes more sense to include it within this period, even though some scholars date it after 218 BC.

Another inscription was found in a rock-cut tomb discovered in Bengħisa, near Birżebbuġa in 1761 (*CIS* 1, 124), to which we have already referred in the previous chapter (p.62). It is now kept in the Bibliothèque Nationale in Paris. The text seems to have been engraved on the rock wall of the burial chamber and mentioned a man called 'Hannibal son of Barmelech (or Bodmelek)' who is thought to be either the buried person or the eponymous magistrate of the year of interment. This funerary inscription is dated to the fourth-third century BC.

A much shorter inscription, formerly in private possession, now housed in the National Museum of Archaeology in Valletta, carries only two words: 'door (or gate) of 'bdl'y'. It is engraved on a rectangular block of stone. Although it is tentatively dated to the fourth-third century BC, some doubts have been expressed as to its authenticity since neither the place nor the date of the discovery are known.

It should be made clear that the inscribed characters on the stone floor paving inside the inner court of the south temple at Ġgantija is only pseudo-Phoenician. Several attempts at deciphering it were made since 1905, without success. As the characters look extremely

THE ĠGANTIJA INSCRIPTION

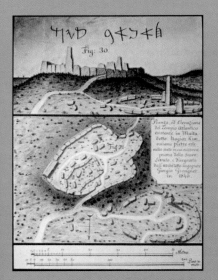

Close-up view of the pseudo-Phoenician inscription on the floor of the south temple at Ġgantija. On the left is a drawing of Ħaġar Qim, by Giorgio Grognet de Vassé, reproduced from his manuscript held in the National Library of Malta. The characters are very similar.

similar to those used in the pseudo-Phoenician script adopted by the nineteenth-century French engineer and antiquarian Giorgio Grognet de Vassé to designate several prehistoric temple sites, like Ħaġar Qim, the suspicion of having forged this inscription falls on him, or one of his followers. De Vassé is better known as the architect who designed the Mosta church, but he also published an extraordinary book linking the Maltese temples with the mythical lost continent of Atlantis.

More Phoenician inscriptions have been recorded which do not survive. One was discovered in March 1885 engraved on a door jamb separating two chambers on one side of a corridor forming the entrance to the catacombs of St Paul. A.A. Caruana tells us that it was 'damaged by dampness, rendered irrecoverable

The inscription with the word Ba'al at the entrance of St Paul's catacombs cannot be traced. This is a detail of the three letters with the word Ba'al from the inscription on the surviving stele found in Rabat (p.42). Note that the vowels are not inserted in the Punic script, creating problems of interpretation.

by scratching of visitors'. But drawings were made and sent to experts abroad for deciphering. A reply was received from Professor Wright who confirmed that the inscription was Phoenician and read the first word as B-L (Ba'al). More inscriptions were observed on the walls of the same corridor which, the author observes, did not originally form part of the catacomb. The same Caruana reported that Phoenician letters could be read on sarcophagi lids found in 'tomb-caves on St Angelo's promontory'.

By this stage, the incised dedications to the goddess Ashtart at Tas-Silġ become numerous; they occur in their hundreds on pottery, mostly on offering bowls, but also on cooking pots. Almost all such inscriptions are dated by Maria Giulia Amadasi Guzzo to the second-first century BC, more recently even down to the 'Roman era (first BC-first AD)'. This dating does not seem to coincide with the dating of the deposits that have been excavated by the Department of Classics and Archaeology of the University of Malta on the south side of the Tas-Silġ site between 1996 and 1999.

For some strange reason no deposits later than the second century BC have been encountered in the three areas investigated so far. Most of the deposits appear to belong to cumulative dumping of organic material and broken pottery ranging from the fourth to the second century BC. A considerable number of pottery sherds (at least 87 up to 1999) carried inscriptions of the same type, of which one was painted rather than incised. This implies that these inscriptions are earlier than the first century BC.

A fragment of a typical cooking pot in crisp ware was retrieved during a very short archaeological investigation made in 1976 inside the remains of an ancient country house in the neighbouring town of Żejtun. The sherd carries the inscribed name of Ashtart, which the late Tancred Gouder and myself found to be quite identical to those discovered at Tas-Silġ. Anthony J. Frendo, however, sees a break, albeit very faint, within the presumed third character of the inscription. In Frendo's view this reading would thus give the name of another goddess, Anat, along with that of Ashtart. Anat was reasonably well known in the Near East but quite unusual in Phoenician-Punic inscriptions of the first millennium BC, particularly in the west. He sees her being venerated in Malta at this very late time as the composite deity Anat-Ashtart. Whichever way it is

Fragment of the rim of a cooking pot found in 1976 during excavations in the remains of a 'Roman' villa in Żejtun. The inscription is almost identical to many others found at Tas-Silġ with dedications to Ashtart.

0 cm   5 cm

read, the significance of the inscription in a domestic context, rather than a sacred one, is very intriguing and needs to be investigated properly.

The study of the Tas-Silġ inscriptions on pottery is rendered more complicated by the occurrence of an even greater number of them consisting of just two incised characters, occasionally even one. These are normally taken to be abbreviations of the name of the divinity to whom the offering is dedicated. At one stage these were thought to be dedications to another female divinity in the Phoenician pantheon, Tanit (or Tin(n)it), who came to replace Ashtart in most western Phoenician colonies; but now there seems to be a change of heart and the scholars expert in the field have ruled out this latter identification and prefer to see abbreviated forms of the name Ashtart, or simply for the word 'offer, present'. Notwithstanding this, according to another scholar, 'it seems inevitable that the inscriptions consisting of the letters TT have to be linked with the name of the goddess Tin(n)it'.

On the basis of the interpretation of three more inscriptions which, together with the name of Ashtart, carry the formula 'nn which is the same as that on the early coins of Malta in Roman times, two Italian scholars, C. Grottanelli and M.G. Amadasi Guzzo, have concluded that the sole divinity to whom the sanctuary of Tas-Silġ was dedicated was Ashtart, with the epithet 'of Malta'. Parallels for this epithet are found in sanctuaries of Ashtart in Cyprus ('Ashtart of Paphos') and Sicily ('Ashtart of Eryx'). The most important inscription of the three was the one carved on a stone architectural element, since the latter could have been a prominent element in the architecture of the sanctuary.

The assimilation of this Phoenician female divinity with her Graeco-Roman counterpart Hera/Juno, rather than with Aphrodite/Venus (as it is at Eryx and Paphos), is documented by just a handful of inscriptions in Greek with the formulas HRAC and HRAI ('of Hera' and 'to Hera').

Two new groups of inscriptions, painted or engraved, on pottery have recently been identified. One has been interpreted as 'belonging to the priest [of Ashtart]' and the other as 'belonging to the sanctuary'. One inscription with the Greek letters OIKOU (literally, 'of the house') has been associated with the second group and, therefore, translated as 'of the sanctuary'

A different kind of inscription was retrieved during the excavations of 1965 from courtyard 8 in the north side. It is incised on the slightly convex side of a rectangular sheet of bone, the left side of which, together with the letters therein, is missing. It has been dated to the fifth-fourth century BC and reads thus: 'To our lady Ashtart…this is the 'bst who has dedicated…son of b'lhls, son of k…[because she heard] the voice of his words.' Other than being a votive inscription to Ashtart, its meaning remains uncertain.

Inscribed sherds from the recent University of Malta excavations at Tas-Silġ. The bottom two sherds bear the full dedication 'to Ashtart'. The meaning of the short, sometimes one-letter, inscriptions is debated.

Phoenician Medals

By their very nature, and inasmuch as they contain inscribed legends, coins also have epigraphic value. Apart from coins of foreign origin, about which more later on in this chapter, there are no locally minted coins before the beginning of the Roman period. But the imagery combined with legends inscribed on the coins struck in Malta in that period testify to the survival of Punic culture in general, of oriental religious beliefs and of the Punic language in particular. All the divinities appearing in those coins were, most likely, the ones worshipped during the Punic period. The word '*nn* inscribed on the earliest of those coins was, most probably, the name by which the Punic inhabitants of the island knew their country of residence.

Drawings from Louis de Boisgelin's Ancient and Modern Malta *(1804) of three different types of bronze coins minted in Malta in the early Roman period, all with the legend '*nn*. Top: veiled head of goddess; three Egyptian divinities. Bottom left: veiled head of goddess; ram's head. Bottom right: bearded head of god; flamen's cap.*

The Material Remains

Although we have reason to believe that at this time the two principal Phoenician settlements, one for each island, had been consolidated further, our presumption is based on the much greater frequency of tombs recorded around them since no structures datable specifically to this period have been so far identified.

Nathaniel Cutajar, the curator of archaeology in charge of archaeological rescue operations, laments the 'apparent absence of Punic (fifth to third century BC) strata at Mdina'; but further on, in his account of recent archaeological discoveries made in Mdina under his direction, he remarks that at Mesquita Square 'the Phoenician remains were replaced and cut into by a massive Punic ashlar wall, possibly - given its topographical positioning - a turreted structure belonging to some type of fortified enclosure'. He also observes that more plentiful Punic remains have been reported in Rabat, outside Mdina; this is taken to mean that the domestic quarters might have already been shifted to the lower town outside Mdina, with the latter assuming more and more the role of an acropolis. This anticipates by a few centuries a similar suggestion I made with regard to Mdina constituting the city's acropolis in the Roman period, even though I did not envisage the exclusion of domestic quarters from it.

Whether this single structural presence in Mdina, fortuitous or otherwise, can be construed to support a purely conjectural existence at this stage of a Punic sanctuary with a fortified *temenos* in the area, even more specifically, one dedicated to Melqart or Baal Hammon, is highly debatable. While such a possibility cannot be ruled out, it would be most unwise to consider it as more than an attractive hypothesis, unsupported by hard evidence.

The deep and wide ditch artificially cut on the west side of the Rabat-Mdina promontory is probably the only visible remnant of the town fortification system of this phase. It is known as the 'Roman ditch' but, like the round towers in the countryside (which will be dealt with further on), it does not really fall within the typical Roman fortification pattern and, what is even more significant, it would make much more sense as a defence necessity in the troubled times of the Graeco-Carthaginian and, later, the Romano-Carthaginian wars, than after the establishment of the *pax Romana* throughout the Inner Sea.

Part of the ancient ditch which was probably cut in the Punic age to reinforce the fortifications of the city of Melite. Some of the adjacent fortifications were still visible at the time of Gian Francesco Abela in the 17th century. The church of St Paul was built partly inside the ditch.

The most important surviving architectural remains of this phase are those belonging to the sanctuary of Tas-Silġ. Here the sanctuary continued to expand with additional structures within an extensive *temenos* which gave it more and more the semblance of a fortified sanctuary. From the fourth century onwards, the sanctuary was further monumentalized and enhanced with architectural features of Hellenistic influence. These probably included Egyptianizing features like those one meets in several North African cities that had been occupied by the western Phoenicians. The evidence

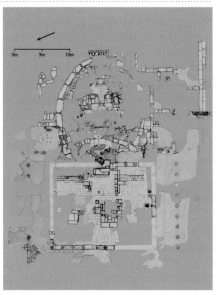

Plan of the Tas-Silġ sanctuary of Ashtart at the height of its development during the Hellenistic age (4th-1st century BC). Sections of the rectangular temenos *(boundary wall) are preserved, as well as the foundations of the four-sided porticoed courtyard in front of the older Phoenician temple.*

Profiles of different cavetto cornices from various buildings and monuments in the Levant, Egypt, and North Africa, compared to that of the Żurrieq 'tower' (far bottom right).

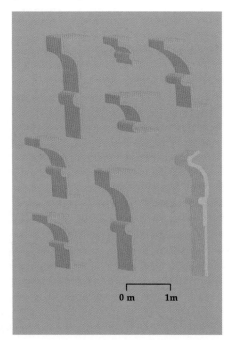

for them comes from several architectural fragments, including sections of a single cavetto cornice and a square pilaster capital with a double cavetto gorge, as well as fragments of a frieze with Egyptian *uraei*.

Another set of architectural remains are those of a partially rock-cut, partly built, religious complex perched most suggestively right on the edge of precipitous cliffs at Ras Il-Wardija on the northwest coast of Gozo. This other extra-urban sanctuary seems to have had a rather short life-span of a couple of centuries, between the third and first centuries BC, when Punic Malta, like the

Aerial view (1974) of the partly rock-cut and partly terraced sanctuary of Ras il-Wardija in Gozo. The sanctuary lies on the edge of a precipitous cliff falling sharply into the sea.

rest of the Punic world was under the pervasive cultural influence of Hellenism, very much like the influence exerted by American culture on practically the whole world today. Unfortunately, the scanty remains of material culture retrieved during the excavations, in particular the absence of epigraphic material, have not made it possible to identify the divinity to which the sanctuary was dedicated. Nevertheless, a hypothetical association of a part of this sanctuary with sacred prostitution, has been proposed, similar to those documented for the temples of Ashtart in Kition, Cyprus and in Eryx, Sicily. This view is far too conjectural and has been contested by other scholars. Whichever deity was venerated here, the location of the sanctuary suggests that it was connected with the sea.

THE SO-CALLED SIGN OF TANIT

A symbol in the shape of a cross engraved on the façade of one of the niches decorating the deep rock-cut chamber of the Ras il-Wardija sanctuary. Though not exactly similar, the symbol has been interpreted by some as the 'sign of Tanit' (left), a symbol commonly found in religious contexts in the Punic world, such as Motya and Carthage. Regrettably, the engraving was detached by unknown individuals sometime in the late 1980s.

The building itself could well have been a landmark for sailors plying the seas in the area.

The most outstanding surviving structure of the Punic period is, however, the curious square building enclosed inside a private garden in Żurrieq. It consists of a single room and stands about five metres high preserving a crowning cornice of Egyptian inspiration, the so-called 'cavetto cornice'. It could well have belonged to a religious building. Some even think it could have been part of the sanctuary of Heracles mentioned by the geographer Ptolemy in the second century AD, along with that of Hera. Much of the rest of the complex survived in relatively good shape in the late eighteenth century when Jean Houel, a French artist from the court of Louis XVI of France, saw it and published a plan and elevation of it all, describing it as a 'Greek house'. This part has unfortunately been destroyed. Excavations were effected inside and outside it on several occasions, without producing any valuable additional information.

The Maltese country landscape must have been dotted here and there with the occasional country house. No such explicitly Punic house has ever been excavated and recorded. But the fact that virtually

The so-called Punic 'tower' in Żurrieq. Originally forming part of a much more extensive building, it now stands on its own, incorporated within the garden walls of the house of the parish priest. Note the dimensions and perfect fit of its ashlar stones, much larger than the modern ones.

every time a Roman country house (better known as 'villa') was archaeologically excavated it was found to have earlier underlying structures, often accompanied by the presence of Punic pottery, suggests that these Roman villas had been preceded by Punic ones. Such is the case with the villa at Ta' Kaċċatura, near Birżebbuġa, that of Żejtun, and that of San Pawl Milqi, the largest of them all. It also appears that the olive-pressing apparatus used in Malta's Roman villas was of Punic typology.

Round Towers

Another enigma of Maltese archaeology are the so-called 'Roman towers'. They consist of five or six cylindrical towers distributed without any apparent pattern in the countryside: four in the south-east of Malta (Ta' Gawhar, Ta' Wilġa, Tal-Bakkari, and It-Torrijiet), one in the north (Ta' Ċieda) and a dubious one in the north-west (Tas-Santi). The one identified by David Trump at Għajn Klieb has been found to be a threshing floor. Only the Ta' Gawhar, Ta' Cieda, and Ta' Wilġa ones have been investigated; the three of them have a rectangular cistern attached to them, just outside the structure.

As elements of defence these round towers, like the defence system of ancient Melite, would not make much sense to be built in the Roman period. As the whole Mediterranean was under Roman control, there was absolutely no

The Ta' Wilġa tower, one of the better preserved of the round towers. Built of large ashlar stone blocks, probably back in the Punic period, these free-standing towers have no parallel in the ancient world.

Tombs

Punic tombs continue the old Phoenician tradition of underground chambers reached by means of vertical shafts. According to a very simplified classification set out at the beginning of the twentieth century by Paul K. Bellanti, followed by Temi Zammit, the original floor plan of the Phoenician tomb, which consisted of a round or oval chamber and a round shaft, is replaced in the early Punic phase by one consisting of a round chamber and rectangular shaft. In the second (or Hellenized) Punic phase and overlapping onto the Roman period, the chamber too becomes rectangular in plan and rooms are placed on several sides of the shaft. This simplified classification has been further elaborated by Claudia Sagona into ten categories which, however, do not all follow each other in chronological order.

need for such an erratic system of defensive towers. An earlier, Punic, date is also suggested by the archaeological stratification of the investigated towers: the Ta' Ċieda, Ta' Wilġa, and Ta' Ġawhar ones. This is further confirmed by their ashlar construction technique which is quite typical of Punic buildings of this late date. Even then, their distribution pattern does not seem to make much logical sense as part of a defence system. An alternative function has, in fact, been proposed for them, namely, that of a system of watch towers intended to guard over the olive estates gravitating around the ancient villas.

The problem with this hypothesis is that very few of the known villas are in the vicinity of these towers, and several towers have no villa remains within sight.

In the majority of cases these underground spaces were hewn in the living rock to accommodate interments, that is, the primary deposition of the corpse, which was laid on a smooth platform on one side of a shallow trench which at first was positioned transversally along the entrance to the burial chamber, later at right angles to it. This trench was intended either for the insertion of pottery items, like amphorae, at the time of burial or, more probably, to take up the rain water which in the rainy seasons managed to penetrate the burial chamber through the sealing slab; or for both purposes.

This does not mean that the other mortuary ritual, cremation, was not practised. On the contrary, it now became statistically increasingly more common; but in this ritual the cremated human remains were placed in special ceramic urns which were introduced in pre-existing chamber tombs without disturbing the previous tomb contents. Occasionally, though, a special type of tomb was hewn out in the same fashion in the rock, this time consisting of a very small square space, similarly accessible by a narrow shaft from the surface. A typical example was discovered in St Catherine Street, Żejtun in 1912.

During this period, underground tombs become increasingly more abundant, testifying to a steady growth of the population, as well as its distribution over most of the islands. We find large concentrations in the immediate vicinity of

Rabat, some just outside the defensive ditch. Some examples are Ħal Bajjada (10 tombs), New Street (27 tombs), Tac-Ċagħqi (almost 50 tombs); Ta' Marcell (40 tombs), Ferris Street (39 tombs), not to mention those further away, such as Tal-Virtù, Nigred, Mtarfa, and Qallilija.

One cannot fail to be struck, in this respect, by the relatively much smaller number of such tombs discovered in Gozo than in Malta - not more than 13 recorded items, mostly in the St Francis Square zone of Rabat, and some datable to other periods. This might be taken to suggest a slower demographic growth in the sister island.

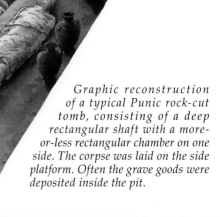

Graphic reconstruction of a typical Punic rock-cut tomb, consisting of a deep rectangular shaft with a more-or-less rectangular chamber on one side. The corpse was laid on the side platform. Often the grave goods were deposited inside the pit.

Material Culture

The material culture of this period, notably pottery, is also comparatively very abundant, probably in direct proportion to the greater number of tombs, since these, being underground, provide the ideal ambiance for the preservation of fragile archaeological objects. On the other hand, compared to other parts of the Punic world, such as Tharros, in Sardinia, the Maltese Punic tombs stand out for their relative poverty in terms of precious objects. Core-wound banded glass

vessels, figurines, engraved ivory, faience, glass and other beads, and ostrich egg shell products are not absent, but they are not as abundant as expected. This poverty of material culture had already been observed by Temi Zammit in his general historical account of Malta. Though tomb-robbing was unchecked up to the end of the nineteenth century, the absence of the *tombaroli* (organized tomb-robbing) phenomenon in Maltese lore in the twentieth century might also be indicative of this. Tombs are not rich enough in 'treasure' to provoke an illegal tomb-robbing industry. Zammit's observation has been found still valid three-quarters of a century later.

This situation is reflected to a certain extent at Tas-Silġ where very little prestige material was

Fragment of a miniature ointment jar made of core-wound glass (faience). From the 1960s excavations at Tas-Silġ. Two whole alabastra of the same material are illustrated on p.26.

Many fragments of gold foil found during the excavations of Tas-Silġ in the 1960s. A small gilt terracotta pendant found in the recent University of Malta excavations at Tas-Silġ (not to scale).

retrieved during the excavations inside the premises themselves and, similarly, few items found their way into the dumps that are in the process of being excavated outside them. Gold and silver are conspicuous by their absence. The only gold items found there so far are fragments of gold foil. Of particular significance is the gilt terracotta pendant found in the latter dumps. It clearly shows that the original donor of the trinket could not afford a solid gold one and made an offering of a gilt one. This contrasts in a way with the picture of relative prosperity given by the written sources, mostly Diodorus and, with more specific reference to the sanctuary of Tas-Silġ, Cicero.

All the above can be interpreted to mean that, unlike other cultures elsewhere, especially those of the Greek cities in nearby Sicily, the Punic inhabitants of Malta did not put much value in what might have been considered a 'wasteful' ritual of depositing precious stuff in tombs and sanctuaries, and accumulated wealth was preferably passed on to descendants. Whichever way we look at it, such an attitude does not really reflect a particularly affluent society, unless, of course, their riches were of a perishable nature, like purple-dyed textiles, perfumes, and ointments and, therefore, might not have survived in the archaeological record.

Coins

For reasons that will be explained in the following chapter, although we have a whole series of 'Punic' coins minted in Malta, these were all struck within the Roman period. Up to 218 BC the only coins that circulated in Malta were ones originating in Carthage and a few coin-minting Punic colonies of the west, particularly Sicily. A few came from the Greek Hellenistic world, again mostly from Greek Sicily. A fair number of these coins were found during the excavations of the Tas-Silġ sanctuary; some came from 'villa' sites (which confirms the existence of previous buildings on these sites); occasionally also from tombs. These coins shed light on the state of the economy and trading relations of the Maltese islands during the Punic phase.

Malta has produced two important hoards of Punic coins of this period, one from Mqabba and the other of unknown provenance.

The coins of the Mqabba hoard date to within the second half of the fourth century BC, more precisely the period of Timoleon in Sicily around 344 BC. They were discovered accidentally in 1921 in a field near Mqabba (see box). The hoard consisted of 267 bronze coins of the Punic typology. The numerical distribution of the different types within the hoard is quite representative of the frequency of similar coins circulating generally in Malta in the same period.

The hoard of unknown provenance is said to have been found in Malta in mysterious circumstances before 1938, the year in which it was donated to Yale University by

THE MQABBA COIN HOARD

One of the major hoards of Punic coins from Malta was found accidentally by a farmer on 26 July 1921. While removing a heap of stones from his field somewhere north of Mqabba, the farmer found a jar full of bronze coins. Temi Zammit, then curator of the Valletta Museum, inspected the find.

The jar had been broken, but a reconstruction of it was made from the surviving fragments. Of the 300 coins claimed to have been found by the farmer only 255 were delivered to Zammit who published a brief note about them in The Antiquaries Journal of 1923. An exhaustive and fully-illustrated study of the

hoard, now numbering 267 coins, was published by G.J. Jenkins in the Rivista di Studi Fenici of 1983. The coins were in good shape. Most of them showed the head of Kore (Persephone) crowned with ears of wheat on the obverse, and a galloping horse on the reverse.

Obverse: head of Tanit facing left   Reverse: head of a horse and Punic letters

Obverse: head of Tanit facing left   Reverse: horse standing right, head facing left

Obverse: head of Tanit facing left   Reverse: horse standing right, palm tree in background

The characteristic iconography on Carthaginian coins consisted of the head of the goddess Tanit on the obverse of the coin; on the reverse, the horse and the palm tree.

The underside of a small complete clay plate from the University of Malta excavation at Tas-Silġ. Several of these plates were marked with incised letters or symbols.

Pottery

Pottery is, as it is to be expected, the most abundant material. Despite the problems inherent in the chronology of Punic pottery it still provides a very useful tool for the archaeologist to date the context in which it is found, and to draw a range of other conclusions, such as the evolution of styles, the trade contacts and movement of commodities between one area and another, as well as social stratification.

Finally, the immense corpus of pottery brought to light from tombs discovered over the last century, and even before, has been extensively and carefully studied by Claudia Sagona to produce a logical sequence of shapes and types. This classification has in turn made it possible to date the tombs in which the pottery was found and to produce a more reliable sequential classification of tomb shapes. The same pottery sequence is now being used to help to sort out in a similar way the pottery shapes from other contexts, such as those from the archaeological strata encountered during the excavations of the sanctuary of Tas-Silġ, even though these are to a great extent different from them.

H. Dunscomb Colt. Until its full publication by P. Visonà in 1990, it received little attention. The hoard, of more than 550 coins, must have been buried in the first quarter of the third century, most probably between 280 and 270 BC, the decade that witnessed the war of Pyrrhus in Italy and the rise to power of Hieron II of Syracuse.

Both hoards, like the rest of the contemporary archaeological record of Malta, suggest that during this period the island was solidly entrenched within the Carthaginian political and economic sphere. Their composition also reflects the importance of Malta's strategic location between North Africa and Carthage's main overseas markets, mainly those of southern Sicily.

Opposite page:
Some of the more prevalent shapes of pottery of this period. Along the more traditional shapes, one notices the introduction of new shapes, like the partly-covered lamp (37) and the askoi (15-16). Not to scale.
(After Sagona 2002)

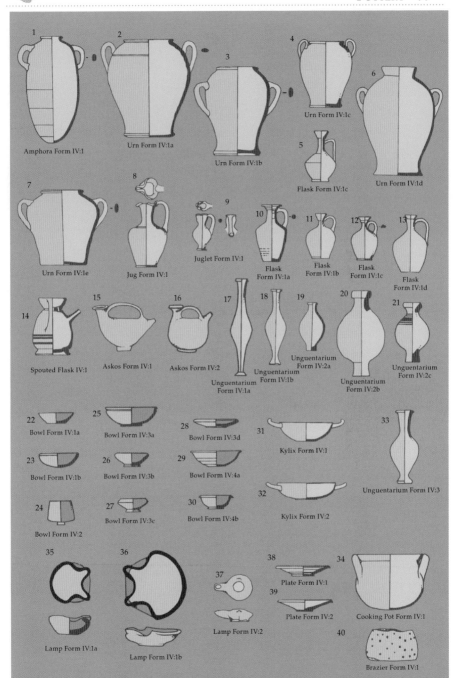

1 Amphora Form IV:1

2 Urn Form IV:1a

3 Urn Form IV:1b

4 Urn Form IV:1c

5 Flask Form IV:1c

6 Urn Form IV:1d

7 Urn Form IV:1e

8 Jug Form IV:1

9 Juglet Form IV:1

10 Flask Form IV:1a

11 Flask Form IV:1b

12 Flask Form IV:1c

13 Flask Form IV:1d

14 Spouted Flask IV:1

15 Askos Form IV:1

16 Askos Form IV:2

17 Unguentarium Form IV:1a

18 Unguentarium Form IV:1b

19 Unguentarium Form IV:2a

20 Unguentarium Form IV:2b

21 Unguentarium Form IV:2c

22 Bowl Form IV:1a

23 Bowl Form IV:1b

24 Bowl Form IV:2

25 Bowl Form IV:3a

26 Bowl Form IV:3b

27 Bowl Form IV:3c

28 Bowl Form IV:3d

29 Bowl Form IV:4a

30 Bowl Form IV:4b

31 Kylix Form IV:1

32 Kylix Form IV:2

33 Unguentarium Form IV:3

34 Cooking Pot Form IV:1

35 Lamp Form IV:1a

36 Lamp Form IV:1b

37 Lamp Form IV:2

38 Plate Form IV:1

39 Plate Form IV:2

40 Brazier Form IV:1

A selection of pottery shapes typical of the Punic period. The most characteristic are: the cinerary urn (top left), the bilychne oil lamp (top row second), and the feeding bottle (bottom row second). The jug with a trefoil mouth (top row fourth) is probably a Greek black-glazed import, and the spherical jug with trefoil mouth (bottom right) is a local imitation of it. (Pots not to scale with one another).

Political and Social Structure

The political situation beyond the islands has been briefly summarized in the introductory paragraphs of this chapter. The instability of the times and the continuous warfare activity between the three powers could not have left the islands unaffected. At face value, one would say inevitably for the worse; but given the opportunistic penchant of the now predominantly Levantine population, it is not inconceivable that, in spite of the odds, the inhabitants managed to eke out a reasonably prosperous economy based on agricultural, industrial, and commercial activity. This is what seems to be implied by Diodorus Siculus' comment that 'the inhabitants of this island, since they received assistance in many

A selection of fine Greek painted pottery imported from Attica. They are claimed to have been discovered in Rabat in the late 19th century, though some of them seem to be illustrated already in Jean Houel's Voyage Pittoresque *in 1878 (p.77).*

aspects through the sea-merchants, shot up quickly in their manner of living and increased in renown'.

This does not mean that the Maltese inhabitants were exempt from taxes. We know from Cicero (*Verr.* II, 3, 12-13) that Carthage exacted tribute both from the Greek cities of Sicily and from those of Sicanian, Elymian, and Punic origin that fell under its control. In the case of the latter cities, it consisted of a tithe of the annual harvest. It is most likely that Malta paid the same tribute to Carthage.

While official foreign policy must have been dictated by Carthage and any available military and port facilities were, on her instructions, negated to the enemy, there must have been a certain amount of free play in trading operations, as revealed by the archaeological record. This is testified mostly by the occasional presence of coins originating in Greek Sicily and other Hellenistic centres further afield, apart from the expected ones from Carthage itself and other Punic centres of the west, such as those contained in the two coin hoards mentioned above (p.96). Further proof of this comes from the presence of a fair amount of Greek pottery, mostly fine, black-glazed table ware, and other luxury items. We now notice much stronger trading ties with Magna Graecia. Malta, in fact, assumes a role of an important trading link on the commercial route between southern Italy and Tripolitania.

There must also have been a high degree of helplessness in front of large naval expeditions. This is made blatantly obvious by the written texts relating to the only two recorded episodes, first when the Roman navy raided Malta during the First Punic War, and then when the island gave itself up to the Roman invader, at the outset of the Second Punic War, in spite of the presence of a substantial Punic garrison of about 2,000 soldiers. The latter episode forces us to conclude that the defensive rating of the island was very low indeed and that the Carthaginians never really bothered even to try to make the island capable of resisting long sieges. The island fortifications must have been very weak, probably compounded by the distance between the harbours and the main urban centres. The rapidity by which the two operations were concluded confirms this.

We have no written documentation relating to the social and political organization of the Punic population in Malta. The Greek inscription on a bronze tablet, which in the past has been proposed as evidence of such organization at the very end of this period or the very beginning of the following one, is now being assigned, on the basis of historical evidence, to the first century BC (see chapter 5). In spite of the absence of any related evidence, it is quite legitimate to assume that Malta had a similar political organization to that of its sister island.

We are, ironically, much better informed on Gozo. The marble Punic inscription described above, datable to the end of this period, shows that by then the population of Gozo must have been organized around a properly-governed urban centre. The island was governed by a political system involving a representative body of the citizens ('the people of Gaulos'), and a senatorial body from which came the two highest magistrates, or governors (*rab*). These were probably eponymous, that is, their name determined the date of the year. The duality of these chief magistrates, called *rab*, is considered by many to be another sign of the Punic character of the political organisation of Gozo, possibly equivalent to the two *suffete* in the Carthaginian constitution.

One important question that comes up in any discussion of the social set-up of the Maltese population in the Punic period is whether one could detect any lingering distinction between natives and colonizers. Although there is no clear-cut evidence in this respect, if I were forced to answer that question, I would say 'no'. Even by the fifth century, possibly earlier, the native population must have been entirely absorbed, both culturally and physically, by the Punic one. There is not a single archaeological feature, not one single tomb that could in any way be identified as evidence of a surviving social group, distinct from the Punic superstructure.

Another important question regarding the same subject is whether Punic society in Malta was slave-based. Although we know that Carthaginian society was so, it is most unlikely that the Maltese one, being so relatively small, depended on slavery. There is no evidence for such a social class either in the written sources or in the archaeological record. The only major public works that suggest the possibility of

One illustration from Jean Houel's Voyage Pittoresque *showing a long wall of large ashlar blocks, some parts of it preserved up to four courses high. Since the accompanying caption describes the site as near Marsaxlokk, it probably illustrates the remains of Tas-Silġ. Alternatively, it might depict the ashlar wall at Safi.*

Obverse of a bronze coin minted in Malta showing a female head with a long, wig-like hairstyle that is normally worn by the Egyptian goddess Isis. On the left is an ear of wheat, possibly a reference to wheat growing as part of the island's economy. On the right is the legend ΜΕΛΙΤΑΙΩΝ.

the presence of slavery are the Rabat defensive ditch and the Tas-Silġ sanctuary. In the latter case, this is suggested by the sheer size of the building blocks used and the monumentality of the building. On the other hand, we already know how, on the very Maltese soil, a limited prehistoric population achieved great feats of architecture, employing immensely large building blocks, without resorting to slave coercion. This does not exclude the possibility, however, that individual families employed slave, or hired, help for domestic and agricultural purposes. Imported, foreign slavery is nowhere apparent in either the historical or the archaeological record.

Economy and Commerce

Although the western Phoenicians, like their eastern ancestors, are known to us, as they were known to their adversaries, almost exclusively as intrepid mariners and sea merchants, they were also accomplished farmers. Both in their homeland and in the west they practised professionally and successfully both agriculture and animal husbandry. A classic textbook in antiquity was the treatise on agriculture by Mago, a third-century BC Carthaginian writer. Its 28 books survived the destruction of Carthage in 146 BC and the Roman senate had it translated into Latin (Pliny *N.H.* xviii. 22).

Whenever the geography of their colonies permitted, the western Phoenicians turned the hinterland into productive agricultural land. The *chora* of Carthage is a classic case. They cultivated cereals (mainly wheat and barley) and flax for linen, but also olives and vines for the production of olive oil and wine, as well as figs and, in the right climatic conditions, date palms.

Given the geomorphology of the Maltese islands, irrigation farming was mostly restricted to the land nearest the perennial springs, that is on the fringes of the coralline capping mass covering the underlying clay layer, and to the valley sides in the rest of the islands. The remaining parts of the islands could only

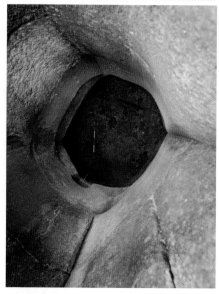

The opening of a cistern on the north side of the Tas-Silġ sanctuary. The cistern is rock-cut with a circular plan tapering inwards toward the top.

The plan of an old tank found at Marsa during the excavations for the erection of the tramway power station in June 1904.

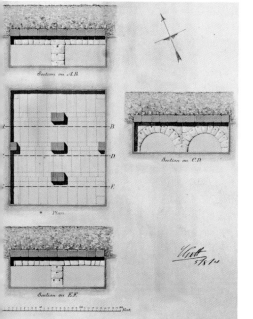

be exploited for dry farming and for pastoralism. Some of this land could be cultivated by farming families living within the urban settlements, but the distribution of tombs and the remains of isolated country residences referred to above are indicative of small farming communities scattered throughout the countryside. As for the main towns, given their situation on high ground, both of them no doubt dominated the agricultural land beneath them, at least within a radius of a few kilometres.

The Tas-Silġ site has also revealed that the Maltese inhabitants of this period had developed the right technology to dig well shafts up to 10m deep, possibly more, to access deep water tables. At Tas-Silġ at least two

Ancient Cisterns

Ancient cisterns are basically of two shapes: bottle-shaped or cuboid. Both are hewn out of the bedrock, at least partially. The first type is simpler in shape and technology: being circular in plan, the walls taper inwards toward the top, thus leaving a very small opening at the surface. The shape can be said to be a larger version of the Bronze Age 'silo-pits'. The most securely dated cistern of this type is the one discovered during the 1983-84 excavations in the square in front of the Domus Romana in Rabat. A cone-shaped heap of pottery sherds deposited on the bottom directly beneath the opening suggested that the cistern stopped being used and was sealed towards the end of the Hellenistic age (1st century BC).

The second type was more spacious and sophisticated. It was square or rectangular in floor plan. As the walls rose vertically without tapering inwards a roof was necessary. The latter consisted of rows of huge horizontal slabs of stone (up to 2m long) supported either by horizontal arches, or by thick stone beams which in turn were propped up by hefty vertical pillars set up at regular intervals. The most daring example of the latter system is the huge cistern attached to the Roman villa at ta' Kaccatura, near Birżebbuġa; the former system (with horizontal arches) is exemplified by several cisterns, like the one situated near the now destroyed villa at l-Iklin, and the still visible one at San Ġwann. Other cisterns of the rectangular type have been recorded at Tal-Hlas and Il-Brolli.

Both types of cisterns were internally lined with a cement-like mortar formed of finely-crushed pottery and lime or hydraulic cement, the latter probably imported from Campania, Italy.

OLD CISTERN AT "TAL HLAS

Scale 1/160

Section on AB

Section on CD

A

C

I

B

Plan

AD

Below: The huge water cistern accompanying the villa at Ta' Kaccatura.

One of several systems of shallow pans in the Mġarr ix-Xini valley, Gozo. It consists of a large rectangular depression, c.30 cm deep. A smaller and shallower rectangular depression on a slightly higher level is connected to one of its sides by means of a small hole.

such wells are present, one on the north side, the other on the south side. This might well mean that whenever such wells were previously attributed to the Roman period, the archaeological context may suggest that these had been perforated already in the Punic period. The same applies to the large cisterns frequently encountered in the grounds of Roman villas. Some of these are impressive for their size and the technology of their roofing systems (see box). Whenever such villas were built over pre-existing country buildings, the chances are that these cisterns had been built in the previous age. Neither the deep wells, however, nor the large cisterns stored enough water for extensive farming; they were probably only sufficient to serve domestic water needs, at most small garden crop cultivation, during the dry months. Some of the stored water was also needed in the processing of olive oil.

Agricultural production was most probably subjected to the tithe system of taxation imposed by Carthage on its subject cities in Sicily. We do not have any reason to believe that Malta was spared this tax.

The Phoenicians were also renowned for two types of industry connected with the sea: *garum* production and purple dyeing. Both involved the use of specially constructed basins, square or rectangular in shape. Such systems of basins are met with in, or near, almost all the coastal Punic colonies in the western Mediterranean, especially in North Africa. The ones on the slopes of the ancient town of Lixus in Morocco are probably the best known examples, though similar ones have been identified within the urban network of Leptis Magna. It is, therefore, quite strange that they have not been encountered in Malta, though there is the possibility that a large group of bottle-shaped pits, albeit of Bronze Age 'silo' typology and circular in shape, located on the sea-shore near Birżebbuġa, were used for dyeing at this age, if not earlier. The existence of the textile industry in Malta is amply documented by the ancient writers both for the Roman and, by logical extension, to the Punic period but we do not know whether it was limited to weaving or whether it involved also the cultivation of the raw material and the dyeing process.

Dyeing brings also to mind a number of strange shallow pans grouped together in an area south of Xewkija, Gozo. They are hewn out in the hard rock surface close to the edges of a deep, canyon-like, valley flowing into Mġarr ix-Xini. The main basin is normally rectangular in shape but it is accompanied by smaller, shallower round basins of different sizes connected to it by perforated holes. A single specimen has also been identified close

to the Misqa Tanks, above Mnajdra. Both their purpose and their age are difficult to establish, but it is very tempting to associate them with either linen retting, and/or cloth dyeing. If this was their real purpose, in which period would they fit better than this one?

Another missing element as evidence for the dyeing industry is the 'mountains' of murex shells one finds elsewhere. This absence could be explained by the intensive occupation and use of the coast in the Maltese islands, which tends to result in a clean sweep of any such material from their shores; on the other hand, single murex shells are frequently encountered in Punic strata in the current University of Malta excavations at Tas-Silġ.

Two examples of murex shells whose flesh was processed to extract the purple dye for clothing for which the Phoenicians, both of the west and of the motherland, were renowned.

One of two burial chambers on either side of a tomb shaft found at Gwardamanġja in 1960. Among the tomb furniture one notices a long Punic amphora and a cinerary urn of the typical Maltese type.

We know that the passion for trade flowed in the very blood vessels of the Phoenicians, and they are not likely to have given up that passion for landlubberly agriculture after settling down in Malta. To pursue with their trading activity, their successors could continue with their middlemen role, exchanging exotic goods produced by others, but that was not to the exclusion of locally-produced commodities. For once, we know from written literature of at least one product they exported, fine textiles that by the first century BC had assumed an international reputation for their sheer quality (Diodorus, V, 12). We have good reasons to believe that they also produced oil and, possibly, wine, but we do not know whether they did so in sufficient quantities

to afford exporting them. One type of egg-shaped amphora is said to be of Maltese origin and could have been the medium for transport for such products. Examples of it have been retrieved from the necropolis of Carthage and that of Lilybaeum and one from Ibiza. But one has to identify and quantify any typically Maltese oil amphorae discovered abroad to be able to verify this. We look forward to this piece of research being undertaken in the very near future.

There is, on the other hand, a certain class of rather fine pottery that is reputed to be of 'Maltese' production, namely, small elongated amphorae and other shapes with brownish-red bands on a light cream slip. These are found in other parts of the central and western Mediterranean, even in Carthage, and have been explained as possible exports from Malta. Quantities of a similar style of pottery have also been found on Ibiza, but they have been assigned to an indigenous production of that island; both productions could, therefore, be separate expressions of the same ceramic fashion.

Finally, a type of small jar which in the Maltese context is normally found in tombs containing cremated human remains has been classified as Maltese. It has a very limited circulation, one was fished out of the sea off the south coast of Sardinia; one came from the necropolis of Lilybaeum and another one kept in the museum of Motya probably from the same necropolis; while a final one came from a tomb in Leptis Magna.

Mention has already been made of the Etruscan involvement in the central Mediterranean in the period immediately preceding and in that following the beginning of the fifth century BC. Although no reference to this involvement in Maltese affairs has survived in the written sources, there are a handful of items that show, at least, that their products reached the Maltese islands. The Etruscans' most characteristic ceramic product is the black *bucchero* ware, a fine quality table ware characterized by its entirely black fabric, from core to surface, as well as its individual shapes. Fragments, albeit no whole pots, of these have occasionally turned up in Maltese archaeological deposits, including the excavations currently conducted by the University of Malta on the site of Tas-Silġ. Were these the surviving remnants of pots given as votive offerings by visiting Etruscan mariners to their divine protectress to secure a safe journey home, or simply highly appreciated objects of trade exchange that might have changed hands several times before ending up as an offering in this international

Below: Small amphorae with brown-red bands on a light cream slip thought to be of local Maltese production, even though similar shapes and decoration occur also in Ibiza, one of the Balearic islands.

Left: A strange pot with an external 'pouch' and handles decorated with heads of Bes in relief.

Bottom: Two small amphorae with red bands on light cream slip, thought to be of local production.

sanctuary? Only more similar, or more intact, finds will tell.

An even earlier object of Etruscan pedigree was unearthed during the unprofessionally conducted excavations at Ras ir-Raħeb in 1962: a small ivory rectangular tablet showing a boar carved in relief on one side. This object has been identified as Etruscan by no lesser an authority in Etruscan affairs than Massimo Pallottino, and assigned to a group of ivories dated to around 500 BC by Martina Martelli. What is odd is that it was found in a structural context which is made to fall by the rest of the archaeological

material towards the end of the period being discussed in this chapter. It could well be another example of heirlooms, objects of 'antiquity' of which the Phoenicians and their Punic successors are known to be very fond - see, for example, the ancient Egyptian objects found in a much later necropolis at Almuñécar in southern Spain.

During his long study visit to Malta in 1970, the late William Culican researched extensively on Maltese Phoenician and Punic antiquities. We are told that in 1977 the above ivory plaque was due to be published by him. I also remember him handling a group of rectangular ivory plaques from a private collection, each about 10 cm in height and representing a male figure. The style of the figures was quite unusual, one which did not fit in either Classical or Oriental art. Professor Culican was inclined to attribute them to Etruscan workmanship. It is a real pity he never published the plaques, and I hope they will re-surface one day.

A small ivory tablet, probably a plaque to be attached to a piece of furniture, found during the excavations of Ras ir-Raħeb in 1962. It shows a recumbent boar within a rectangular frame. Experts on Etruscology have dated it to the late 6th century BC and attributed to it an Etruscan origin. Prima facie, the dating does not fit well with the traditional dating of the Ras ir-Raħeb remains.

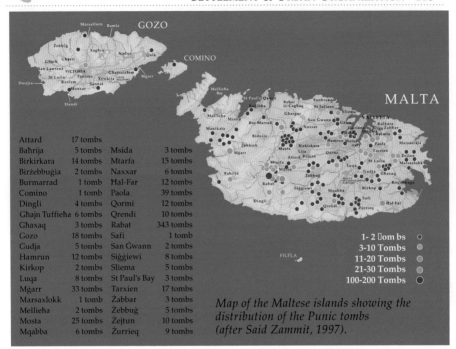

Attard	17 tombs		
Baħrija	5 tombs	Msida	3 tombs
Birkirkara	14 tombs	Mtarfa	15 tombs
Birżebbuġia	2 tombs	Naxxar	6 tombs
Burmarrad	1 tomb	Ħal-Far	12 tombs
Comino	1 tomb	Paola	39 tombs
Dingli	4 tombs	Qormi	12 tombs
Għajn Tuffieħa	6 tombs	Qrendi	10 tombs
Ghaxaq	3 tombs	Rabat	343 tombs
Gozo	18 tombs	Safi	1 tomb
Gudja	5 tombs	San Ġwann	2 tombs
Hamrun	12 tombs	Siġġiewi	8 tombs
Kirkop	2 tombs	Sliema	5 tombs
Luqa	8 tombs	St Paul's Bay	3 tombs
Mġarr	33 tombs	Tarxien	17 tombs
Marsaxlokk	1 tomb	Żabbar	3 tombs
Mellieħa	2 tombs	Żebbuġ	5 tombs
Mosta	25 tombs	Żejtun	10 tombs
Mqabba	6 tombs	Żurrieq	9 tombs

Map of the Maltese islands showing the distribution of the Punic tombs (after Said Zammit, 1997).

Settlement Organization

The increasing number of tombs datable to this period dotting the area around Rabat, outside the rock-cut ditch discussed above, as well as the ditch itself, are a good indication that the size of ancient Melite had already extended this far on the Mdina/Rabat promontory. This implies a considerable demographic growth. Indeed, the tombs are no longer found in single units, as in the previous period, but clustered in minor necropoleis (such as those of Għajn Klieb and Qallilija) and major ones (like that of Tac-Ċagħqi). Titus Livius' account of the Roman invasion in 218 BC also implies that by then this urban centre had become an *oppidum*, which normally means

'a fortified town'. We may safely assume that the 2000-odd soldiers forming the Punic garrison mentioned by Livy were stationed inside the *oppidum*, thus straining further the limited food resources produced by the local agricultural economy. No wonder the island succumbed and capitulated without resistance.

Population estimates based on the distribution of tombs have revealed that by the end of the Punic period, probably much earlier, another major nucleated centre had taken shape on the island of Malta, that at the very inner end of the Grand Harbour. A similar one appears to have emerged at Rabat, Gozo. The Punic tombs found in the immediate surroundings of

Rabat (Victoria) point to the most likely topographical feature, the Citadella rock and the area immediately around it as the site for the emerging main town of Gozo, even though this does not correspond to the typical classical location of early Phoenician colonies, that is, small islands or promontories providing sheltered harbours at the same time.

Isolated farmsteads must have dotted the Maltese countryside. In some places they precede the later Roman villas that were built over them. Their existence is often suggested by the presence of tombs dated to this phase. Antonia Ciasca states that the Punic predecessor of the large villa of San Pawl Milqi had its own private cemetery, as suggested by some tombs and a Punic inscription.

Aerial view of the inner harbour of Marsaxlokk with a peculiar rectangular artificial basin. There are no records as to when this feature was built and there are suspicions it might date back to the Phoenician period since it looks very much like the 'cothon', or enclosed small harbour, on the island of Motya.

Ports and Harbours

For Malta we have already observed that Marsaxlokk must have established itself as the main harbour in early Phoenician times. This position was further strengthened in the Punic period, when the extra-urban sanctuary of Tas-Silġ, dedicated to the divine protectress of mariners, was increasingly enlarged and monumentalized. Excavations inside and outside the main building have shown that an intensive ritual activity must have taken place involving sacrificial offerings of both marine and terrestrial creatures, as well as the offering of objects of overseas origin, such as items of fine black-glaze ware originating in Greece or in the Greek production centres of southern Italy. A number of small *lekythoi* of this ware could have been offered more for their contents, like perfumed oils, than for their own sake.

What is still apparently missing in this respect is evidence for harbour activity in this area, both in terms of settlement and of port-related structures. I have elsewhere expressed my amazement at the fact that there is not a single indication of any Punic settlement in this part of the harbour - the Benghisa tomb is indicative of the presence of at least a country house on the opposite side of the large harbour - even more so, on the hill-side between the shore and the Ashtart sanctuary on top of it. As to port-related structures, as we noted already, these might not have been necessary for simple mooring since it was customary to beach boats rather than berth them.

For long, the small enclosed rectangular shelter at the innermost head of the Marsaxlokk harbour was the subject of much speculation connected with the Punic presence in Malta. The obviously man-made feature was strikingly similar to the *cothon* (or artificial harbour for the repair and maintenance of ships) of Motya, the island colony between Marsala and Trapani on the western tip of Sicily. It was equally similar to the square-shaped artificial harbour of Carthage itself, though this seems to be of a later, Roman, date. All this, the absence of any record of its construction within documented history, and the position of the imposing sanctuary of Ashtart on top of a steep hill overlooking it, generated the plausible hypothesis that this was the Maltese version of the Phoenician *cothon*, to which the late Tancred Gouder fully subscribed. Unfortunately, no archaeological investigations have ever been undertaken on the spot to verify this hypothesis, not even during recent dredging and restructuring operations. One can only hope it is still not too late for such

The two enclosed harbours of Carthage: the round one was for war ships; the rectangular one was for merchant ships.

investigations to take place and that some original deposits and structural remains still survive under the modern structures for future archaeologists to discover.

On the other hand, an increasingly thicker concentration of Punic tombs of this period recorded during the last hundred years in various areas around the inner harbour, like Marsa, Ħamrun, Tarxien, and Paola, as well as the occasional find of the remains of domestic structures, such as water cisterns, tend to suggest that this part of the Grand Harbour was emerging as an alternative port centre.

Aerial view of Xlendi Bay, one of a few small inlets that provided at least temporary shelter from rough seas. A number of ancient ships have foundered outside the mouth of the bay, including a Punic one.

The Grand Harbour has several deep creeks which offer excellent shelter in bad weather. Aerial view of the two creeks on either side of Senglea.

For Gozo, the situation is different. Although it does not have either the deep, well-sheltered, and fjord-like channels, such as the Grand Harbour and Marsamxett harbour, or wide and deep gulfs like the Marsaxlokk harbour, Gozo has a number of short narrow inlets with a sand bed at the head. The best examples are Mġarr, Mġarr ix-Xini, Xlendi, Marsalforn, and, possibly, Ir-Ramla l-Ħamra, the latter being rather wider and less sheltered. Being conveniently located all around the island, they provided at least temporary, very opportunistic shelter and beaching facility for small boats, whose use had to shift with the direction of the winds and the swells.

A small Hellenistic marble statuette representing Artemis, the hunting goddess. When whole she was shown running, with a quiver behind her back and accompanied by a dog against her left thigh.

Culture

Malta's geographical position, almost the easternmost of the western colonies, on the same longitude as the Tripolitanian ones on the southern mainland, must have played a decisive role in the formation of the character of its culture at this time. Its position between Greek Sicily, officially enemy territory, and the Tripolitanian colonies of Sabratha, Oea, and Leptis Magna was ideal for the passage of the commercial traffic between the two culturally and politically distinct areas. Hellenization was getting more predominant and pervasive in the whole Mediterranean, not least in the western Phoenician colonies, including Carthage itself. It was becoming a culturally unifying factor even though perhaps not as comprehensively as in the east.

GREEK AND PUNIC CITIES TO THE NORTH AND SOUTH OF MALTA

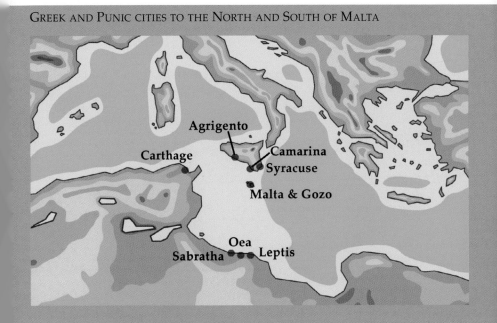

There is, no doubt, a striking difference between the still predominantly utilitarian, somewhat drab, material culture of the Maltese Punic population of this time and the exuberant, high quality cultural expressions of the Greek centres to the north, even as close as Camarina and Gela on the southern shores of Sicily. But one does occasionally come across the odd Greek *objet d'art*, say a piece of marble sculpture; more frequently, products of refined craftsmanship, such as fine pottery items and terracotta figurines, both among the tomb furniture and in the archaeological deposits of the Tas-Silġ sanctuary.

The oriental (or orientalizing) component, on the other hand, cannot be overlooked. Most of the Egyptianizing architectural elements, such as the elaborate pilaster capital from Tas-Silġ and the various cavetto cornices both from Tas-Silġ and elsewhere, including a couple of silo pits at Mtarfa and the recent rescue operations at Mdina, as well as that on the splendid Żurrieq 'tower', belong to this period.

Sabatino Moscati has noted a number of linguistic anomalies in Maltese inscriptions which continue to link Malta with the Orient rather than with Carthage, and which endure down to the second century BC. While in the remainder of the Punic world the suffix of the

A capital of a square pillar, probably of one of two pillars that flanked the monumental entrance to the temple. It consists of two Egyptian cavetto cornices surmounted by a convex, cushion-like abacus.

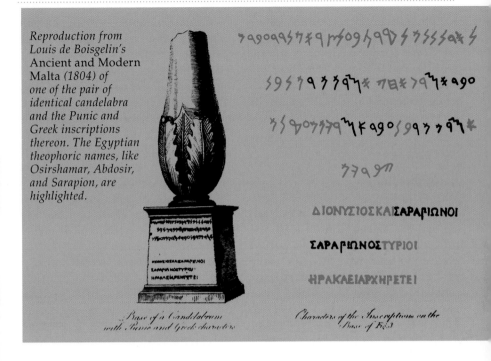

Reproduction from Louis de Boisgelin's Ancient and Modern Malta *(1804) of one of the pair of identical candelabra and the Punic and Greek inscriptions thereon. The Egyptian theophoric names, like Osirshamar, Abdosir, and Sarapion, are highlighted.*

pronoun *y* evolves very early in ', in Malta it is preserved down to the second century BC. In the structure of the inscriptions, contrary to what is found more generally in the Punic area, the name of the divinity to which the dedication is made is placed just before the concluding formula, as in the earlier Phoenician dedicatory inscriptions. Also noteworthy is the survival of the cult of Astarte as the main female divinity, while elsewhere she is replaced by Tanit. Even the theophoric names Osirshamar and Abdosir on the late bilingual inscription underscore the eastern, in this case Egyptian-inspired, connection. The latter, however, given the late date of the inscription (second century BC), could be more plausibly explained by the invading Egyptianizing influence in the Hellenistic age, while the former linguistic and religious aberrations can be easily attributed to a certain tendency of remote islands like Malta to lag behind in linguistic conservatism, a phenomenon that is found most notably in the survival of Arabic in the present Maltese language.

In pottery this period seems to have laid the cultural and technical foundations of pottery-making for centuries to come. The preparation of the paste, the covering slip, the painted decoration and the firing technique seems to have changed very little, even in Roman times, especially with respect to thick-walled, unrefined ware. Tomb furniture continues and consolidates a typical funerary repertoire which had been in use in the previous period. Some forms will survive long into the following, Roman, period. One particular shape of the cinerary urn is endemic to the Maltese islands and undergoes its own evolution. The only examples known outside Malta have already been listed above.

Religious Beliefs

Very symptomatic of the general cultural set-up, and a very important aspect of it, is religion. Indeed, the religious expressions of this period and of the first two centuries of the next are very informative on the current cultural order. In brief, the latter is characterized by conservatism which sees the survival of the major old divinities of the Phoenician pantheon, namely, Ashtart and Baal. The new component is determined by the infiltration and eventual affirmation of Egyptian divinities, often undergoing a process of syncretism with the established Phoenician divinities. This is best recognized in the early coinage of the following period which should be read as an expression of vigorous religious beliefs surviving throughout the Punic period and well into the following one.

This is mostly the case with Isis. We had already met Isis in her own right in the sixth-century papyrus from a tomb at Tal-Virtù. The representation of a female head wearing the typical Isis hairstyle on some of the early coins can only be explained as the assimilation of the traditional principal goddess Ashtart with the new Isis. The new Egyptian component can best be seen on the most singular reverse of coins showing Osiris between Isis and Nephthys. Perhaps typically of that period, the obverse of the same coin shows a completely Hellenized female divine profile, which is in turn interpreted, according to the Graeco-Roman interpretation, as the assimilation of Ashtart with Hera/Juno.

That Ashtart remained the main divinity in the Maltese pantheon is confirmed by the frequent inscriptions on offerings, and even on architectural fragments, at Tas-Silġ, as well as by the marble inscription from Gozo that lists a shrine/temple dedicated to her. As we have already mentioned, certainly one inscription (and, possibly, two others) from Tas-Silġ raise the status of that goddess to a national, even international one, proclaiming her to the world as the Asthart of 'nn (i.e. Malta). The reading of the name of the god Milk-ashtart on a fragmentary inscription is somewhat dubious.

The name of Baal is documented for this period on an inscription in a tomb found in the necropolis of Taċ-Ċagħqi, Rabat. The figure between Isis and Nephthys on the above-mentioned coin has also been identified as Baal Hammon.

Of more uncertain identification is the bearded male head appearing on the obverse of what is generally considered to be the earliest Maltese monetary issue. Some see in it Eshmun, the Phoenician equivalent of Asklepios, the Greek god of healing, on the basis of the caduceus depicted beside his head. According to one interpretation, Eshmun is also to be seen in the kneeling figure with four wings on the reverse of one coin issue with Isis on the obverse.

The Gozo marble inscription, then, mentions other divinities, whose identity is the subject of much scholarly controversy.

The affirmation of a fully-fledged Egyptian cult seems to have been fully realized in the following period at the Tas-Silġ sanctuary. It is suggested by the presence of an architectural feature symbolizing another Egyptian triad: Isis, Osiris, and Serapis. That process too must have had its beginning in the Punic phase.

The immediate and voluntary surrender of Malta to the Roman invader was probably a decision dictated by *realpolitik*, a piece of pragmatic logic so often associated with the Levantine character, perhaps the earliest one the Maltese inhabitants were destined to take. They most probably saw the writing on the wall and perceived the inevitability of a Roman domination.

Enlarged image of a Maltese coin with the legend 'nn on top of a scene showing an Egyptian male divinity (Osiris) in the centre, flanked by two female Egyptian divinities (Isis and Nephthys).

The End of Carthaginian Rule

The Roman occupation in 218 BC brought to an end, at least politically, a long historical chapter of Semitic identity that lasted more than half a millennium. There is no question that it left its indelible mark on the formation of the Maltese people, whether or not the second Semitic chapter, that of the Arab occupation, brought about a real hiatus in the continuity of Maltese historical, cultural and ethnic development.

It was inevitable that one day or another Malta should fall to the Romans. In this chapter a brief account is given of the history of the Romans: the legendary origin of the city and its territorial expansion; the historical divisions based on the city's changing constitutional set-up. This is followed by a brief overview of the historical vicissitudes of Malta under the Romans.

CHAPTER 4

THE ROMANS AND MALTA

Who were the Romans?

In the same way that I gave a brief overview of the Phoenicians, the first sea power that ruled over the Maltese islands, it would seem to be in order to do the same for the Romans, if only to maintain a certain balance, even if some readers' greater familiarity with the latter might render this task superfluous for them.

According to legend, the city of Rome was established in 753 BC. The Romans themselves were so convinced of this event as a historical fact that the whole of their history down to the beginning of the empire was dated from the year of the city's foundation (*ab urbe condita*). That date coincides to a great extent with the beginning of the great colonization boom on the part of the Greeks, which saw the establishment, from 750 onwards of scores of Greek

The Capitoline she-wolf (Lupa Capitolina). *An early 5th-century* BC *bronze sculpture now housed in the Museo Capitolino, in Rome. From the earliest times, the legendary she-wolf suckling the twins Romulus and Remus became the emblem of Roma.*

cities along the northern coast of the central and western Mediterranean, as well as a limited stretch of the North African coast (Cyrenaica) and all along that of the Black Sea. It is to be expected that, given its encounters with the Greek world, this ambitious young nation should have, or should create for itself, an origin at least as ancient as the earliest Greek colony on the Italian peninsula, namely Cumae. On the other hand, the Greek colonies in the west must have influenced the emergence of Rome as an individual city-state, the Italian version of the Greek *polis*.

It was at this same time, we should keep it in mind, that to the south of Rome, beyond the mists of the Tyrrhenian and Ionian seas, the islands of Malta were inhabited by similar farming and pastoralist

A section from the frieze that once decorated the Basilica Aemilia in the Forum Romanum. It depicts one of the episodes of the legendary history of Rome, the Punishment of Tarpeia.

Iron Age communities who were making their first contacts with the Phoenicians, the Semitic traders visiting their islands in search of tradable goods.

The first three-and-a-half centuries of Rome's history are peopled by legendary heroes and villains that provided the offspring of the Roman higher and middle classes with *exempla* to emulate or to shun. There is no doubt that, although there is a kernel of historical truth in many of these legendary accounts, they were, in reality, made-up stories intended to boost the morale of the Roman people in general, and of their leading elite in particular. Thus, in the period of the Kings, the story of the first King Tarquin (Tarquinius Priscus) probably reflects a strong and very influential Etruscan presence in Rome if not, as frequently suggested, an Etruscan political domination of Rome and Latium. The story of the last king of Rome, another Tarquin (Tarquinius Superbus), embellished as it is with the romance of the beautiful and virtuous Berenice, reflects the end of the same Etruscan hegemony, as well as the end of the Regal period and the beginning of the Republican age. The latter period was characterized by a different constitution which brought about a certain amount of gradual devolution of political, religious, and social power among the inhabitants of this city.

It was more than two centuries after this radical change in their political set-up, a period in which the republican idea continued to mature gradually, that the Romans started earnestly on a programme of territorial expansion which eventually saw them asserting themselves as rulers of all the lands bordering the Mediterranean sea and of many others beyond.

Topographical map of Rome showing the city limits in the 4th century BC and the contours of the seven hills that came to form the city. Note the change of the course of the river Tiber from the seventh century BC to the present.

Geographical Setting

In reality Rome arose as a city when a group of villages of farmers and pastoralists occupying the hills around a common valley on the side of the river Tiber came together to form a common urban centre governed by a common political order. This valley, situated some 30 kilometres from the Tiber's estuary on the western coast of the Italian peninsula, roughly halfway along its length, was initially a burial area and a market place where the different villagers came to exchange their wares. Eventually, the same valley was properly drained by a major piece of civil engineering (the *cloaca maxima*) and itself became the famous Roman Forum, the very hub of Rome's social, commercial, religious, and political life.

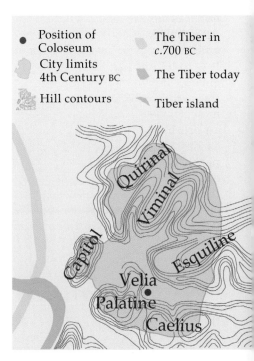

- Position of Coloseum
- City limits 4th Century BC
- Hill contours
- The Tiber in c.700 BC
- The Tiber today
- Tiber island

Quirinal
Viminal
Capitol
Esquiline
Velia
Palatine
Caelius

At first, the city of Rome occupied only the east, or left, side of the river Tiber at a spot where a crossing from one side to the other was relatively easier. This was probably what gave Rome its strategic position, controlling the movement of salt along the north-south trajectory and reflected in the name of one of the major roads emanating from the city, the *via salaria*. A city wall was built of regular masonry to enclose and protect the city sometime in the fourth century BC, even though its name (the 'Servian wall') associates it with Servius, one of the kings of the previous Regal period. With the expansion of the city, a sizeable area of land on the left bank of the river, the *Campus Martius* was incorporated.

Ancient Rome suffered its worst invasion in 390 BC when it was sacked by the Gauls. Even this episode is adorned with legendary details which imply that what was destined to become the eternal city was saved from obliteration by a hair's breath, literally by the cackling of the sacred geese on the Capitoline hill. This invasion is presumed to have caused the total destruction of the city's archives and whatever other historical records that existed at the time. This event is probably responsible for the revisionist legendary version of Rome's history prior to the fourth century.

Satellite image of central Italy showing the position of Rome in relation to the Tiber and the Tyrrhenian coast.

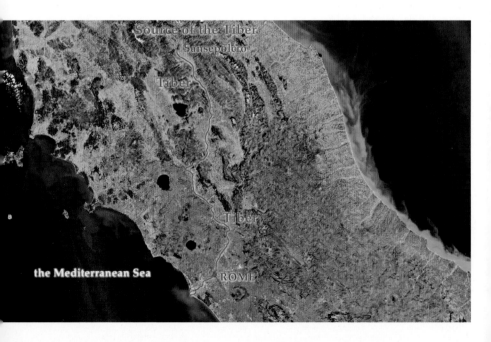

the Mediterranean Sea

ROME

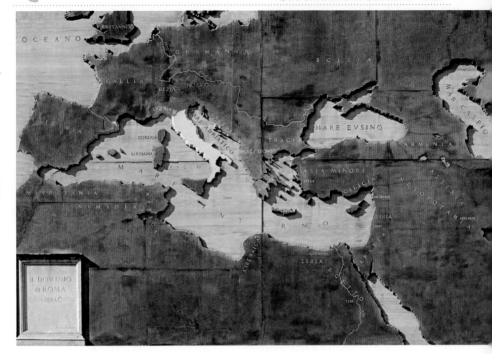

Image of the Mediterranean showing Rome's annexed territory by 264 BC. One of the large-format maps affixed to the boundary wall of the Roman Forum on the Via dei Fori Imperiali in Rome.

In spite of what the Romans themselves wrote, and what present history writers still write, in defence of their territorial expansionism and their conquests, these were hardly ever forced on them as they were on the their vowed enemies, the Carthaginians. This expansion materialized gradually but steadily, engulfing first the immediate Latin-speaking neighbours, then the indomitable mountain tribes of central Italy, as well as the more civilized Etruscan cities to their immediate north and Greek colonies to their immediate south. The only foreign invasion which could be said to have twisted their arm and forced them to war was that of King Pyrrhus; and even then, he had come to the rescue of a Greek ally, the city of Tarentum, which was being harassed by the Romans.

To cut a longish story short, since it is outside the purpose of this work, by 264 BC the Romans controlled the whole of the Italian peninsula from Etruria and Umbria to the southern tip of Calabria. That year was a fateful one because it brought about the pretext for waging the first of a serious of three long-drawn wars (the Punic wars) against the Carthaginians. By 146 BC, when Carthage was razed completely to the ground, the Romans had incorporated not only the former territorial possessions of that city, but had embarked on a series of wars on other fronts, which eventually made them masters of the whole of Italy south of the Alps, the larger islands of the western Mediterranean, parts of Spain, and North Africa, Greece, and the previous Macedonian possessions. The Punic wars are of direct relevance to our subject because they brought about the first incursion by the Romans on Malta and their eventual possession of it.

From this point onwards, a much more complex mosaic of historical vicissitudes saw the Romans taking possession, by hook or by crook, of an empire which incorporated the whole of western and central Europe west of the river Rhine and south of the river Danube, all the lands bordering the Mediterranean,

Top: Modern portrait bust in relief of Cicero on a bronze plaque set up on the side of the Cathedral Museum in Mdina.

Below left: A portrait head of Alexander the Great.

including Egypt and the whole of North Africa. At intervals it even encompassed the remoter provinces of the Persian empire that had been conquered by Alexander the Great, but these turned out to be a harder nut to crack even for the Romans. Again, however, these are beyond the scope of this volume.

Historical Divisions

As hinted above, the history of Rome and of the Romans is divided broadly into three periods characterized by different constitutional regimes: the Regal period, from the city's foundation to 510 BC, during which time Rome was ruled by a succession of kings; the Republican age, from 510 to 27 BC, when

Rome and its expanding territory were administered by a constitution which strived to develop and uphold a relatively democratic order, with the required checks and balances; the Imperial age, from 27 BC to the final collapse of the western Roman empire in AD 476, during which the same were ruled by a succession of autocratic rulers, some benign and beneficent, others mad, vicious, and murderous.

Malta under the Romans

The Maltese islands were occupied by Rome towards the middle of the Republican age. According to Livy (xxi. 51) the Romans replaced the Carthaginians as political masters of the Maltese archipelago in 218 BC, at the outset of the Second Punic War, when Tiberius Sempronius Longus,

Marble bust of Emperor Trajan (emperor from AD 98 to 117) at the British Museum. During his reign, the Roman empire experienced a major expansion with the conquest of Dacia and Mesopotamia.

Model of archaic Rome from the Museo della Civiltà Romana, in Rome.

The Tiber and the Isola Tiberina are in the foreground; beyond them are the Capitol (centre), the Quirinal (left) and the Palatine (right).

Reverses of some of the coin types minted in Malta, including: a flamen's cap; cauldron on tripod; three Egyptian divinities; a kneeling winged divinity; curule chair.

one of the two consuls for that year, captured the islands without encountering any resistance. They came to form part of the province of Sicily. During the Republican age Malta, as an extension of the Sicilian province, was controlled by a propraetor who was supposed to look after the interests of Rome on behalf of the Roman Senate. Some of these propraetors in different provinces abused of their position and we hear of a number of such magistrates arraigned in court for such corrupt practices. One of them was the notorious Caius Verres who was governor of Sicily from 73 to 71 BC. We shall hear about him in greater detail in the following chapter.

Within this same period there appear to have been a number of changes with regard to the internal administration of the islands. The fact that Malta, almost throughout the Republican age, was allowed to mint coins for local circulation is taken by many to imply a certain amount of autonomy. But other cities and small islands, whether Greek or Punic, which had fallen to the Romans in similar circumstances, are known to have issued their own coins. In every case these were limited to copper coinage. Even Gozo issued its own coins, but only towards the very end of the Republican age, and this too is taken to signify a certain amount of autonomy of that island with respect to Malta.

There are indications that for a brief period towards the middle of the first century BC Malta, possibly independently from Gozo, had a privileged political status in that it could manage its internal government by means of properly-structured, republican-type decision making bodies, namely, a people's assembly and a senate. This seems to have been withdrawn with the rise to power of the first emperor, Augustus. In early imperial times both islands, together, may have been the personal property of the emperor and were administered by a person who was his personally-appointed 'procurator'. It is later, towards the middle of the second century AD that we hear for the first time of a municipal set-up, with its specific government officials, and not only for Malta, but also for Gozo. In the late Empire, then, at the end of the third and the beginning of the fourth century we have notice of a different terminology which probably involved a different set-up. There is no doubt that, although we have no specific references to them, with emperor Diocletian's reforms, the islands had to take on board a number of bureaucratic measures which were destined to change the economic, social, and administrative structures.

The Arian Baptistry, Ravenna, built by Theodoric, the Ostrogothic regent of Italy (AD 493-526) appointed by emperor Zeno of Byzantium. The central medallion shows the Baptism of Christ. The encircling ring shows the twelve apostles led by St Peter and St Paul.

It is at this time, from the fourth century AD onwards, that we start to see the rise and rapid growth of another force, a spiritual one this time, but which is known to have frequently spilled over the temporal one. The rise and rapid growth of Christianity in Malta is attested to by the relatively vast number of collective tombs scattered throughout the islands, that seem to respond to a 'Christian' typology. This typology appears to overlap into the following period, from AD 535 onwards, when Malta formed part of the Byzantine empire. Since, according to established historiographic conventions the Byzantine period is considered part of the Middle Ages, its treatment will be taken care of in the next volume of this series.

One of the major flaws of past publications dealing with the Roman period of Malta's ancient history is their treatment of the period as one whole block, without any distinction between different sub-periods. This has resulted in clearly erroneous and very misleading attributions of political, economic, and cultural situations, that were specific to particular sub-periods, indiscriminately to the whole Roman period. The Roman occupation of Malta spans close to seven centuries, a long stretch of time which saw drastic changes and upheavals in various facets of the empire. On occasion, new rulers sought to undo their predecessors' dispositions, changing overnight the political status of cities and large territories. It is wise, therefore, to distinguish between one period and another, if possible between one century and another.

We have to be careful, on the other hand, not to stretch our expectations too far. We have to keep everything in its proper perspective. Compared to Rome and other parts of the Roman empire, which are endowed with a vast array of documentary evidence, enough to fill volumes, Malta was a rather remote, almost insignificant corner of that same empire, about which only a handful of writers bothered

The catacombs of St Callixtus are among the greatest and most important of Rome. They originated about the middle of the 2nd century AD and are part of a cemeterial complex which occupies an area of 90 acres, with a network of galleries about 12 miles long, in four levels, in some parts more than 20 m deep.

to write. To strike a 'happy medium', therefore, it seems to me essential to distinguish at least between the Republican age and the following Imperial age, as I have done in the previous paragraphs, and to apply certain generalizations accordingly. Along the same lines of argument, we need to distinguish the late Roman period because it is characterized by a cultural development, Christianization, that separates it from the previous one, the high empire, and joins it with the following one. This explains the separation of the treatment of the Roman period in several chapters.

I also find unacceptable an increasing tendency in archaeological literature to lump a considerable portion, if not the whole, of what we defined as the Roman period with the 'Punic' period. This is done on the pretext that the Punic material culture of the previous period survived quite conspicuously in the first two centuries of Roman occupation. While recognizing this not unusual phenomenon in the history of nations and succession of civilizations, I do not believe the nomenclature is justified, and I shall continue to insist on 218 BC as the landmark that separates quite distinctly the Punic period from the Roman one. We are rarely so fortunate in being regaled with a precise, historically-significant, date such as this. While I look favourably on the current flourishing interest in the long neglected Phoenician-Punic legacy, I do not think we should throw that date overboard simply to render this legacy more voluminous.

Having been conquered by the Romans, Malta was incorporated within the first Roman overseas province, that of Sicily. Thus Malta came to share with that island a common destiny for centuries. It shared the same treatment from the Roman masters with the majority of the cities of the larger island. At one stage they came very close to enjoy the privileges (and responsibilities) of a full Roman citizenship.

CHAPTER 5

THE FIRST TWO CENTURIES OF ROMAN DOMINATION: THE REPUBLICAN PHASE

Historical Background

The breakdown of the balance of power between Greeks, Etruscans, and Carthaginians at the outset of the fifth century paved the way for the gradual emergence and eventual rise of another power in the central Mediterranean, one that was indigenous to the Italian soil and one that was destined to dominate not only the peninsula itself but the whole Mediterranean and beyond.

By 264, by a series of wars and forced alliances, Rome had extended its control virtually over the whole of the Italian peninsula; the outbreak of the First Punic War in that year was clearly directed towards the domination of Sicily. During that war the Romans had to fight several sea-battles and by the end of it they had become a sea power as

View of the Roman Forum, the commercial, religious, and political hub of Rome. In the background are the foundations of the Basilica Iulia. The three Corinthian columns of the temple of Vespasian and Titus occupy the foreground. In the middle ground stands the Ionic portico of the temple of Saturn.

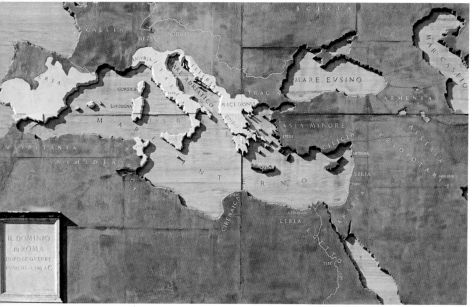

well as a land power. In 255 BC Malta, being enemy territory, was raided and its countryside devastated.

As yet, however, Rome did not estimate the position of this group of small islands highly enough to try to secure them from the enemy; their main and only concern throughout that war (264-241 BC) was Sicily, though the two other large islands of the west (Sardinia and Corsica) were annexed very soon after (238 BC). The Carthaginians, on the other hand, in view of these heavy losses, took some measures to avoid a second Roman invasion and, possibly, an occupation of the Maltese islands: in 218 BC Malta was guarded by a Carthaginian garrison of almost 2,000 men under the command of Hamilcar, son of Gisgo. But this proved to be inadequate, certainly not enough to ward off a naval

Map of the Mediterranean showing Rome's conquered territory by 146 BC.

expedition by one of the Roman consuls who won over the archipelago, apparently without even having to fight for it (Livy, xxi, 51).

In 218 BC, therefore, Malta was incorporated within the Roman commonwealth. This prevented it from being used by the enemy as a possible base for naval military action in the Sicilian channel. Most naturally, it was included in the newly-formed province of Sicily which had been set up in 241 (or, more probably, 227) BC. From then on and for many centuries to come, as noted by the sixteenth-century French writer Jean Quintin, Malta's destiny was inseparable from that of the larger neighbouring island.

Though most of the Second Punic War (218-202 BC) was fought on Italian soil, and towards the end on African soil, close to Carthage itself, one feels that the Romans must have taken some pains to prevent any of the islands from being recovered by the enemy. With the loss of all of Carthage's territorial claims outside North Africa at the end of the Second Punic War, even more so with the complete annihilation of the city itself in 146 BC, and the ensuing creation of *provincia Africa*, which was paralleled by that of *provincia Achaia* in the east in the same year, Malta lost its last shreds of strategic significance and, as it has been observed, it hardly figured any more in ancient history.

Nevertheless, if threats from outside the Roman empire were, to a great extent and for a long time, eliminated, those from the inside were still lurking. We do not know what role, if any, Malta played in the slave-revolt that we mostly associate with the figure of Spartacus. Nor do we know whether it was involved in any way in the civil wars that brought about the collapse of the Republican constitution in Rome in 27 BC. Most probably it was away from it all since Cicero was considering, at one stage, going into voluntary banishment on the island, but coin evidence seems to imply support given to Sextus Pompeius and his fleet in his resistance against Octavian. We have also a clear statement from the same Cicero that before and during his time (second half of the second to the beginning of the first century BC) Malta was regularly used as a winter base for pirates. Piracy infested the Mediterranean and jeopardized commercial sea-faring on all seas surrounding Italy until Pompey put a definitive stop to it in 67 BC.

Cicero again, followed by Diodorus Siculus, with reference to Malta, gives us a picture of a quiet prosperity which is reflected in the archaeological record - in particular

A graphic reconstruction, signed by Architect E.L. Galizia, of the Doric columns and architrave of the peristyle of the Rabat Domus that had been excavated by Dr A.A. Caruana in 1881. The colour scheme is based on surviving traces of coloured plaster.

that of the villas scattered over the Maltese countryside. They also infer some degree of sophistication both in the industrial production of refined textiles and in the artistically ambitious constructions, of which the Roman *domus* of Rabat is a concrete and prominent example.

When Agrippa, the right-hand man of Augustus was compiling data for his *mappa mundi*, towards the end of the first century BC, Sicily appears to have been divided into 68 *civitates*, or communities. These included the islands of Lipari and Malta. This situation must reflect in many ways that of the previous two

A satellite image of Sicily showing the various Roman cities (civitates) *and the main road system connecting them. Most cities are listed by name by the Latin writer Cicero.*

centuries. At the time of Cicero only two of these *civitates* were *foederatae* and five were *liberae atque immunes*, and Malta does not figure among them; neither does Agrigento with which Malta was paired by the two bronze tablet inscriptions found in Rome before 1549 (about this pairing of Malta with Agrigento see below p.155). These seven *civitates* were autonomous, at least theoretically, and exempted from the tithes. The remaining cities of Sicily, and their territories, were subject to that tax.

The Latin term *civitas* was used by the Romans to denote the administrative concept of a community, such as those of Malta and Gozo. From the point of view of Rome, the main function of the *civitates* was to provide the essential data on which to base the accounts of taxes. The collection proper of the tithes was

An illustration from Jean Houel's Voyage Pittoresque *(1787) with the so-called 'Temple of Concorde' in Agrigento. This temple of the 5th century BC, together with other temples of the Classical Greek age, still survived in good condition in Roman times. Agrigentum, like Melite, had no privileged status after its conquest by the Romans. Around the mid-1st century BC, however, it also had a similar local administrative set-up.*

assigned by tender by means of an auction which was held annually in each *civitas*. A list of the landowners and of those that worked the land was prepared by the *civitas* for the purpose. The tithe was collected on the ground immediately after the harvest. This meant that to a large extent the taxation system remained in the hands of local businessmen.

Administration

Except for periods of war or special tension when consuls or proconsuls were placed in charge of the province, Sicily was governed by a praetor, certainly from 227 BC onwards, the real date when, according to some, Sicily became a province. After the reforms of Sulla, it became normal practice to send an ex-praetor to the province.

The local administration was also left in the hands of the locals, even in the *civitates* that were not *liberae atque immunes*. Rome simply did not have the human resources or the motivations to take up this burden. From the little evidence we have, it appears that there was a great variety of administration systems in use in different communities and that these resulted from previous centuries of individual developments. The most marked differences were between the old Greek *poleis*, like Agrigento and Syracuse, and communities, like Palermo and Trapani, that had never been Greek. This is what makes the strong parallelism between Agrigento and Melite in the inscriptions on two bronze tablets found in Rome so perplexing. There are many indications that the model consisting of councils and popular assemblies continued to function everywhere; these bodies continued to meet and conduct

business, even on a lower scale. In the ordinary management of these communities Rome was represented by the local tax collectors, by two Roman quaestors (officials of the exchequer residing one in Syracuse and one in Lilybaeum), and by the Roman governor.

Culturally, Malta presents itself at this point in time as the melting pot of three diverse cultures and languages. The Roman administration was in no hurry to impose its own language (at least for official transactions), its own official religion, and, inevitably, its own artistic fashions on the Punic ones. Some of these appear to have survived well into the first century BC; the previous non-Greek language, probably Punic, was still spoken (but not written on official documents) in the first century AD (*Acts*, XXVII). Together with

An aerial view of the present archaeological park of Marsala (ancient Lilybaeum). It is from Lilybaeum that the consul Tib. Sempronius Longus left with his fleet to invade Malta in 218 BC.

these two currents another one was mingled, the Greek Hellenistic one, which had started to filter in Malta, as it did in the whole Punic world in the late fourth century BC, but which grew stronger now as a result of the more intensive intercourse between Sicily and the Maltese islands.

The Sources: Literary Sources

Our literary sources for the first 200 years of Roman occupation are probably the most numerous, compared to other periods. This does not always mean they are the most informative on the goings-on of this phase, because some of them seem to refer to times anterior to this one (like Diodorus) and many of them are concerned with subjects, such as Maltese dogs, which do not impinge on the history of these islands. The most generous source is Marcus Tullius Cicero, the first-century BC lawyer and politician who wrote on diverse subjects, including philosophy, but his many references to Malta are found in his prosecution speeches against Verres, the outgoing governor of Sicily.

For the sake of chronological sequence, however, we cannot but start with another writer, Titus Livius, a historian, who lived half-a-century after Cicero, but who gives us a clear-cut account of the historical episode which saw Malta's apparently bloodless passage from a Carthaginian occupation to a Roman domination (Livy, XXI, 51, 1-2). It all happened rather suddenly and, perhaps, unexpectedly. The consul Tiberius Sempronius Longus, one of the two most powerful Roman magistrates for the year 218 BC, decided to leave Lilybaeum (today's Marsala) in western Sicily and to cross to the island of Malta 'which was held by the Carthaginians'.

The war against Carthage, the Second Punic War, had just been declared. At first the Romans allied themselves to Hiero II, king of Syracuse, because he was still a force to be reckoned with in Sicily and it was convenient to have him on their side. In the passage dealing with Malta we are told that Hiero was allowed, or asked, to leave with his regal fleet, whereas the praetor was left to protect the Sicilian coast, before the consul left Lilybaeum.

As soon as he arrived in Malta, Hamilcar, son of Gisgo, who was in charge of the garrison (*praesidium*) of about 2,000 troops, surrendered together with the town (*oppidum*) and island. After a few days, the consul returned to Lilybaeum. There the prisoners, except those of noble

Close-up of the modern portrait bust of Cicero on a bronze plaque fixed on the side wall of the Cathedral Museum, Mdina.

birth, were sold into slavery. Being satisfied that from that side Sicily was safe enough, the consul set out for the islands of Lipari (*Vulcani*) because rumours had it that the Punic fleet was stationed there.

The reference to prisoners of noble birth makes one wonder whether the Hamilcar in charge of the garrison was the brother of Hasdrubal, son of Gisgo, whose daughter Sophonisba married Syphax, king of Numidia, sometime during the Second Punic War (218-201 BC). The timing is right, but it all depends on how common the Carthaginian name Gisgo was. Sophonisba lured her husband to support the Carthaginians against the Romans. He was defeated by a Roman army under another Numidian prince, Masinissa, who eventually fell in love with Sophonisba. According to the same Livy, she was spared the disgrace of being taken captive to Rome by drinking poison sent to her on purpose by Masinissa.

The *Verrines* are a series of books of speeches Cicero wrote in 70 BC for the prosecution of Caius Verres, accusing him of corruption and other crimes and wrongdoings

An artist's impression of Cicero writing his prosecution speeches against Caius Verres; Cicero actually delivering those speeches in court; and slaves piling up on a cart goods and precious objects from the sanctuary of Juno in Malta on behalf of Verres.

during his three years of governorship of Sicily, between 73 and 71 BC. As soon as Cicero delivered his first speech for the prosecution, Verres gave up his case and withdrew into exile. But in order not to waste all his labours in gathering evidence for the case, Cicero published all the speeches, including those parts which he never pronounced. One has to keep in mind, therefore, that the whole of *actio secunda*, which was never delivered, and which contains the references to Malta, was never subject to the scrutiny of the jurors and the counter-statement by the counsel of the defence. The whole purpose of Cicero's speeches was to put Verres in the worst light, as well as to establish a reputation for himself as Rome's leading advocate. We can only rely on Cicero's word and general sense of rectitude for the correctness of the information he imparts.

At this stage, I shall limit myself to listing his most important references to things Maltese. Each reference will be discussed under separate topics as the occasion arises.

Cicero's mention of Maltese *legati* ('delegates') during the hearing of the case, and his referring to the Maltese in general as *socii* have been inflated disproportionately to upgrade the political standing of the Maltese islands (Cic., *Verr.*, II, 4, 104). *Legati* does not have to mean ambassadors, as often implied, but merely representatives; *socii* ('allies') too is probably used in its wider, non-technical, meaning.

Cicero also makes repeated references to Maltese textiles, which shed light on the economy of the islands. At one stage, he states that Verres had the city of Melite turned into one whole factory of such textiles (*textrinum*) to produce women's clothing for his own sake (Cicero, *Verr.*, II, 4. 103).

Cicero reveals in no uncertain terms the international fame of the sanctuary of Juno which had been revered by pirates and Numidian princes, but which the covetous Verres had despoiled of all its treasures (Cicero, *Verr.* II, 4. 103-104). A story of considerable interest is

Ivory or bone bobbins and needles found during the excavations of the Roman domus and the houses in the vicinity. Together with the stone loom-weights found in the same area, they attest to the intensive weaving industry in the town of Melite mentioned by Cicero.

the one about some ivory tusks of enormous size which were removed from the sanctuary by the admiral of Masinissa, king of Numidia, to make a present of them to his king. Massinissa, on hearing where they came from, respectfully ordered their immediate restitution after inscribing the record of this act 'in Punic letters' on the tusks themselves. Cicero adds that the sanctuary housed a great quantity of ivory and many ornaments, among which ivory statuettes of Victory of great antiquity and the finest artistry. All of which were ordered by Verres to be plundered and taken to him in Sicily.

In another passage he narrates how Diodorus, a Maltese gentleman who was asked to give testimony in the trial, and who lived in Lilybaeum, had in his house in Malta a collection of silverware, among which some

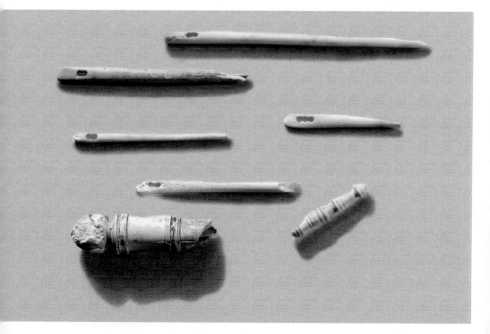

Two anthropomorphic bone hairpins (10.5 and 12.5 cm long). Bone hairpins were commonly used by Roman women to hold their elaborate hairstyles in place. Roman female hair styles changed almost as frequently as today and imperial ladies played a crucial role in introducing new hairstyle fashions. Numerous hairpins, some plain, others with spherical, segmented, or thistle-shaped heads were yielded by the excavations of the Roman Domus remains.

cups, known as *Thericlia*, were wrought by the hands of Mentor, a well-known Greek silversmith (Cicero, *Verr.*, II, 4, 38-39). To have an idea of the value of these collector's items, L. Licinius Crassus (consul in 95 BC) paid 100,000 sesterces for two cups by the same Mentor (Pliny *N.H.* 33.147). When he got to know about the Diodorus collection, Verres wanted to take possession of them, but their owner managed to trick him out of it.

Two passages in Cicero's speeches against Verres (Cic., *Verr.* II, 2, 176 and 183) are often misread and misquoted to attribute to Malta a predominant position in the production of honey, almost on the same level as that of fine quality textiles. In the first passage Verres is being accused of smuggling out of the harbour of Syracuse - therefore, not stealing it from Malta - a large quantity of Maltese draperies (*plurimam vestem melitensem*), together with a variety of other products originating from a variety of places, including a large amount of honey (*vim mellis maximam*). He does not specify a Maltese origin for the honey. So it is not correct to say that Malta was famous for its honey on the basis of this passage. Similarly, in the second passage, Cicero rhetorically asks Verres where he got 'those 400 amphorae of honey (*CCCC. amphoras mellis*), where all that Maltese cloth (*tantum Melitensium*), or those fifty dining-room couches, or all those candelabra', referring to what he has just stated in the previous passage.

Cicero also mentions Malta in his private correspondence. In one letter to his friend Atticus (*Ad Att.* III, 4), Cicero debates with himself the possibility of going into voluntary exile on Malta. Things got so bad for him in the political scene in Rome and a raging civil war, that Cicero was seriously considering taking this step. In Malta he had friends, in particular a certain Aristoteles whom he calls *hospes* (which can mean either 'guest' or 'host') in another letter (*Ad Fam.* XIII, 52). At the end he realized that Malta was not a possible venue because, according to the bill of exile, while he was allowed to stay in exile in a place not less than 400 miles away from Rome, he was declared an outlaw from the date of the passage of the law. This was in April 58 BC. In April 49 BC he was again thinking of settling in Malta and to stay out of

Four silver vessels with embossed figurative decoration in relief. It is likely that the silver cups belonging to Diodorus, Cicero's Maltese friend, were of this type.

politics and the civil war. But in May he received word from Antony that he had received instructions from Caesar not to allow anybody to leave Italy (*Ad Att.* X, 7,8,9,18). Cicero met his end soon after Caesar's death, by Antony's proscription of 43 BC.

The references to Malta in Ovid's *Fasti* (3. 567-568) concerns the legendary past (see box on Battus) but the opening two lines probably refer to contemporary geographical realities: the first one, that Malta was fertile, compared to sterile Cossyra (Pantelleria); the second one that it was lapped by the Libyan sea, therefore the African geographical identity of the island. The latter is further emphasised by the geographer Ptolemy two centuries later (see following chapter, p.196).

The Greek geographer Strabo (64 BC-after AD 24) also mentions Malta briefly, but only to give the distance (500 stadia) between Malta and Cossyra (Pantelleria) (*Geog.* XVII, 3. 16), and the distance (88 miles) that separates Malta and Gozo from Cape Pachynus (*Geog.* VI, 2.11). His *Geography* was finished by 7 BC, so his remarks apply to the period in question, apart from the distances which, naturally, have not changed since. In the author's own words, his geography was intended for political leaders and to impart practical wisdom, such as distances between landfalls, for the sake of navigators. From this we may assume that there were frequent connections between Malta and these two destinations.

Similarly, the information of a geographical nature given by Diodorus Siculus, who wrote between 60 and 30 BC, is valid for his own time, that is, the first century BC. He gives us the Greek names of the islands by which they were then commonly known. The attribution of a city and harbours to each island, harbours

that provided safety for ships in distress, must have remained valid even in his time. He extols further the number and exceptional qualities of the harbours of Malta, compared to those of Gozo. He also gives the distance that separated Malta from Syracuse, an indication (if there was need for one) that there was a regular navigation route between the two destinations. Diodorus also praises the inhabitants for their skills in many crafts, the most important of which was linen-weaving, as well as the noteworthy dwellings that were ambitiously constructed with cornices and finished in stucco with unusual workmanship. As for Gozo, his remark about its harbours is that they were well situated; which seems to apply to what we observed already

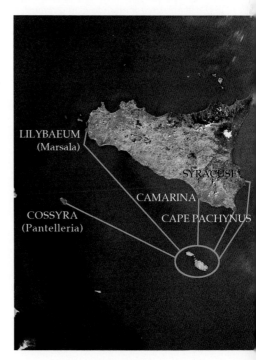

Regular sea routes between Malta and other destinations suggested by the distances between them given by the ancient writers: 500 stadia between Malta and Cossyra (Pantelleria); 88 (Roman) miles between Malta and Cape Pachynus (nearest point in Sicily); 800 stadia from Malta to Syracuse; 87 (Roman) miles to Camarina; 113 (Roman) miles to Lilybaeum.

with regard to the location of small inlets around the whole island, even though they are not exactly as suitably sheltered as those of Malta.

Inscriptions

Probably the most internationally-renowned inscribed monument of this period is the pair of marble candelabra which found their way in Giovanni Francesco Abela's collection of antiquities at Marsa (see box). This is so because the inscribed Punic and Greek texts were used in the eighteenth century, particularly by Jean-Jacques Barthélemy, for the

One of the plates illustrating the monumental work by Jean Houel, the Voyage Pittoresque des Iles de Sicile, Malte et Lipari *of 1787. In it we see a group of antiquities he came across on Malta, including the two candelabra and a sculptured marble base of dubious antiquity.*

decipherment of the Phoenician script. Later, this was rendered easier because one of the identical pair was given to King Louis XVI of France by Grand Master De Rohan in 1780; eventually it was incorporated in the Louvre collection. The original provenance of the two candelabra is still unknown, but they are generally believed to have been found in Marsaxlokk and often connected with a presumed temple of Hercules in the area.

Each of the candelabra contains a Punic inscription and what seems to be a Greek version of it, though not exactly a faithful translation. While the Punic version records the offering made to the god Melqart by two brothers mentioned by their respective Punic names (Abdosir and Osirxamar), the Greek version records the same offering made to

A gold ring from the necropolis of Gordj-Djedid in Tunisia, now in the Bardo Museum, in Tunis. The ring carries an image of a god/hero striking down a lion, probably Melqart. The god, wearing a conical tiara and a short tunic, presses his left leg on the lion. With his right hand he holds down the lion's head while raising a double-axe with his left hand, ready to strike.

Heracles by the same two persons carrying different, theophoric, names (Dionysios and Sarapion). Melqart/Herakles was the protective divinity of the Phoenician city of Tyre. In spite of the Punic inscription, these two ex-votos are currently dated to the second century BC, mostly on the basis of the letter style of the Greek script. This is why we are considering them in this chapter. Assuming the date is right, they also yield significant data about the general culture and the religious beliefs of the Maltese inhabitants in the period in question.

Less known than the previous one, but of equal importance is the Demetrios inscription (*I.G.* XIV, 953). It has reached us intact. It is inscribed in Greek on a bronze tablet and records a decision taken by the Maltese senate and people to award a proxeny, the equivalent to our honorary consulate, to a certain Demetrios from Syracuse. This inscription has an enormous historical potential, because it can enlighten us on the political status of Malta at a determined time and on the social and cultural backdrop against which the recorded episode was enacted. But it is essential to determine with some precision the date of the edict, because things must have changed extensively during the century-and-a-half between the dates variously allocated to it by different scholars. The fact that the tablet was found together with another one carrying a similar decree to the same person, but by another city, the Sicilian Agrigento, helps greatly the dating process.

THE PAIR OF CANDELABRA

One of the most important monuments of Maltese antiquity is the marble 'candelabrum' bearing a bilingual inscription, an identical twin of which was donated by Grand Master de Rohan to King Louis XVI of France in 1780. An undocumented provenance from Marsaxlokk has been wrongly inferred for them merely because the inscriptions commemorate a votive offering to Herakles/Melqart.

Each candelabrum consists of a square base, with moulded horizontal edges, surmounted by a fusiform shaft enclosed within alternating four lanceolate and four acanthus leaves. The shaft is broken at the top in both specimens. From comparisons made with other objects of the same shape housed in various collections of Greek and Roman art, it can be established with certainty that these objects were candelabra of a Greek Hellenistic pedigree. They usually support a wide, splayed receptacle which is often shown containing fire. At times they are topped by a round, flat shelf intended to hold a lamp. They could also have been used for incense burning. Given the foreign material, marble, the objects were probably carved into shape abroad; but the inscription was probably engraved in Malta.

THE BILINGUAL INSCRIPTION

Each candelabrum has two inscriptions, the main one in Punic followed by a Greek synopsis.

Punic inscription:

> To our lord Melqart, lord of Tyre, offering by your servant Abdosir and his bother Osirxamar, sons of Osirxamar, son of Abdosir, for hearing their voice; let him bless them.

Greek inscription:

> Dionysios and Sarapion, sons of Sarapion, to Tyrian Herakles, lord of that city.

Judging by their names, Abdosir and Osirxamar, and the language of the main inscriptions, the dedicators were Punic. But the addition of a synopsis of the dedication in Greek, with Hellenized equivalents of their names and that of the god, suggests a strong Hellenistic influence.

The Egyptianizing element is even stronger if one had to see a budding lotus motif in the lanceolate leaves on the shaft.

Far left: The marble 'candelabrum' of the National Musuem of Archaeology.
Left: A plaster copy of the 'candelabrum' at the Louvre Musuem, Paris.

At the top, distributed on either side of an inscribed crown, the tablet carries the title of the decree: 'Regarding the Proxeny to Demetrios of Syracuse, son of Diodotos, and to his progeny'. Then follows the body of the text, incised with a steady hand and in very impersonal capital letters. It follows the established proxeny formula. It starts by giving the year of the decree, which was determined by the eponymous high priest (Hiketas) and the two magistrates (Hereas and Kotes). This is followed by the decree itself as emanated by the two legislative organs of the *civitas*: the senate (*synkletos*)

Detail of the engraved central crown and part of the text of the original Demetrios inscription with the word ΜΕΛΙΤΑΙΩΝ *('of the Maltese') highlighted.*

A graphic illustration of the engraved text of the Demetrios inscription (see opposite page) as reproduced in Onorato Bres's Malta Antica Illustrata *(1816).*

and the people (*demos*). This includes also the motivation, namely, in recognition of and appreciation for Demetrios' kind services towards the Maltese community, and the decision to register the decree on two copper tablets, one of which to be given to Demetrios himself.

Dating of the decree oscillates between the end of the third century and the first century BC.

In my book on *Roman Malta* of 1992, I was already supporting the date of around 40 BC, suggested by the epigraphist Giacomo Manganaro and others before and after him. The results of recent research conducted by myself in recent years induce me to confirm it with more stringent evidence.

According to Maria Giulia Amadasi Guzzo, many of the short inscriptions incised in Punic script on pottery vessels unearthed during the excavations of the Tas-Silġ sanctuary have been specifically dated to this phase. If the dating is correct, it confirms the uninterrupted continuity of function of the place as the most important sacred shrine on the island, as suggested by Cicero, as well as the survival of the Punic language way into the Roman period. The few ones inscribed, or painted, in Greek characters with the name HERA date almost certainly from this phase.

The discovery of ivory objects, one inscribed with a Punic inscription, during the same archaeological excavations appears to confirm Cicero's claim about the abundance of

A whole saucer retrieved from the recent University of Malta excavations at Tas-Silġ. It carries a one-character inscription, possibly an indication of the identity (or weight) of the offering.

THE DEMETRIOS (OR PROXENY) INSCRIPTION

The matrix on which this curious inscription was engraved is of bronze and consists of a flat sheet framed by a projecting temple facade. This in turn consists of an empty pediment with a horizontal fascia below it made up of four oblong sunken metopes, the whole being supported on two side columns. These stand on a raised platform. They are fluted and have a plain base with torus and four-sided capitals with large everted leaves - one could say that the capitals are of Egyptian typology. The entire tablet is 0.37m high and 0.235m wide.

Ironically, it was not unearthed from Maltese soil but in Rome, near the ancient Curia, a few years before the mid-sixteenth century, together with another bronze tablet containing another proxeny decree for the same person, this time issued by the senate and assembly of the Sicilian city of Acragas (I.G. XIV, 953). In the Greek world the proxeny was an honorific title, very similar in concept and function to our honorary consulate awarded to a foreigner for his services to the awarding community.

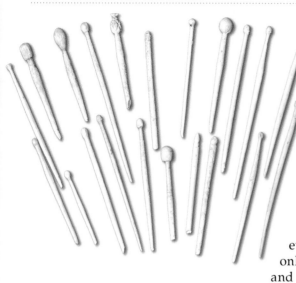

A large quantity of bone (some of ivory) hairpins found during the excavations of the Roman domus and other houses to its north. Some of the examples illustrated here have spherical heads; one has a pomegranate-shaped one.

ivory objects deposited in the sanctuary and his story of the elephant tusks returned to the sanctuary on the orders of Masinissa, king of Numidia, shortly after the Second Punic War.

Coins

Coins are extremely important for the archaeologist. Besides shedding light on the economic history of a people, they turn out to be very helpful in dating the archaeological context in which they are found. They could be the very source for the dating of the associated pottery which is in turn used to date other archaeological contexts. This is possible, however, only when the coins themselves contain internal dating evidence, such as the image and inscribed name of the Roman magistrate governing a province, or of the reigning emperor. Unfortunately, the ancient coins of Malta

and Gozo do not contain such direct, internal dating evidence. What they show are only variations in their imagery and legends whose evolution can be construed as a linear chronological progression. A notable exception is the very last issue which carries the name of C. Arruntanus Balbus, the propraetor of Sicily for 35 BC, towards the end of the Republic.

In view of the oriental, or rather orientalizing, iconography of the majority of the ancient Maltese coin issues and the Punic inscriptions (or legends) on many of them, it does come as a surprise to learn that these coins were not minted in the period when the islands formed part of the political sphere of Carthage; they were struck during the first two centuries of Roman rule. They thus reflect the cultural setting of the islands rather than their political status. They show a cultural admixture that is hardly ever met elsewhere, not even in the Punic cities of Sicily. In their temporal development, they show two or more of the following traits overlapping each other, more or less in this order:

Egyptian religious imagery, Punic language, Punic divine iconography, Greek language, Hellenized divine iconography, and, finally, Roman images and Latin language.

As many as twenty different coin types have been identified. At first, the coins show an entirely non-Hellenic character: the images are derived wholesale, or with little modification, from the Egyptian and Levantine repertoire, with a Punic legend. Soon after, a Greek legend starts replacing the Punic one, while the Punic iconography is maintained. In time, even the latter is transformed into a Hellenized version of (presumably) the same goddess. The image of Isis/Astarte becomes a Hellenistic female divinity whose identity is more difficult to determine. It is also possible, albeit less probable, that these variations were more or less contemporary

and that they reflected the mixed population and culture of the island at the time. Or else, they reflected the ambivalence of the local community's commercial interests: one addressed towards Greek Sicily to the north, while the other was oriented towards the still Punic (certainly until 146 BC) cities on the North African littoral.

At the end of the Republican period, the introduction of Latin in the legend points to a more advanced process of Romanization which becomes even more obvious in the epigraphy of the first two centuries of the empire. In this particular issue the script becomes Latin but, strangely enough, the ending of the name of the island is Greek (*MELITAS*).

The reverse of a Roman coin with the representation of a tripod and the legend MELITAS.

Semis. Obv.: female head (prob. Ashtart/Isis) and ear of wheat; Rev. Four-winged fig.

Semis. Obv.: female head (prob. Ashtart/Isis) and sign of Tanit; Rev.: Four-winged fig.

Sextans. Obv.: male head (prob. Herakles/Melqart); Rev.: sacrificial cap.

Sextans. Obv.: male head (prob. Herakles/Melqart)and caduceus; Rev.: sacrificial cap.

Quadrans. Obv.: veiled female head; Rev.: ram's head and Punic letters 'nn.

As. Obv.: veiled female head; Rev.: tripod and Greek letters ΜΕΛΙΤΑΙΩΝ

Quincunx. Obv.: helmeted female head above crescent; Rev.: warrior holding shield and spear, and Greek letters ΓΑΥΛΙΤΩΝ

Coins that were locally-struck, for reasons that are still not completely within our grasp, appear for the first time after Malta's annexation with the Roman province of Sicily. Most probably, it reflects a radically different policy in this respect practised by the new Roman masters, as opposed to that of the old Carthaginian one. What is even stranger is the oriental (Punic) character of both the iconography and the legend on the early issues.

In line with their policy elsewhere, the Romans seem to have tolerated these harmless expressions of local tradition, as long as they distanced themselves from those of the Carthaginian domination.

A number of different issues were struck over the next two centuries until this autonomous coinage ends with the close of the Republican period at the end of the first century BC.

No one has really sorted out a proper chronological sequence but the main line of development seems to be from the oriental to the Hellenized. What is very striking is their resumption, along with other contemporary Punic issues in other parts of the Mediterranean, of Egyptianizing themes that had been conspicuous by their absence in previous Punic editions.

Architectural Remains

There is not much in terms of remains of buildings that can be dated firmly to this phase. With respect to the two main towns, no structures have been identified in that of Gaulos, while for Melite the only structure, whose construction is firmly dated to this phase, is the fine *domus* discovered just outside Mdina by A.A. Caruana in 1881, with further extensions uncovered by T. Zammit in 1922. Its construction had been dated to around 80 BC on the basis of the style of its architecture, namely the fine

Fragments of painted plaster from Temi Zammit's excavations of 1922 on a further extension of the Rabat domus as well as other houses to the north. The motifs are imitation of marble and, in one instance, a summary representation of a Corinthian capital.

Hellenistic peristyle, with Doric columns and entablature in local limestone, and the fine-quality set of mosaics that decorated its floors. But recently a wider chronological range has been assigned to these mosaics, starting from the last quarter of the second century to the middle of the first century BC. Of course, there is always the possibility of the mosaics having been laid years after the construction of the house, but there is nothing to indicate this, and it is more than likely that the construction and the mosaics are contemporary. Even the few fragments of painted wall plaster mentioned in the excavation reports suggest that they belong to the First Pompeian Style of wall painting. This house survived well into the next phase and it will reappear in the next chapter.

The corner of small structure in Globigerina limestone discovered during trenching works in Villegaignon Street, Mdina. The top and bottom mouldings, its size, and its position in relation to the rest of the remains of buildings discovered in the same exercise, suggest that it was a base of an honorific monument.

It is a real pity that no more architectural remains of the same level have been discovered anywhere else. One was hoping that the archaeological investigations conducted during the trenching exercise in the streets of Mdina would yield some such remains. So far only sections of walls made up of well-dressed ashlar blocks in Coralline Limestone have been encountered, apart from the isolated fluted-column drum and other loose architectural fragments. The only exception is what appears to be a free-standing structure, probably the base of an honorific monument - perhaps a statue group - of which the whole height of one corner was discovered in Villegaignon Street. It looks Classical in style, but it could belong to this phase as much as to the following one. Just part of one block forming the moulded upper frieze survived *in situ*. The lowest course was also moulded and it seemed to be intact. The road surface on which it rests indicates that the road level in Roman times was from three to four metres below the present one. A considerable amount of pottery was also discovered during these rescue operations. Unfortunately, these structural remains had to be covered over again on completion of the investigations.

Many of the country villas seem to have been built during this phase, in some cases, as noted earlier, constructed over previous Punic ones. The Żejtun and

Birżebbuġa villas produced pottery of this phase. At the villa of San Pawl Milqi, besides pottery, even the large sections of painted wall plaster, belonging to the First Pompeian Style, confirm a date within this phase. All three villas were equipped with elaborate apparatus for the pressing of olive oil, as evidenced by the surviving stone parts of the olive crushers (*trapeta*) and presses (*prela*). By far the largest and most complex of these industrial plants was that of the villa of San Pawl Milqi which traditionally is associated with the country house of Publius, the chief man of Malta who gave shelter to St Paul, after the latter's shipwreck on the island.

As expected, the Tas-Silġ sanctuary continued to thrive in this phase and the structures and

A view from the roof of the chapel of part of the large courtyard of the Roman villa at San Pawl Milqi. The olive crusher (trapetum) is one of several found on this site. It was quite intact when excavated in the 1960s (see p.179); it has broken since then.

stratigraphy there do not indicate any significant changes or discontinuities with the change of political power. Similarly, the sanctuary of Ras il-Wardija, Gozo, continued to function during this phase, at least for the next two centuries.

A good number of rock-cut underground tombs date to this phase. As we observed earlier, even in Roman times they continue the same Punic tradition, including the practice of both burial rites of inhumation and cremation and the use of the cinerary urn so typical of the Maltese islands. It appears that the tomb plan with rectangular shaft and rectangular chamber became predominant in this phase. Once more, the major concentration is in groups around Mdina, Malta, and Rabat, Gozo; a scatter of single family tombs in the countryside suggests the presence of isolated country houses both in the vicinity of these two centres and beyond.

Material Culture

It is a well-known fact that, apart from architecture and feats of engineering, the Romans were rather slow in taking up original artistic production. Beyond wall paintings and mosaics, portraiture and commemorative relief sculpture, there are hardly any other art products that one can call, in the strict sense of the word, 'Roman', as distinct from Hellenistic. But from this phase onwards, a number of products from various workshops in Italy, and to a certain degree in Sicily and elsewhere, are given the generic epithet 'Roman', really meaning that they were produced in the Roman empire.

As far as sculpture is concerned, a number of statuary pieces housed in various Maltese national and private collections can be dated to this phase of the Roman period, mostly

from their style. Among these are a couple of Hellenistic female heads housed in the Mdina Cathedral Museum and a very eroded one from Tas-Silġ, a couple of nude male torsos in the National Museum of Archaeology, the Amazon torso retrieved from the sea near Marsa, and the mysterious female draped figure with a strange elaborate necklace over her breast, probably representing Isis. The major problem with these sculptures is that, except for the Amazon torso and the head from Tas-Silġ, we do not know the exact provenance of the other pieces and it is hard to tell to which building they belonged.

A detail of the elaborate necklace worn by the statue of Isis. It displays two horizontal rows of rosettes above a curvilinear row of rams' heads.

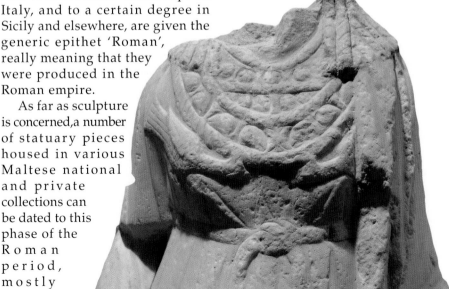

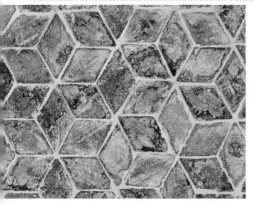

On the contrary, the series of mosaics adorning the Rabat *domus* are clearly anchored to that building. They can be dated quite closely on iconographic, stylistic, and technical grounds to a span of time of 70 years from *c*.125 to *c*.50 BC and thus provide a *terminus post quem non* for the building. They show close connections with slightly earlier mosaic art in Alexandria of Egypt.

The mosaics form a coherent cycle even if they were rendered in a variety of subjects and laying techniques. The large outer borders, normally intended to frame the central panels, are either plain white, red or black, or show geometric designs with a preference for *tromp l'oeil* effects. They are in *opus tessellatum*, that is, formed of standard-size coloured stone cubes (*tesserae*). The most pleasant geometric one is the frame surrounding the central theme in the peristyled courtyard (A). It shows a maze-like motif based on the three-dimensional meander. A similar one in the larger of the two side-rooms (B) frames an equally illusionistic design consisting of a pattern of cascading cubes in perspective formed by lozenge-shaped tiles of three different colours (*opus scutulatum*). While a black-and-white 'wave-crest' frame is enclosed within the larger polychrome

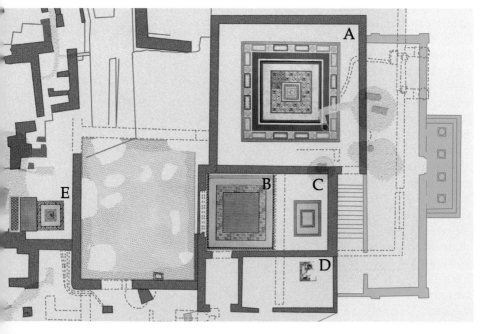

Detail from the central mosaic panel (emblema) depicting the punishment of a satyr. The upturned bearded head displays the snub nose, pointed ear, and short horn typical of this mythological creature. The woman in front of him is clutching his hair and brandishing a pair of shears.

Top opposite page:
Section of a pavement (reconstructed) from the Roman domus of Rabat. It is formed of lozenge-shaped clay tiles of three different colours, thus producing an illusion of cascading cubes or cubic steps.

Bottom opposite page:
Plan of the Roman Domus.

meander frame in the courtyard, the much larger 'wave-crest' design in the side-room frames the whole floor on three sides. The fourth side of the same room is decorated by an intricate stylized lyre motif.

The same lyre motif in *opus vermiculatum* (laid with very tiny stone cubes) is also used in the larger frame of the smaller side-room (C), commonly referred to as the dining room (*triclinium*), as well as in the border of the central panel (*emblema*) from room D. The same technique (*opus vermiculatum*) is used pictorially in all three surviving *emblemata* (prefabricated central panels) and in the square border originally framing the 'satyr' panel in Room E. This border shows an elaborate festoon carrying a variety of fruits, with different theatrical masks in the corners and at the centre of each side. The panel itself depicts a unique mythological scene involving a nude male figure (identified as a satyr) held captive by two female figures (possibly nymphs or maenads) one of whom brandishes menacingly a pair of shears in her right hand.

The panel still *in situ* in the centre of the courtyard depicts a rather hackneyed motif, consisting of two doves perched on an elaborately worked basin, while the panel from Room D portrays a cute dishevelled young child holding a bunch of grapes in his right hand and a pomegranate in his left hand. The composition is balanced by a bird in flight at the top and a duck at the bottom of the picture.

Disappointingly little survives of the fresco decoration of this house. Only a few fragments are on show in the museum attached to it. Most of the fragments are in the so-called 'First Pompeian Style', consisting of panels in imitation marble. But one fragment depicts the top part of a stylized column with a sketchy pseudo-Corinthian capital.

Central panel of the peristyle.

Section of an illusionistic maze.

The three different central panels (emblemata) in opus vermiculatum *and a selection of parts of other mosaic floors from the Roman domus in Rabat. Apart from the emblemata, which could have been imported as finished products, all the other floors were laid on the spot. (mosaics are not to scale)*

Three sections of festoon originally bordering the satyr emblema.

The *satyr* emblema.

Section of a scrolled border.

The *'Autumn'* emblema.

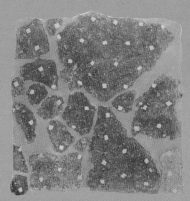

Section of an opus signinum *floor.*

Part of a black-and-white mosaic.

Section of a pavement with lozenge-shaped tiles.

A fragment of a 'Magarian' bowl
found during the 1922 excavations
of the Roman Domus by Temi Zammit.

Pottery

What has just been stated with regard to Roman products of material culture applies even more effectively to pottery in general, and to the 'Roman' pottery found in Malta during this phase in particular.

We have already seen how occasional items of fine, black-glazed pottery from Greek south Italian workshops reached Malta during the Punic phase. Some of them were found in tombs, others were retrieved, mostly in a fragmentary state, from the deposits of Tas-Silġ. During this phase plates and other shapes of tableware characterized by their metallic black glaze, the so-called 'Campanian ware', become more common. It is this type of ware that during the first half of

the first century BC sheds its black glaze which is replaced by a darkish red slip which characterizes the fine tableware production of several Italian workshops, known as Italian *terra sigillata*. Foremost among these centres of production was Arezzo (*Arretium*) and its product is widely known as Arretine ware.

Many of the potters were so proud of their work that they stamped their initials at the bottom of the vessel. Often the initials of the potter were enclosed within a foot-shaped stamp, whence the term *'in planta pedis'*. Up to some decades ago all fine ware of this type used to be called 'Arretine' but now more and more workshops are being identified in other parts of Italy, foremost among them in Pisa. In fact, fragments of vessels inscribed with the stamp of C. Rasinius Pisanus (CRASINPIS) found in the 1922 excavations of the Rabat town-house were originally identified as 'Arretine', but should now be assigned to a Pisan potter of that name. Similarly those found at Tas-Silġ and one stamped with the mark of L. Rasinius Pisanus (L.R.Pi) found in a tomb in Gudja Road, Tarxien.

During the same 1922 excavations of the Rabat house, Temi Zammit found large quantities of Italian *terra sigillata* decorated in relief, among which fragments of twenty bowls which he called 'Magarian', but which are more probably Italian versions of this eastern Mediterranean typology. One plain fragmentary saucer of Italian *terra sigillata* found during the 1922 excavations is incised with the Greek word ΜΕΛΙΔΟΤΟΥ, probably the name of its owner.

This fine Roman pottery, both from ancient Melite and from other sites, in the Maltese national and private collections is crying out for a proper study. Such study will undoubtedly shed important light on the social and economic history of this and the following period.

The same applies to coarse Roman pottery, thick-walled containers used for transportation and storage of liquids, such as water, oil, and wine, as well as solid food, like fish-sauce (*garum*), besides ordinary domestic purposes. This is the most common material to be found in archaeological excavations of sites of this period, including shipwrecks.

A fragmentary bowl in Italian terra sigillata with the word ΜΕΛΙΔΟΤΟΥ *('of Melidotos') inscribed on the rim. Clearly, the owner wanted his bowl to be identified with his name. In view of the Greek script, he was probably a slave of Hellenistic origin.*

Temi Zammit, in his short account of his excavation of the Rabat house in 1922, states that: 'The amount of potsherds obtained from the debris was astounding; cartloads of them were disposed of after a careful examination. Most of the fragments were of ordinary domestic Roman pottery, amphorae, jugs, pots, basins, etc.' It is regretted that all that material is no longer available for study. The 'disposal' of pottery fragments is, I am happy to say, no longer customary in archaeological practice; it has not been so for the last 50 years. The Tas-Silġ excavations

Map of the Mediterranean showing the distribution of Tripolitanian amphorae of all types. The green dots show where they have turned up, implying trade routes between them.

have produced, and continue to produce hundreds and hundreds of boxfuls of course pottery; but nobody would dream of disposing of any of it. It is a precious tool for the study of economic and social history. Rhodian amphorae, to give just one example, recognizable both from their shape and their stamped handles, occur on several sites in Malta; they indicate the importation of wine or olive oil from that island. So do south Italian, Spanish, and North African amphorae.

John Riley has already put Malta on the shipping trade routes of the period; in his study of the Roman coarse ware from the excavations of Sidi Khrebish (ancient Berenike) in Benghazi, Libya, he made frequent references to amphorae of various origins housed in Maltese collections. The course pottery (mostly

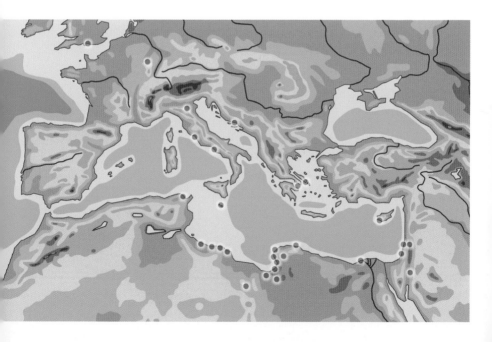

Two examples of cooking pots. Note the rebate on the rim of the pot on the left, intended to receive a fitting lid.

amphorae) from Tas-Silġ has already been studied and classified by Brunella Bruno. The cooking wares, which are mostly of local production, have been studied by Alessandro Quercia, who has published a short synthesis in the *Malta Archaeological Review* of 2000.

Politics and Social Structure

The inhabitants of the Maltese islands were subject communities controlled by Rome. With the creation of the first province of Sicily, the Romans started to develop an efficient and effective system of controlling and administering a fast-expanding territory. Malta was taken care of as part of the Sicilian province. It belonged to the majority of Sicilian *civitates* who enjoyed no

special privileges and were subject to an established taxation system. Innumerable statements made, suggesting the opposite, have no sound basis and are mostly grounded on false or anachronistic premises.

Whatever foreign relations the Maltese people had were dictated by Rome. Thus, they were definitely not allowed to provide any assistance to enemy fleets; officially, the same applied to pirates. Pirates were constantly a real nuisance in the Mediterranean, periodically a serious threat not only to maritime trade and traffic and to coastal towns in general but also to the smooth management of the empire; and we know of several naval campaigns sent out specifically against pirates, the major and most successful one being

[DECREE] OF PUBLIC HOSPITALITY AND GOOD-WILL TOWARDS DEMETRIOS, SON OF DIODOTOS OF SYRACUSE, AND HIS DESCENDANTS. [ISSUED] AT THE TIME OF THE HIGH PRIEST IKETAS AND THE ARCHONS [CHIEF MAGISTRATES] DEREOS AND KOTETOS.

AS DEMETRIOS, SON OF DIODOTOS OF SYRACUSE, ALWAYS STROVE FOR THE BENEFIT OF OUR CITIZENS IN THEIR PUBLIC AFFAIRS, IT SEEMED PROPER TO THE SENATE AND PEOPLE OF MELITE [MALTA] TO DECREE, THAT BECAUSE OF HIS MERIT AND THE GOOD-WILL HE ALWAYS SHOWED TOWARDS OUR PEOPLE, DEMETRIOS, SON OF DIODOTOS OF SYRACUSE, BE HONOURED BY THE PEOPLE OF MELITE AND THEIR DESCENDANTS.

THIS DECREE IS TO BE INSCRIBED ON THE TWO BRONZE TABLETS ONE OF WHICH IS TO BE GIVEN TO DEMETRIOS, SON OF DIODOTOS OF SYRACUSE.

that of Pompey in 67 BC. Cicero's allusion to the presence of pirates on Malta surely refers to the first three decades of the first century BC when the threat posed by these corsairs had become very serious and had extended to the western Mediterranean. One wonders to what degree the central administration was just tolerant of their regular presence in Malta - they sheltered there regularly in winter - or simply helpless in face of this adverse situation.

One needs to remember that in antiquity sea traffic was virtually at a standstill in the winter months, and the Maltese archipelago was distant enough from the mainland to render it inaccessible throughout most of the stormy season. We all know how precarious the crossing between Sicily and Malta and vice-versa remained even up to early

The English translation of the text of the proxeny inscription, as published by Louis de Boisgelin in his Ancient and Modern Malta *(1805).*

modern times. It must have been even more so in antiquity. Cicero himself tells us how dangerous the sea that separated the two islands was (Verr., II. 4. 103). The propraetor and the quaestors of Sicily did not have much incentive to make the crossing either. From Cicero we learn that Verres never made it to Malta in his three years of governorship and he organized all his spoliations by means of agents and slaves. Cicero does not manifest any particular familiarity with the Maltese landscape; he himself probably never visited Malta so that his Maltese friend Aristoteles was more probably his guest in Sicily or in Rome rather than his host in Malta. So that both praetor and quaestors administered Malta mostly by proxy.

There must have been more than one occasion when things became rather tough for the Maltese, such as in the term of Verres' mischievous administration, when the inhabitants needed to send representations to Rome to lobby at the right quarters or to defend their claims directly at the heart of things, where it really mattered. Cicero tells us that there were Maltese delegates (*legati*) in Rome to assist him with details of Verres' maladministration, in preparation for the latter's trial. Such delegations, whether official or otherwise, needed someone to host them in this overpowering metropolis. One can only imagine how estranged people coming from a tiny island hundreds of miles away would have felt in a huge city like Rome. Things would be infinitely easier if they could rely on someone of the place who could host them, look after them and open the right gates for them. This seems to be the kind of service given to the Maltese population by Demetrios of Syracuse in the couple of decades after Verres' trial, for which they decided to bestow on him the title of *proxenos*, a sort of honorary consulate

as we know it today. The decree was two-pronged: it manifested its gratitude for services already rendered and endeavoured to secure similar services for the future.

The same decree, which is inscribed on a decorated bronze tablet, sheds precious light on the internal administration and legislative set-up prevailing, roughly, between 60 and 27 BC. The decree itself reveals only one type of transaction that this set-up could perform, the conferment of a proxeny on a foreign benefactor, but it also mentions official posts, both civilian and religious, and decision-making bodies. There was a *hierothytes* (a sort of high priest), Hiketas by name. The fact that he is mentioned in the context of a decree suggests that he was eponymous,

A section from the model of ancient Rome in the Museo della Civiltà Romana *in Rome. At the top one can easily identify the Coliseum, while at the bottom the theatre of Marcellus stands out close to the Isola Tiberina.*

that is, he probably gave his name to the current year. Then there were two chief administators (*archontes*), Hereas and Kotes. The duality of this highest executive post could be, as has been suggested, reminiscent of the dual *rabs* mentioned in the Gozo third-century BC Punic inscription and, indirectly, of the dual *suffetes* in Carthage; but they more probably reflect the duality of the consuls in the Roman republican constitution.

Finally, the decision-making bodies are the council (*synkletos*) and the assembly of the people (*demos*) who declare to deem it fit to confer the honour on Demetrios. So we have a two-chamber legislative body, in perfect parallelism with the *senatus populusque* of the Roman metropolis. They represented the inhabitants of Malta, or of both islands, who were free-born, but not Roman citizens. The constitutional format described by the inscription could, possibly, indicate a special status, that of the *ius Latii* (that is, Latin citizenship), which is known to have been granted by Caesar to a number of Sicilian *civitates* before his demise, and which was withdrawn by Augustus as soon as he had himself declared sole ruler of Rome and of the empire.

Statue of Julius Caesar from the Museo della Civiltà Romana, *in Rome. Caesar, just before he was murdered by his fellow senators in 44 BC, had extended the Latin citizenship to all the Sicilian* civitates *(including Malta and Gozo). After his death, Antony claimed that Caesar had intended to award them full Roman citizenship.*

I have frequently made reference to the possibility that Caesar granted municipal status to both Malta and Gozo before he was murdered in March 44 BC. This grant did not make it in time to come into effect because of Caesar's untimely death; but only two days after that event, the Roman senate decided that his *acta* were to be treated as law. It seems that this decision gave Marcus Antonius, his lieutenant, discretion to validate by publication decisions, including alleged ones, of the dead dictator. One of these concerned the granting of full Roman citizenship to the Sicilians; the Maltese would have thus obtained the same privilege, since Malta was part of Sicily. The most direct evidence on this comes from Cicero in a letter to his friend Atticus (*Ad Att.* 14.12.1): 'You know how warm a feeling I have for the Sicilians and what an honour I consider it to have them as my clients. Caesar was generous to them and I was not sorry that he should be - though the Latin franchise was intolerable, but let that pass... But look how Antonius, following a huge bribe, has published a law, passed by the dictator in an assembly, which makes the Sicilians Roman citizens.' That right, however, was only enjoyed by the Sicilians (consequently also by the Maltese) for a few years, if at all. If not already by 36 BC, certainly by 21 BC, Octavian had changed all that. The political status of the Sicilian *civitates* after that date is defined by Pliny the Elder (see the following chapter).

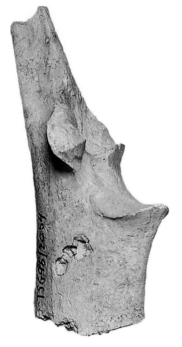

One of the purposes of the University of Malta excavations at Tas-Silġ is to establish what types of sacred rituals took place inside the sanctuary by studying the organic remains from its excavations in the dump outside it. This ulna of a sheep or goat carries the imprint of a dog's teeth.

Once more we have no indication of any full-scale use of slaves in Malta, though their presence is very likely, both in the stone quarries and in the households of the rich, in their country villas and on their estates.

At the other end of the social spectrum, the remains of the splendid *domus* discovered outside Mdina in 1881 demonstrate that there was at least one man of substance who could afford to build a sizeable town-house with the highest architectural specifications and to transfer to Malta master mosaicists with their specialized equipment and raw materials to decorate its floors with the finest specimens of mosaic art available on the market. At this stage the house does not have any features which connect it with officialdom; so its owner could be just a wealthy private individual, a local gentleman, or a foreign resident, with very up-to-date Hellenized tastes. On the other hand, such foreign magnates preferred the quiet life in villas out in the countryside or close to the sea, like the Ramla Bay one. I would rather imagine a Maltese gentleman like Cicero's acquaintance, Diodorus or Aristoteles, inhabiting this and similar houses in town. After all Diodorus could afford a collection of precious silver vessels, some of high artistic value, as well as another residence in Lilybaeum.

In terms of social differentiation based on financial resources, the economic system seems to have provided the majority of the population with just enough for a decent survival, mostly a subsistence economy. Many were in an economic position to afford sharing their modest surplus with their gods, offering a proportion of their harvesting of sea resources (from fish to molluscs and sea-urchins) or of their agricultural crops or farm animals (mostly sheep and goats). The abundant remains of all these creatures yielded by the recent excavations by the University of Malta in what must have been the dumping area of the Tas-Silġ sanctuary imply that such offerings were regularly made there by the humbler population.

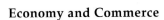
Economy and Commerce

We have no direct evidence as to whether Carthage imposed any taxes on the inhabitants of the Maltese islands during the previous period; the Romans certainly did. According to Cicero (*Verr.*, II, 3, 12-13), however, the Romans did not impose any new taxes on the land in Sicily, and the Roman tax system was a continuation of that imposed by the Carthaginians on the cities under their control, that is, a tithe of the annual harvest, which was similar to that levied by Hiero II, king of Syracuse, on the territory of his subject cities in south-eastern Sicily. The tithe-paying cities of Sicily included, at the time of Cicero, some of the cities that had been 'most loyal' to Rome in the Second Punic War as well as the cities that had supported the Carthaginians, including Agrigento and Morgantina (*Verr.* III, 100-104). But Cicero lists only 35 tithe-paying cities (*civitates decumanae*); the rest were, according to some scholars, *civitates censoriae*, which probably meant that their taxes were farmed by the censors in Rome rather than by the Roman governor in Syracuse. Since Cicero states that these cities were very few in number (*perpaucae*) and since they tended to be those that had been captured by force (*vi captae*) during the Second Punic War, Malta has never been identified among the latter.

In the province of Sicily, of which Malta formed part, the Roman taxation system imposed the submission

Graphic reconstruction of the seaside villa in its natural setting at Ramla Bay in Gozo.

in kind of a tenth of the grain and barley harvest, which was shipped directly to Rome, and a tax in cash (probably also equivalent to a tenth) on olives, fruits, and vegetables, as well as on wine and herds. The collection of these dues was normally farmed out to contractors in Sicily by the quaestors of that province. Besides, the Roman senate reserved the right to exact a second tithe in case of necessity, of which we know of at least two cases (in 190 and 171 BC). In 73 BC this additional contribution was turned into a regular one. Rome also imposed a customs

duty (*portoria*) of 5 per cent on all cargoes entering or exiting from all Sicilian harbours; this helps us to understand two often misquoted and misread passages by Cicero concerning Maltese draperies and honey that Verres smuggled out of Syracuse without paying the relevant customs duty (Cicero, *Verr*. II, 2, 176 and 183; see above p.147).

Various communities were also obliged to furnish the ships of a small fleet with the appropriate crews to protect the ports from pirates. One wonders how the Maltese community handled this predicament when pirates seemed to be regular visitors in their harbours. Someone must have closed one eye, if not both eyes, when the subject came up for discussion, at least until the problem of piracy was eradicated completely, or almost.

An aerial view of St Paul's Bay, undoubtedly one of the Maltese bays and harbours that, according to the orator Cicero, were frequented by pirates in late Republican times.

Olive mill from San Pawl Milqi just after it had been excavated in the 1960s.

While they had no armies to keep, the Sicilian communities, including those of Malta and Gozo, had to shoulder all the expenses involved in public works (roads and water supplies) and buildings (civil and religious) and other public utilities. Some of these were paid for by rich benefactors; the rest had to be seen to by taxes. For this purpose two censors collected the relevant data of each community every five years

The major industrial activity that transpires from the frequent references to it in ancient sources, including Diodorus and Cicero, is the textile industry. Diodorus praises the sheer qualities of Maltese drapery; Cicero infers that it was widely renowned and sought after. Given the frequent mention of Maltese fabrics, one wonders whether *Melitenses* referred simply to a type of drapery, originally produced only in Malta, but later produced also in other parts, very much like our muslin, calico, or denim. But Cicero implies that between 73 and 70 BC virtually the whole population of the city of Melite was kept busy by Verres weaving drapery for women's clothing. According to him, a specially sheer (*perlucidus*) Maltese cloth was used for cushions, stuffed with rose petals, such as those Verres used for his carriage. This passage (Cicero, *Verr.*, II,2, 27) has also been often misread to mean 'Maltese roses', again erroneously attributing Malta with rose production.

An industrial activity which implies an agricultural produce is olive-oil production. It is only testified by archaeological evidence, a score or so of complex structures (*villas*) spread out in the countryside

with sections equipped with stone apparatus for the pressing of olive oil. Whether enough was produced to satisfy the local demand, or whether the production was so much in excess as to permit export we cannot tell; certainly 10 per cent of it had to be paid to Rome in kind or in cash as tax. Olive-oil production implies extensive olive groves surrounding these country villas, no trace of which survived in the twentieth century.

Grain production could, until recently, only be inferred from the representation of an ear of grain to the left of the head of Isis/Ashtart on the obverse of one of the coin issues of Malta of this time. From environmental studies carried out in connection with the recent archaeological exca-

An artist's reconstruction of an olive press (prelum) based on evidence forthcoming from the San Pawl Milqi villa and other sites. In this model the horizontal beam, which presses down on the wicker basket containing the olives, is drawn down by means of a capstan. An olive crusher (trapetum) is visible in the background.

vations conducted by the University of Malta, while it was confirmed that cereals were the staple agricultural product, it transpired that the economy was also based on animal husbandry and the exploitation of coastal resources and fishing. Several ashy deposits were encountered, clearly dumped in the area outside the sanctuary, which contained large quantities of animal bones, predominantly sheep and goat, of fish bones, sea-urchins and sea-shells, including

Two fragmentary items of Campanian A ware from the excavations of the Roman domus or the houses adjacent to it.

the odd murex shell. While tax was statutorily paid on land produce, one wonders whether tax was also exacted on such sea products.

The local coin production is indicative of a sufficiently complex market economy to require a local substitute for coinage of Roman provenance. It should be kept in mind that the 'privilege' of issuing their own coins was also enjoyed by more than half of the cities of Sicily, including the island *civitates* of Cossyra (Pantelleria) and Lipari. It was limited to copper issues of lower denominations. Transactions with the outside world, including the payment of taxes, were made in silver and gold coinage for which Rome held to its almost total monopoly. Specimens of Maltese-struck coins, however, have reputedly also turned up on archaeological sites outside Malta, for example Agrigento, Morgantina, and Sciacca in Sicily. A coin from the Gozo mint has been reported to be found as far away as Martigny in France , together with a Jewish coin from Palestine of AD 67-68. These imply trade activity which is confirmed by the presence on Malta of imported pottery, normally of fine table ware, mostly from Campania

and later from Arezzo and other north Italian workshops producing their typical *terra sigillata* ware. Shipwrecks, such as the second oldest one (second-first century BC) outside Xlendi bay in Gozo, also confirm these commercial connections, even though this could have been merely the wreck of a ship plying Maltese waters but directed to some other destination.

According to numismatists, the series of Maltese coins point to a progressive inflation and rising standards of living. In time, smaller denominations give way to higher denominations. As many as three issues in the AS denomination in the early first century BC could reflect a sharp rise in the cost of living following the social war in Italy and the slave war in Sicily. Then, a debasement in the coinage after 75 BC is attributed to a scarcity of metal for minting purposes resulting from the various wars, including the civil war.

In the lawsuit against Verres we learn of all his pillages. At the end of the first Verrine, Cicero estimated that Verres had stolen approximately forty million sesterces from the Sicilians. What we are not told is whether the Sicilian plaintiffs, including the Maltese community, received compensation. Apparently they did not, certainly not an adequate one. We have noted above that Verres gave up his case halfway through the trial and retired in exile. We are not told of the disastrous consequences of this cunning decision, which is likely to have been advised by the defence council, the consummate lawyer Hortentius.

Parts of the original Doric peristyle of the Roman domus *reconstructed in situ. The triglyph frieze preserves traces of the original plaster colour scheme.*

We know that if the accused retired into exile before condemnation and the official seizure of his property, as happened in this case, it was extremely difficult to obtain adequate compensation. Since the historian Plutarch gives us a much lower figure for Cicero's estimate, namely, 750,000 denarii (equivalent to three million sesterces), it is quite possible that this represents the actual amount collected and shared out, that is, seven per cent of the claimed amount.

Settlement & Urban Organization

The two main urban centres already in existence in pre-Roman times and documented in the mid-fourth century BC by Pseudo-Skylax (111) must have continued to develop further in the Roman Republican phase. Diodorus Siculus indicates that the two towns had already been firmly established by his time. Apart from Livy, a century-and-a-half after the Roman conquest of the Maltese archipelago, Cicero referred on several occasions to a fortified town (*oppidum*) in Malta, but not in Gozo. At one stage he claimed that it had been turned by Verres into a textile-producing factory (*textrinum*) for three years (*Verr.*, ii. 4. 103). Diodorus adds a further comment in praise of the Maltese dwellings which seems to find a perfect fit in the Roman *domus* inside Melite mentioned above. He states that 'the dwellings on the island are worthy of note, being

Opposite:
An artist's impression of a typical Roman market scene.

ambitiously constructed with cornices and finished in stucco with unusual workmanship.' In fact, the architectural decoration of the Doric peristyle of that house manifests a very elegant cornice supported by columns, all of which were in local soft limestone, but covered with a thin coating of stucco and painted in the standard polychromy.

The ancient sources and the geography of the islands leave no doubt that the political and administrative jurisdiction of each town extended to the rest of the territory of the respective island. The Maltese coins discussed above must have been struck in some special building inside Melite; and coin minting must have been administered by a special body under the authority of the local government, whatever form

A coin issued by Gozo with the legend ΓΑΥΛΙΤΩΝ *(Gauliton).*

the latter might have had. Coins with the legend GAULITON struck locally at the end of the Republic suggest some degree of autonomy for Gozo and its town already by then, at least for the short period in which they circulated.

SAN PAWL MILQI

Aerial view of the site of San Pawl Milqi. The site was excavated by an Italian expedition in the 1960s which revealed extensive remains of a Roman villa equipped with at least two olive presses (prela) and several olive crushers (trapeta). On a section of the remains a small church was constructed in early modern times, which was replaced by the present one in the 17th century.

What has been stated regarding small rural settlements with respect to the Punic period applies also to this period. The existence of such settlements, in particular the one at the head of the Grand Harbour, is indicated by the frequent discoveries of rock-cut tombs dated to this period. The much more intensive use of this harbour in this phase must have been one of the reasons for an increasing settlement in the area.

Country villas belonging to well-off gentlemen also increase steadily in number, sometimes replacing previous country houses. The large villa at San Pawl Milqi is likely to have been constructed on the remains of a Punic building at this stage.

Ports and Harbours

Whereas Marsaxlokk harbour seems to have been preferred for use in Phoenician and Punic times, it seems that the deeper and narrower harbours on the north coast were used much more extensively in Roman times.

Given that ancient mariners, after what must have been each time a thrilling, but necessary, adventure in the open sea, preferred to hug the land after the first landfall and to enter the first safe anchorage beyond it, it is understandable that harbour activity should shift in this period to the harbours facing Rome. These were the two well sheltered harbours flanking the Mount Sceberras peninsula on the eastern side of Malta and Salina Bay further west.

THE GRAND HARBOUR

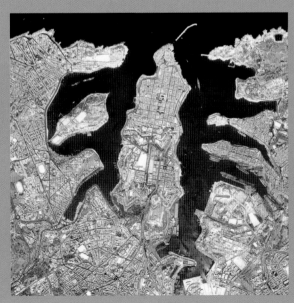

Aerial view of the two harbours on the north-east coast of Malta. Note how convenient both harbours were as shelters for ships reaching Malta from the north. They are separated by the Mount Sceberras peninsula. Given the prominence of the peninsula between the two harbours it might well have been recorded by ancient mariners as an important landmark in their periploi (or portulans)*, so important as to end up being registered in the* Geography *of Ptolemy as a* chersonesos.

Culture and Religious Beliefs

Religious beliefs, as transmitted to us by the material remains of cult imagery and religious ritual, are the most articulate and enduring expressions of any culture. This is the case with Malta's glorious prehistoric temple culture; it is the same with the culture of the Maltese islands in the Roman period. It is for this reason that the two, culture and religion, are dealt with together in this section.

Punic culture, being rooted in Semitic culture and traditions, was anti-classical by definition. In spite of that, even before Alexander's titanic achievement, but more intensively after it, Hellenic culture percolated through most aspects of the life and culture of the Phoenicians, both in the east and in the west. Witness the splendid Alexander sarcophagus, dated 332-30 BC, removed from an underground necropolis of the Phoenician rulers outside Sidon, and now housed in the Museum of Archaeology of Istanbul, and the sculpture from the Mahdia shipwreck now in the Bardo Museum in Tunis. So it is not surprising that the Hellenization process started to permeate life in Malta already in the last century of the Punic occupation. With the severance of the umbilical cord with Carthage in 218 BC, Hellenization becomes the most prominent feature in the acculturation process of the islands during the Republican age.

This is best seen in the locally-struck coinage, where the oriental iconography of the earliest series is replaced by Graeco-Roman imagery in Hellenistic style. Even the Punic legend is replaced by a Greek one. It can also be seen in sculpture, most of which is without a specific Maltese provenance, such as the two celebrated inscribed candelabra, a couple of marble heads in the Mdina Cathedral Museum, and the enigmatic draped statue of 'Isis' in the Domus Romana Museum in Rabat, but a few pieces are from secure provenance, such as a statue of Amazon from the Marsa harbour and a marble female head from Tas-Silġ.

The Egyptianizing element in the coin imagery and in the sculpture forms part of the general Hellenistic influence. Alexandria is thought to have played a leading role in the propagation of Hellenization in general, and of the Egyptianizing part of it in particular.

During the late Punic period Malta had borrowed extensively from Alexandrian art and architecture, often with an Egyptianizing iconography. This artistic current gathers momentum in this phase. A close connection between the Egyptianizing imagery on coins and statuary can be seen in the ram's head on the reverse of one coin issue, which has the same typology as the series of ram's heads on the strange necklace worn by the unique marble statue, probably representing Isis. I do not think this analogy is coincidental and the link deserves further investigation.

As far as architecture and mosaic art are concerned the Roman *domus* excavated by A.A

RAMS' HEADS

The head of a ram on the reverse of one of the Maltese coins of the late Republican phase is paralleled by similar rams' heads both on the elaborate necklace hanging on the chest of the statue of 'Isis' in the Domvs Romana Museum (top right) and on an oscillum *in the Gozo Archaeological Museum (bottom right).*

Caruana outside Mdina's Greeks Gate in 1881 stands out as the finest example of domestic architecture and interior decoration found on the island. The mosaics date it to the late-second or the first half of the first century BC, a time when Rome itself was embroiled in some of the worst episodes of civil war. The fine architectural standards of the house are best expressed by the decoration of the peristyle which was in the Doric order. The columns, faceted in the lower third and fluted in the rest of the height, and the entablature, were in local limestone coated with stucco and painted with a colour scheme in fashion at the time. The great nineteenth-century architect E.L. Galizia has left us a splendid graphic reconstruction of the elevation of the peristyle.

The group of mosaics decorating the floors of the peristyle courtyard and the surrounding rooms are often quoted by the most authoritative scholars in the field (such as Erich Pernice) as some of the finest examples of Hellenistic mosaic art. Itinerant mosaicists must have been present on the island to lay the large schemes of *opus tessellatum* on the floors. The materials used to form

A sherd of a plate or saucer with the Greek word HRAC (meaning 'of Hera') inscribed on it before firing. This implies that the Greek goddess Hera had already started to be identified with Ashtart at the Tas-Silġ sanctuary.

these geometric and figurative designs must have been imported as well. Some of the geometric borders show extraordinary optical illusions of depth. One particular border depicting festoons loaded with fruits and nuts is formed of tiny cubes of coloured stones and glass (*opus vermiculatum*), and the effect is very life-like. This border and another one in the adjacent room show a deep interest in the theatre, as they portray several theatrical masks.

The central *emblemata*, self-contained pictures made in *opus vermiculatum*, are likely to have been pre-fabricated in some far-away workshop, probably on the explicit specifications of the owner of the house. One surviving *emblema* shows a mysterious scene which shows a muscular male figure being held captive by two female ones against an idyllic country backdrop. Surviving in a slightly worse condition is the second *emblema* which depicts a putto-like child holding grapes and pomegranates, accompanied by a bird and a duck.

Romanization and Resistance. Survival of Punic Traditions

In spite of the direct control from Rome and more intensified cultural and commercial, as well as political, intercourse with Sicily, we have good reasons to believe that Punic religious beliefs and practices survived for centuries after the Roman annexation. Although the literary sources are not in the least informative on the matter, inscriptions and archaeological evidence suggest clearly that the Maltese inhabitants continued to practise actively the worship of the Phoenician pantheon of divinities. Religious differences were generally resolved by syncretism, linking local gods with those of the Graeco-Roman pantheon. This is the time when syncretism assumes an accelerated pace. Thus Melqart is assimilated with Herakles in the bilingual inscription. He is qualified by the epithet *Archegetes* (city founder) in the Greek version.

Ashtart is assimilated with Isis in the earlier coin issues, with a veiled divinity of a purely Hellenistic typology and style in later ones. I am inclined to believe that the divinity most suited for this latter image, given the accumulated evidence for her worship in Malta, is Hera. At Tas-Silġ, in fact, Ashtart gradually assumed also the name Hera and eventually Juno, though this last name is only found in Cicero in his court speeches against Verres. Although the name Hera appears on a handful of pottery sherds, no inscriptions with Juno's name have ever turned up in the excavations on the site.

Less easy to define is the assimilation of the oriental-looking bearded male divinity on the obverse of one coin issue, mostly because there is even lack of agreement as to which Punic divinity it represents. As many as three male divinities have been suggested: Eshmun, Melqart, and Baal Hammon. Unlike that of his female counterpart, his image does not evolve into a Hellenized one. In spite of that, suggestions of assimilation with Graeco-Roman gods have not been lacking. Eshmun is identified with Aesculapius, the god of healing, on the basis of the *caduceus* depicted next to his head; as usual Melqart is identified with Herakles.

The survival of Punic religious traditions should not come as a surprise because the Romans are well known for their liberal attitude towards their conquered subjects when it came to religious matters. On one hand, this attitude is characterized by a next to total absence of a policy of religious acculturation of subject peoples; on the other hand, not only

were the Romans tolerant of foreign creeds but, on several occasions, they went to the point of importing cults, albeit under very tight controls by Senate. This phenomenon started with the early adoption of new Greek gods into the pantheon of Roman deities. In 204 BC the Phrygian cult of Cybele was ceremoniously and officially introduced into Rome itself. The cults of Mithras, Isis, and Serapis eventually became widespread both in Rome and in the empire. It was much later, within imperial rule that the autocratic system felt itself so seriously threatened by an imported foreign religion that it found it necessary to resort to the most drastic measures of persecution to try to ward off that threat.

An oriental-looking bearded head on the obverse of a Maltese coin type. The caduceus in front of the head has led some scholars to identify the head with Eshmun, the Punic equivalent of the Roman Aesculapius.

In reality the Romans hardly ever tried to enforce their own culture on their subject peoples, least so on that of these two small islands. It is still not possible to say to what degree the development of the two towns followed the new Graeco-Roman model. An urban-based system of local government following the approved model seems, however, to have affirmed itself, even though a pre-existent one, on the Carthaginian model, is not to be excluded. It is believed by some scholars that the dual magistrate system (*Archontes*) in the Greek bronze inscription referring to Melite echoes the typical Carthaginian one of two *suffetes* reflected in the two *rabs* of the third-second-century Gozitan inscription. It should not be forgotten, however, that even Rome had a similar system, this time of two consuls, and several contemporary inscriptions from Sicilian cities refer to similar dual magistracies.

Roman tastes in luxuries were probably encouraged. They could be satisfied through the growth of trade and cash economy centred on towns. Beyond this, the cultural complex of the islands may be described as 'Romano-Punic'. There might have been a few Italian settlers, and the Greek names of two known personalities, Diodorus and Aristoteles, suggest Sicilian origins; in particular Diodorus, since he had a second house in Lilybaeum. Military presence must have been minimal, especially after the complete elimination of Carthage. Because of this, the indigenous

(that is Punic) cultural substratum remained vigorous.

This might be the reason why we do not see much change at the sanctuary of Tas-Silġ; it seems that life there continued uninterrupted from the Punic phase. On the other hand, the sanctuary of Ras il-Wardija, for some unknown reason, comes to an end. A temple to a Graeco-Roman divinity without a local Punic predecessor (at least a documented one) is the one of Proserpina, celebrated by the Chrestion inscription. Since the temple was restored between 27 BC and AD 14, when it was about to collapse because of its antiquity, it must have been built sometime in this phase. The cult of Proserpina suggests influence from Sicily, where the cult of Demeter and Persephone was very deeply rooted and widely diffused, though Carthaginian coins with a representation of 'Persephone' are not lacking.

An artist's impression of a typical Roman cargo ship berthed against a built wharf. Ships like this must have stopped frequently at any one of the Maltese harbours to load or unload cargo. Grain was transported in sacks, while amphorae were used for wine and oil, as well as for salted fish and fish sauce (garum).

MARE GERMANICO

BRITANNIA

OCEANO

BELGIO
GERMANIA
COLONIA
Reno
GERMANIA

GALLIA
NORICO
REZIA

LIONE
MILANO
AQUILEA
DACIA

LIGVRIA
PANNONIA
ISTRIA
MESIA

SPAGNA
ITALIA
MARE ADRIATICO

MERIDA
TARRACONA
CORSICA
ROMA
TRACIA

SARDEGNA
CAPVA
EPIRO

CADICE
MARE
TVSCO

MARE

MAVRITANIA
SICILIA
CRETA

CARTAGINE
AFRICA
MALTA

NVMIDIA
INTER

AFRICA PROCONSOLARE
CIRENAICA

CIRENE

FASANIA

L'IMPERO
ALLA MORTE DI
AVGVSTO
IMP. a 14 D.C

With the new organization of the Roman empire by its first emperor, Augustus, the clock of the aspirations of the inhabitants of the Maltese for a better political status was turned backwards. Like the inhabitants of many other Sicilian cities, they returned to their status of stipendiarii, *and it was only one-and-a-half centuries later that both Malta and Gozo were individually raised to the status of municipium.*

CHAPTER 6

MALTA UNDER THE ROMAN EMPIRE

In 27 BC, having eliminated all his enemies and suppressed all opposition, Octavian brought about the end of the civil war and initiated a period of peace not only at home but also throughout the now vast empire. He brought about the *Pax Romana*. The empire now covered all the lands that stretched from Spain and northern Morocco on the west side, to Turkey and the Red Sea on the eastern side. On the eastern front he coerced the Parthians to a peace treaty, while on the German frontier he kept up the offensive and lost his young potential successors in the process. He set up an extremely efficient bureaucratic and propaganda machinery which held the empire together and assured the capital, Rome, of a regular food supply and of an incredibly immense revenue.

One of the large-format maps affixed to the boundary wall of the Roman Forum on the Via dei Fori Imperiali *in Rome. The extent of the Roman empire in* AD *14, the year Augustus, the first emperor, died. By then all the lands washed by the Mediterranean, except Mauritania, had been annexed.*

On the home front he changed quite radically the constitution and political setup. While pretending to uphold almost all the previous Republican institutions, such as the senate, the consulate, and the tribunate of the people, he had the majority of the most powerful posts vested in one person, his own. Significantly, apart from reserving for himself three key provinces, he was also commander-in-chief of all the armed forces. Though technically he shared the power with the senate, Octavian became effectively the sole ruler; and so were his successors. He had by 27 BC assumed the name of his adoptive father, Caesar, as his official title, and in that year the senate conferred a further one with a religious connotation, Augustus (meaning 'revered'). Though at home Caesar Augustus himself shunned

The Ara Pacis (Altar of Peace) of Augustus. Voted by the senate in 13 BC and inaugurated in 9 BC, the altar was intended to celebrate the end of the long-drawn civil war that characterized the last century of the Republic.

any pretension of deification and suppressed all attempts to confer on him any divine title during his lifetime, in the rest of the empire, especially in the east, where the soil was most fertile for the culture of such ideologies, the divinity of the person of the emperor was already on the political agenda.

According to Tacitus (*Annals* 1.2), the provincials did not reject the new state of affairs, 'since they regarded with suspicion the sovereignty (*imperium*) of the senate and the people [of the old regime] on account of the feuds of dynasts and the greed of magistrates. The protection they had received from the laws was feeble, since these were subverted by violence, intrigue and ultimately money'. The Maltese, together with the whole of Sicily, had had a very bitter experience of the consequences of 'the greed of magistrates' barely fifty years before the accession of Augustus to the imperial throne. Tacitus implies that the provincials had high hopes that the new political structure would change their lives for the better.

With the reform and re-organization of the provinces that had started before Augustus' accession to the imperial throne, however, it appears that many of the *civitates* of the Sicilian province lost their ephemeral citizen status, normally attributed to Caesar and Antony (see previous chapter). Malta and Gozo seem to be among the number of unfortunate ones. Some writers attribute this reversal of fortune to the cities' involvement in the civil war by siding with the wrong party, namely that of Antony or that of Sextus Pompeius, the son of the great Pompey who for months had deprived Rome of its essential grain stocks with his navy. These cities were punished also by having to pay a heavy indemnity

(Appian, *bciv*. V, 129). According to Michael Grant that indemnity was partially levied in bronze coinage and the C. Arruntanus Balbus, whose name appears with the title PRO PR. on one of Malta's last coin issues, was the naval officer stationed there in 36 to superintend the subjugation of the island and collect the indemnity. Like many other Sicilian cities, therefore, Malta and Gozo returned to their peregrine status and lost their local self-government (as limited as it could be) and the right to issue their own money.

In 27 BC the various provinces of the empire were divided between the emperor and the senate, and Sicily became a senatorial province. It was governed by an ex-praetor, with the title of proconsul, assisted

The reverse of the penultimate coin type, a semis showing a curule chair with the legend C. ARRUNTANUS BALB. PRO. PR. The obverse shows a veiled female head facing left with the Greek legend ΜΕΛΙΤΑΙΩΝ *(of the Maltese).*

by quaestors and legates. This did not prevent the emperor from intervening directly in this and other senatorial provinces, both through his 'vast and undefined powers of consul' and by virtue of his *maius imperium*. Moreover, both Augustus and his successors had their own personal agents known as *procuratores* in these same provinces, of which Chrestion, the *'procurator Augusti'*, recorded in the earliest Latin inscription of Malta, seems to be an example. Originally the *procurators* were private agents of the emperor, looking after his private property and estates in various parts of the senatorial provinces. They were used, however, to keep an eye on the goings-on in these provinces, on which he did not have direct control, and to keep him informed on them.

After the relatively extensive account of St Paul's shipwreck of AD 60 in the *Acts of the Apostles*, a curtain of silence falls on Malta in ancient literary texts. It is almost as if it did not exist. We only find the occasional mention in geographical texts, like that of Pliny (first century AD) and Ptolemy (second century AD) and the odd portulan, like the *Itinerarium Antonini*, but nothing much else of significance before the references in Byzantine texts. Since it is unlikely that more texts will ever be discovered, we can only resort to epigraphic and archaeological evidence. Our only hope is that significantly more evidence will be produced by future archaeological discoveries.

This situation appears to have endured with little change till the beginning of the sixth century AD when Malta was absorbed, together with Sicily and its islands within the eastern empire. This impression, I hasten to add, is determined by the total absence of literary evidence to the contrary and is liable to change with the discovery of new archaeological evidence, preferably also epigraphic. The available epigraphic evidence, in fact, already provides us with hazy glimpses of the involvement of the islands, more precisely of Gozo, in the political intrigues and hostilities in the imperial court: the struggle for power between the two sons of Septimius Severus in one inscription (*CIL*, X, 7503) and that between the two tetrarchs, Constantius and Galerius, in two other inscriptions (*CIL*, X, 7507-7508).

Sources
Literary sources
The earliest recorded event connected with Malta occurring after the rise of imperial rule is the fateful shipwreck of St Paul in AD 60, as narrated by Luke, Paul's companion on his voyage from Caesarea to Rome (*Acts*, xxvii, 37-44, xxviii, 1-12). This is not the place where to discuss the intricacies of the arguments in favour or against the historical truth and value of the episode. It is important, however, to be aware of the current controversy on this subject. On my part, for the purposes of this book, I shall take the narrative at face value.

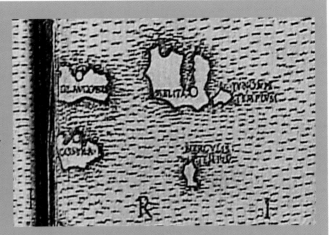

A section showing the central Mediterranean of a map from an incunabular edition of Ptolemy's Geography *(Rome, 1490).*

Top: Detail showing the area of the islands of Gaulos and Melita and the temples of Juno and Hercules.

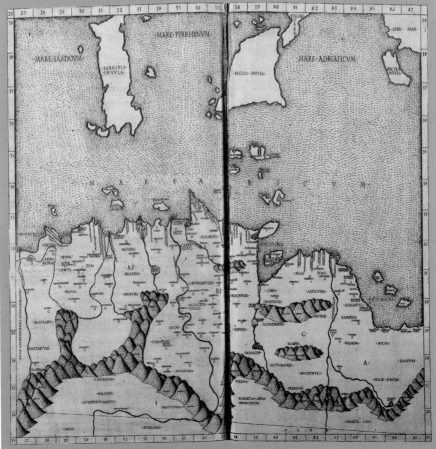

Paul, together with many other prisoners, was being taken to Rome on board an Alexandrian ship to stand trial there. After leaving harbour in southern Crete, the ship was caught in a violent storm and, after fourteen days being tossed about in the Adriatic sea, it was wrecked on an island called 'Melite'. In spite of the violence of the impact, Paul and all his companions on board the ship, some 275 of them, miraculously survived and reached the shore. There they were rescued by the inhabitants who lit a fire for them to warm themselves. At this point a miracle is supposed to have taken place. Paul was bitten by a viper. The local inhabitants, who were *barbaroi*, expected him to die instantaneously; but he did not. Whereupon they thought he was a god. Paul and others were given shelter in the country house of the chief man of the island, a certain Publius, whose father was soon after cured by Paul of fever and dysentery. Hearing of this many others brought their sick to be cured. After three months Paul and his companions left Malta for Syracuse on another Alexandrian ship which had wintered in Malta.

An artist's impression of the shipwreck of St Paul in St Paul's Bay, illustrated in Gian Francesco Abela's Della Descrittione di Malta (1647). *Paul and his fellow apostle Luke (with haloed heads) are shown close to the fire. Presumably the building in the background refers to the country estate of Publius where the latter hosted Paul and some of his companions.*

About the identification of the 'island called "Melite"' of the text with Malta few still harbour any doubts. All the geographical factors of the narrative point to Malta. It makes absolutely no sense to sail for Rome via Syracuse from either Meleda (Mljet) in Dalmatia or Cephallonia in Greece, two other proposed identifications for the Melite in question; Brindisi would have been their most logical destination.

The words *topon dithalasson* ('a place where two seas meet') have been the centre of frequent and long debates trying to determine the exact location of the shipwreck. Malta is full of such headlands; but I do not think it matters that much which one the ship hit on, unless we had any hope of discovering the remains of that shipwreck in Maltese waters.

Much more important is the issue of the Christianization of the Maltese people so early after the death of Christ; mostly because the notion of this Apostolic conversion to Christianity is deeply and solidly rooted in the Maltese historiographic tradition. No mention is made of preaching, converting, or baptizing in Luke's account. On the other hand, given Paul's character and the mission he had so actively and enthusiastically embraced since he saw light on the road to Damascus, it is hard to believe that he spent three months in Malta idling away without even trying to win over sections of this small Gentile population. After all, he started his stay on the island by praying over and curing several people. Consequently, it is more than likely that Paul left behind him at least a nucleus of new converts to the new religion, evidence for which, I hasten to add, is completely lacking. Whether we should expect to find evidence for their presence in the archaeological record is a moot point.

The tradition of the appointment of Publius as the first bishop of Malta, on the other hand, is the result of a confusion with another Publius, bishop of Athens, several generations later. And it would serve no purpose to continue to uphold it.

After the *Acts* the next reference is found in the *Natural History* of the Elder Pliny (AD 23-79) who mentions Malta and Gozo in his geographical overview of Italy and Sicily. For the latter, Pliny starts by asserting (*NH*, III, viii, 88) that in Sicily there were five colonies and sixty-three cities and states (*civitates*). He first lists the cities of the coast, specifying the ones that were colonies and saying nothing on the rest. Then he lists the three towns of the interior having Latin rights, the rest being tributaries (*stipendiarii*). Finally, he refers to the islands 'on the side towards Africa' (*insulae ad Africam versae*) and those on the Italian side of Sicily (*citra vero Siciliam*). Among the first group he lists Gaulos and Melita (*NH*, III, viii 92) specifying their distances from Camarina (87 miles) and Lilybaeum (113 miles). This last piece of information relative to

Publius being ordained bishop of Malta in a painting on the vault of the church of St Publius in Floriana. This alleged episode is deeply rooted in Malta's Pauline tradition.

distances from Malta is repeated verbatim by the fourth-century AD writer Martianus Capella, possibly implying that these were regular routes between Malta and these two destinations both in the first and in the fourth centuries AD, even though the town of Camarina had been abandoned, but not completely, since 258 BC.

In the second century a very informative source is the geographer Ptolemy (*c*. AD 100-178). In his *Geography* Ptolemy lists about 8,000 places with their latitudes and longitudes, among which five concerning the Maltese islands. These were: two cities, Melite for Malta and Gaulos for Gozo; two sanctuaries, one dedicated to

The Pauline Tradition

St Paul's Grotto

There are many places in the Mediterranean which claim an apostolic conversion to Christianity, that is, a conversion by one of the Apostles in the first century AD. Malta is not the least among them, though if one examines the only available contemporary written source, there is absolutely no mention of preaching or of conversions by St Paul. Nor is there any written reference before the fifth century AD to Christianity in Malta (St Jerome). Even in the archaeological record, there is a total absence of any evidence of Christianity prior to the fourth century.

The Pauline tradition seems to have taken deep and strong roots among the Maltese people well before the arrival of the knights of St John in 1530. This fact comes out clearly in the 1536 account by Jean Quintin who reported the convictions of the Maltese regarding St Paul's shipwreck and stay on Malta. While expressing scepticism on this matter, since he favoured the identification of the Biblical Melita with the Dalmatian Meleda, he reported the beliefs of the locals in locating the site of Paul's shipwreck on the spur of land jutting out of St Paul's Bay, opposite St Paul's church. He also testified to the veneration of the Maltese and foreigners alike for St Paul's Grotto where Paul was said to have spent his three months' custody in Malta healing islanders from all sorts of diseases and preaching to them the Christian message. The stone cut from this grotto had already an international reputation (Quintinus cites Africa, Italy, and Rome) for its virtues of healing from bites of poisonous snakes and scorpions. In addition Quintin recorded the current belief that no poisonous serpents existed in Malta and that those brought from abroad also became harmless.

Herakles and the other to Hera; and a landmark called *Chersonessos* meaning 'headland', to which some editions add, in my view erroneously, the word *'polis'*, implying that there was a third city by that name. The co-ordinates given by Ptolemy for these landmarks are not precise, but given the primitive methodology available at that time to determine them, compared to that of today, they are not far off the mark.

The list of Maltese landmarks relating to Malta in the incunabular edition of Ptolemy's Geography *in the National Library of Malta, Valletta. Under the heading of 'The Pelagic islands of Africa', the list includes one item for Cossyra (Pantelleria) and as many as five for Malta and Gozo.*

Contemporary with Ptolemy is the *Itinerarium Antoninianum* (or *Antonini Augusti)* even though it has survived in a fourth-century AD copy. It only mentions Malta as a station for ships plying from Italy to Africa. So is Lucian of Samosata who in his *The Ship* suggests that Malta was a port of call for heavy cargo vessels carrying corn from Egypt to Pozzuoli in Italy.

After these references, we have a long silence which is broken only in the sixth century with the important changes in the geopolitical scenario of the central Mediterranean which saw the fall of the Roman empire of the west to the Visigoths from the north, the occupation of North Africa, including Carthage by the Vandals, followed by its *reconquista* by the Roman empire of the east, that is, Byzantium.

Pelagiæ insulæ aphrice hæ sunt		
Cosyra insula & ciuitas	37⅔	34
Glauconis insula & ciuitas.	36 ⅓	34
Melita insula in qua ciuitas		
Melita	38½¼	34
Et cherfonesus	38 ⅓	38
Et iunonis sacrum	39	34
Et herculis sacrum	28½¼	34

The marble inscription commemorating the restoration of the temple of Proserpina by a certain Chrestion, a freedman of Augustus and his procurator for Malta and Gozo. Found at Mtarfa in 1613, the inscription was still intact when it was reproduced by Gian Francesco Abela in 1647. Only fragments of the original survive.

Inscriptions

Epigraphy is a little bit more generous than literary sources for the Imperial age and Gozo has produced even more inscriptions than Malta

The first inscription in Latin is the one reputed to have been found in Mtarfa in 1613. It is now recomposed of many fragments. Some of the original parts are missing but Abela records virtually the whole text, which is reproduced in the *Corpus Inscriptionum Latinarum* (*CIL*, X, 7494). It commemorates a certain Chrestion, the freedman of Augustus and procurator of the islands of Malta and Gozo, for his generosity in restoring the temple of Proserpina. He had the columns and the pediments restored, as well as the walls which were on the point of collapsing from old age. The last sentence is not clear and has been variously read as 'at the same time he gilded the pillar' (which pillar?) or as 'he also gilded the cult statue.'

There were two types of imperial procurators in a senatorial province like Sicily: the provincial (or praesidial) procurator (e.g. the *procurator provinciae Siciliae*) and the lesser *procuratores* who managed the personal property of the emperor. The former were officials normally appointed from the equestrian ranks, preferably after a reasonable number of years of experience in the administrative career. The latter could be either knights or freedmen. No doubt, our Chrestion was one of these lesser imperial agents.

One of the plates illustrating Jean Houel's 1787 Voyage Pittoresque. *It shows a draped female statue inserted in a rock-cut niche on the outside of the Gozo Citadel. The life-size statue still survives and is exhibited in the Gozo Archaeological Museum (see p.255).*

These originally private agents of the emperor, however, eventually attained judicial and administrative functions.

The dating of the inscription is intricately connected with the changing role of the procurators and thus, of this particular procurator. There are various expressed opinions on the latter aspect. For the purpose of the present work, I shall cut a long story short. The size of Malta and Gozo combined does not warrant the role of a praesidial or provincial procurator. So Chrestion must have been a purely financial official responsible for the management of the imperial properties or revenues of the two islands, under the general supervision of the *procurator provinciae Siciliae*. Although freedmen of later emperors are also designated

in other inscriptions, the reference to Augustus in isolation, without the name of the emperor concerned, appears to me to point to *the* Augustus, the first one of the series, who reigned between 27 BC and AD 14.

Almost contemporary with the above Latin inscription, but slightly later, is an inscription in Greek commemorating a certain Lucius Castricius Prudens (*IG*, 601). He was not only a Roman citizen but also a Roman knight on whom the title of 'Protos (chief citizen) of the Maltese' had been conferred. At some stage in his career he had also been chief magistrate (*archon*) and priest (*amphipolos*) of the god Augustus. The latter designation places the inscription after the death and deification of Augustus. Castricius, or an ancestor of his, may well have obtained his Roman citizenship on an individual basis since he was inscribed in the Quirine tribe, the tribe reserved for Greeks and other foreigners who obtained Roman citizenship by special grants.

The inscription, now lost, was found in a tomb outside Mdina and later incorporated in the basin of a fountain in the ditch, beneath the main gate of Mdina.

Another important inscription of the time of the Julio-Claudian emperors is the one dedicated to Julia Augusta, wife of Augustus, identified with Ceres, the goddess of agriculture and abundance (*CIL*, X, 7501). The mention of her son, the emperor Tiberius, and the divine titles awarded to her and her husband, place the inscription firmly during Tiberius' reign (AD 14-29). The text is inscribed on the face of a marble plinth with a narrow moulding all around. The upper surface has a hollow, clearly intended for the insertion of a statue. Since the female draped statue in the Gozo Archaeological Museum is of the right size and of the same age, the plinth was very probably the base for that statue, a portrait statue of the same imperial lady.

The inscription, as well as the statue above it, were set up by a lady of some consequence, a certain Lutatia, a priestess (*sacerdos*) of the same Augusta and wife of Marcus Livius Optatus, a high priest (*flamen*) of Gozo (possibly also of the same goddess). An important element in this inscription is the reference to the divine nature of the emperor and of members of his family. We have already stated that Augustus himself resisted the attempts to confer on him the title of *divus* in his homeland. But his wife Livia (Julia's real name), his grandsons Caius and Lucius Caesar, and Agrippa Postumus, as well as his son-in-law Marcus Agrippa, were awarded divine honours in his lifetime. When he died, however, the senate decreed the erection of a

A marble statue base with an inscription dedicated to Julia Augusta, wife of Emperor Augustus, in the guise of the goddess Ceres, by Lutatia, a priestess of the same Augusta.

temple for him in Rome. Under his successor, Emperor Tiberius, the cults of Augustus and Livia were combined.

A member of Lutatia's family of origin (or *gens*), a certain Q. Lutatius Longinus, at some point in time raised an inscribed gravestone for himself and his virtuous wife Iunia, daughter of Caius Iunius (*CIL, X,* 7511). The inscription cannot be dated more closely on grounds of style of the lettering because its present whereabouts are unknown.

No inscriptions survive from the second half of the first century AD. The next group take us into the second century, of which the Gozitan ones are the more numerous. A very informative inscription, probably dated to the early part of that century, is the one inscribed on what looks like a large statue base in white marble. The base was discovered accidentally around 1747 near the Benedictine monastery in Mdina; it is now housed in the Domus Romana in Rabat. The text (*CIL, X,* 8313) commemorates the construction of a marble temple and its dedication to the god Apollo. It describes in some detail the various constituent parts of the building: the podium, the floor, the four columns of the front portico, and the flanking pilasters. The name of the generous benefactor who spent a large sum for this construction is regrettably missing, but he is described as the chief man (*primus omnium*) of the Maltese municipium. The base and, presumably, its statue were set up in his honour by public subscription.

Another marble inscription was reputedly found near the same Benedictine monastery at Mdina in 1868; it is now preserved in the Cathedral Museum at Mdina (*CIL, X,* 7495). From the style of the lettering it seems to be contemporary with the previous one. It records the construction of another marble temple, this time with its cult statue and other ornaments. The name of the deity is missing but the benefactor is named as Claudius Iustus who is described as patron of the Maltese municipium. The sum he spent on this project is not specified but is said to have been higher than the amount he had promised.

Of a less public nature is a second-century funerary inscription incised on a local hard stone block discovered in 1951 in the necropolis zone of Tac-Ċagħqi in Rabat. The Greek text commemorates the untimely death of a 25-year old comic actor and lyre-player, P. Aelius Hermolaus, who hailed from Pergamon in Asia Minor.

Two of the Gozitan inscriptions of the advanced second century AD concern two members of the same family, the father and the son. C. Vallius Postumus is the first one to be honoured by the people of Gozo for his many merits and as benefactor and 'patron of their municipium' (*CIL, X,* 7507). Caius held many important posts in his political career. He was a high priest (*flamen*) for the cult of the deified emperor Hadrian in whose court he had conducted a delegation out of his own pocket. He had also been elected into the

A large marble statue base carrying an inscription commemorating the construction of a marble temple dedicated to Apollo at the personal expense of the chief man of Malta's municipium. His name has not survived. Discovered around 1747 near the Benedictine monastery of Mdina.

college of *quadringenarii* (magistrates of equestrian rank in possession of a large capital) by Emperor Antoninus Pius, for 'having honourably held every public office of his city'. The reference to the deified Antoninus Pius tends to suggest a date after the death of that emperor in AD 161 for the engraving of this inscription on a marble slab.

Caius was to see more honours heaped on his family through his son Marcus Vallius Rufus. The latter was commemorated by an inscription on a long block of hard stone which was

A large ashlar block of hard Coralline limestone, incorporated in the inner corner of the old gate of the Gozo Citadel, which carries a Latin inscription on its shorter end. The inscription honours a certain Marcus Vallius Rufus who had been elevated to the rank of knight by Emperor Antininus Pius.

inserted in the wall on one side of the old gate to the Gozo Citadel some time before 1534, when it was seen there by Jean Quintin d'Autun (*CIL*, X, 7508). Again the inscription was set up by the Gozitan people (*pleps* [*sic*] *Gaulitana*), but the only honour recorded in it, at least in the surviving part, is the rank of a knight to which he was raised by the divine Antoninus Pius. The reference to the deification of Emperor Antoninus Pius again points to a date soon after the latter's death in AD 161.

Towards the end of the same century, precisely in AD 195, the municipium of Gozo erected a monument, possibly a statue, documented by an inscription which seems to have gone lost (*CIL*, X, 7502). The monument was dedicated from public donations to Julia Domna, wife of Emperor Septimius Severus, as 'mother of

An inscription on a marble statue base set up by a certain Marcius Marcianus in honour of his friend Cestius Gallus Varenianus Lutatius Natalis Aemilianus, a patron of the municipium. *It is now exhibited at the Gozo Archeological Museum.*

the military camp'. Julia Domna was given this title in April 195. In the same year, however, Severus assumed other titles (*Pius* and *Adiabenicus*) which are not mentioned in the inscription. This means that the inscription was engraved sometime between the two dates. Given the geopolitical position of Gozo, away from any stationed Roman army, the title of 'mother of the military camp' appears rather odd. The name of the eponymous curator is missing.

An even more intriguing inscription regards Geta, the younger of two sons of Iulia Domna and Septimius Severus (*CIL*, X, 7503). It is also missing, but the text has been preserved for us by early writers, including Abela. For a reason that will be explained later, Geta's name

had been chiselled off; but it was reconstructable from the accompanying names of his brother (Caracalla) and of his father (Septimius Severus). This time it is the college of the decurions (*ordo decurionum*) who dedicates the inscription, or the monument in question, to Emperor Caesar Publius Septimius Geta Pius Augustus, brother of Emperor Marcus Aurelius Antoninus Pius Augustus (better known as Caracalla), and son of Lucius Septimius Severus Pius Pertinax, Augustus, Arabicus, Adiabenicus, Parthicus, Maximus. Even on this inscription, the name of the eponymous curator is missing.

This inscription must have been set up at the end of Septimius Severus' reign because it carries all the titles he assumed after each

war campaign. It also describes both Geta and his brother Cara-calla as emperors; that is because Severus in 209 associated Geta with Caracalla as co-heir to the imperial throne. On his death in 211, however, the feud between the two brothers rekindled and in 212 Caracalla murdered his younger brother and ordered his *damnatio memoriae*, which saw to the cancel-lation of all his images and names from public monuments.

The *gens* Lutatia resident in Gozo reappears in an inscription which, from the style of the lettering, seems to be datable to the third century (*CIL, X, 7506*). It is inscribed on a marble plinth with a moulding fram-ing the edges. The plinth is hollow at the top, probably for the insertion of a statue. In it a certain Marcius Marcianus records his raising a

Several fragments of Roman marble inscriptions of which at least four, judging from the thickness of the marble and the size and style of the lettering, seem to have belonged to the same inscription.

monument (probably a statue) at his own expense to his best and dear-est friend (*amico optimo et karissimo* [*sic*]) Cestius Gallus Varenianus Lutatius Natalis Aemilianus who is also described as patron of the municipium.

Besides the above there are a handful of other inscriptions whose record is not beyond question or which are too short or too fragment-ary to shed any significant light on Malta's ancient history. Others, like potters' stamps on amphorae or *terra sigillata* can be used to estab-lish Malta's commercial links with the outside world.

Material Remains

While most of the literary evidence sheds light on the Republican phase, apart from the building of the Roman *domus* outside Mdina, most of what survives in terms of material evidence relating to life in the two cities in the Roman period belongs to this phase. These include the few structural remains found accidentally in the past during trench cutting in the roads of Mdina and Rabat, Malta, and, on one occasion, in the main square of Rabat, Gozo.

Regarding ancient Gaulos, there are several unofficial reports of more finds of ancient structures, such as those found during the construction of a band club and adjacent houses beneath the walls of the Gozo Citadel, and others during the construction of the St George basilica and its annexes. These were hardly ever properly documented and most of them have been destroyed or built over. We are told by the Gozitan historian Agius de Soldanis (1712-70) that many pieces of ancient columns, some fluted, could be seen in different parts of the Citadel and Rabat in his own time. Some of these are still preserved in the Gozo Cathedral Museum, others in the Gozo Archaeological Museum. One piece of such a col-

umn is housed in a souvenir shop in Fosos Street on the side of the cathedral, and the base of a Roman column serves as a well head inside the Folklore Museum round the corner. The eighteenth-century historian was convinced that these columns belonged to the ancient temple of Juno which he believed once stood where the cathedral now stands. The grounds on which Agius de Soldanis bases his convictions and opinions are, however, completely false.

A single ashlar block raised against the outside wall of the oratory of St George basilica is the only relic salvaged and preserved from the finds made there in 1976-77, which consisted of foundation remains of a Roman building (see p.248). Previously, two cisterns had

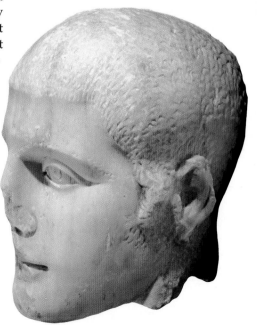

A very fine quality marble portrait head of a young man of the early third century AD. The style and the iconography of the portrait, in particular the hairstyle, are very similar to those of a portrait of Emperor Alexander Severus in the Uffizi Gallery, Florence. Unknown provenance, but probably from Malta.

The L-shaped wall of large ashlar blocks uncovered accidentally in 2000 in St George's Street, Rabat, Gozo. Some later brick-work and evidence of burning were also encountered.

been encountered in 1937 while laying the foundations of the basilica itself. One of them, located under the western aisle of the church, was cylindrical in shape and was built of terracotta slabs embedded in clay; next to it a large jar was found containing 4,000 bronze coins of the third century AD (259-273). The other, located under the eastern aisle, was barrel-shaped and built of irregular stones embedded in clay. It contained fragments of 'very late Roman pottery' and some lozenge-shaped tiles.

Regrettably, even as recently as in 2000 the remains of 'an L-shaped huge masonry wall', identified while digging for foundation works for a building behind the same church, have been reburied. At least this time the find was documented by

an official report drawn by George Azzopardi, the assistant-curator of archaeology for Gozo. Earlier on, in the summer of 1993, I had the occasion of seeing a large, barrel-shaped, Roman cistern in the courtyard of a nunnery in Palm Street, Rabat, after it had been cleaned of its contents and roofed over in concrete. Two of my then students, the same George Azzopardi and Godwin Vella, took measured drawings of the cistern, which was built with regular courses of large ashlar masonry, just in time before it filled up again with water. Pottery salvaged by the nuns from the cleaning operation was handed over to the Museums Department for further study. No doubt, the cistern must have been associated with some ancient building in the immediate vicinity.

The 3m-deep trench cut through the whole length (*c*.52m) of It-Tokk square in 1961 revealed cultural layers ranging from the Bronze Age to Early Christian. It also cut into 'Roman period floors and walls, including a cellar containing wine amphorae, some with stamps'. I tend to believe that an examination of the pottery produced by that trench against the field notes of the find by David Trump, curator of archaeology at the time, will pay good dividends.

The purpose of a very thick wall of large masonry blocks (about 2.0 x 0.75 x 0.75m) found on the western slope below the citadel, about 20 m above Foreman Street, is hard to guess. In view of its location and construction technique, it is possible

that it was intended simply to retain the shifting clay, rather than for defence purposes. Extensive parts of it have clearly been destroyed by building activity. An exploratory trench excavated by the Museums Department in 1999 revealed abundant pottery deposits.

The situation is slightly better with regard to Melite. Almost a whole *insula* of houses, bounded by two roads was excavated by Temi Zammit in 1922 and 1923 in the area adjacent to the 1881 domus. Apart from further rooms belonging to the same house, he identified a series of others of inferior workmanship, involving the re-utilization of older building materials, which he dated to the third century AD on the basis

Part of the section of a trench which cut through the whole length of It-Tokk square in Rabat, Gozo (from a drawing by Dr David Trump). The trench cut through layers representing various periods, including a Roman cellar.

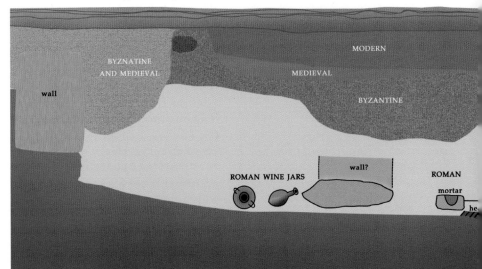

of some coins. In 1920 he had extended his excavations even beyond the road leading to the railway station, as far as the foot of the knights' period rampart. There he discovered, among other features, an odd structure with column-like pillars set thickly together, a water cistern, water channels, and a vaulted gallery. In the cistern he found a quantity of pottery, both of 'coarse household pots' and 'the finest Samian ware', 'Samian' being a term used at the time to denote *terra sigillata* table ware. From the cistern he also found a strange head of an oriental-looking bearded man. As noted by Zammit, 'neither its features nor its workmanship appear to be Roman'. It belongs to a much earlier, probably Phoenician tradition, with strong similarities to Archaic Cypriote art.

In his report of the 1922 excavations Zammit came to conclude that the 'magnificent Roman residence was proved to have stood during the first and second centuries AD, and to have been patched up and utilized by rustic dwellers when it had fallen into decay.' This conclusion, however, contrasts with the date of the range of pottery he retrieved, (which included Campanian ware of the first century BC) and the taphonomy of the ruins he investigated. The fact that a statuary cycle of Julio-Claudian personalities still adorned the house when it collapsed seems to suggest that it was not lived in after the first century AD. Moreover, it seems that Zammit thought that the house extended much further beyond its real size.

After these excavations no proper large-scale excavations were undertaken on ancient Melite before 1983. In that year and in 1984 a small team of archaeologists from the University of California Los Angeles (UCLA), with the

A series of closely-set columns discovered below the knights' period fortifications during Temi Zammit's excavations beyond the road leading to the railway station near the Roman domus, Rabat.

have been sealed and remained unused after the first century BC. The pottery had accumulated as a conical heap right underneath the opening of the cistern. It contained numerous broken pots with a strap handle bridging the mouth known as bale amphoras; these were clearly fragile, and therefore very expendable, containers for extracting water from the cistern.

Further to the south, Francis Mallia had in 1970 excavated two adjacent building plots in the Saqqajja area, one on the road to Buskett, in front of Ta' Saura Hospital, the other round the corner into Main

Left and Top: A limestone head of an oriental-looking bearded man found by Temi Zammit in a cistern during his excavations of the area beyond the road leading to Mtarfa.

A section of a trench dug in Museum Esplanade, Rabat, by a team from the University of California Los Angeles in 1983-84. The mouth of a bottle-shaped water cistern is visible on this side of a large ashlar block.

collaboration of local archaeologists and volunteers, conducted a limited excavation in Museum Esplanade, the wide open space in front of the Domus Romana. Only two large trenches were opened up, which hit on what appeared to be a narrow Roman street with houses on either side. On the lowest floor of one of the rooms a large Italian *terra sigillata* plate was retrieved (approximately 50 BC-AD 50). The excavation was not taken any deeper, mainly because the UCLA team never returned to proceed with the excavations. An interesting feature that was thoroughly investigated was a bottle-shaped water cistern which, from the analysis of the pottery contents by the present writer, appears to

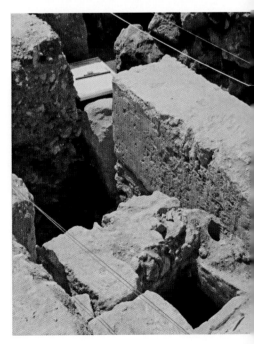

Street, Rabat. In the first plot he came across a tower-like square structure which could be part of the ancient fortifications of the town, being so close to the edge of the cliff on this side of the town. Mallia identified another building close-by as a mosaic workshop; in it he also retrieved a small statuette representing Isis. In the second site he revealed a room whose floor was supported on thick-set rows of up-side-down amphorae, probably a damp-proofing device. A similar one had been discovered in the eighteenth century in Mdina, and another one in Zammit's 1920s excavation outside Greeks Gate.

An exploration of a site on Is-Saqqajja, corner with Main Street, Rabat, revealed a room whose floor was supported on thick-set rows of upside-down amphorae.

A section of a wall built of massive ashlar blocks was discovered in 1988 behind the telephone exchange on Is-Saqqajja, Rabat.

Other sections of the fortifications surrounding Roman Melite have been encountered and recorded on various occasions, right from the seventeenth century. Gian Francesco Abela mentions various sections on the city side along the ditch which bounded the town on its west side. Nearer to us, thick masonry was encountered in 1963 during works beneath the knights' fortifications behind Vilhena Palace, while part of a thick wall was uncovered in 1988 during building works for the telephone exchange in Saqqajja. After they collapsed during a heavy rainstorm the massive masonry blocks were rebuilt on the same spot where they can still be seen.

Perhaps one should not fail to mention sporadic accidental discoveries of structures and buildings made over the years. The most significant seems to be that of the 1950s when parts of a house with columns and a mosaic floor are said to have been uncovered in the area now covered by housing to the west of the Domus Romana.

More remains have been encountered during proper archaeological investigations conducted at key spots during the recent intensive trenching activity along the streets of Mdina. These remains, as I have already noted in the previous chapter, could belong to either the Republican phase or the Imperial one; but the pedestal of some large public monument, possibly a statue group, is more likely to belong to this phase.

MDINA RECENT EXCAVATIONS

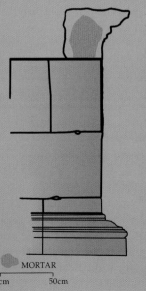

Full-scale rescue excavations were conducted in the streets of Mdina during a trenching operation in the years 2002-03. The operation was conducted by Katya Stroud under the direction of the Museums Department. Several stretches of ancient walls of large masonry blocks were encountered in various places, in particular in the vicinity of the Carmelite church. In St Paul Square walls of late Medieval houses were discovered, which in part rested on ancient masonry.

In Villegaignon Street, near the north-eastern corner of the Benedictine monastery, the corner of this structure came to light. Only one stone that formed part of the upper moulding survived in situ, but the rest of the structure appears to be intact. Its size suggests a monumental pedestal, some three metres in height.

MORTAR

0cm   50cm

Tombs

The various necropoleis outside Melite continued to grow and expand in this phase. But what is even more significant is the frequent opening and re-use of older tombs, some going back various centuries. The Imperial age of these burials is easily recognizable from the presence of blown glass bottles and phials since the technique of blown glass was introduced around 50 BC. Tombs that overlap the Republican and Imperial phases contain several cinerary urns covered with a plate with a lamp on top. Several such tombs were found, for example, in New Street, Rabat. New burials were of both inhumation and cremation rites. Occasionally, even amphorae were deposited containing bone remains of children. Coins dating from the first to the second century AD occur on rare occasions. An interesting observation made by Claudia Sagona is that isolated rock-cut tombs had largely fallen out of use by the second century AD. This might mean that people were either making increasingly wider use of sarcophagi placed out in the open, or they were burying their dead in more complex collective underground systems like the later Palaeochristian hypogea. In the latter case we might have to push the date of these hypogea (not necessarily Christian at this stage) to as early as the third century AD, if not earlier.

In contrast with its rich array of inscriptions of this phase, the town of Gaulos continues to lag behind that of Melite with regard to evidence of burial. No proper necropolis has ever been found and on the few occasions that groups of rock-cut tombs were found, they were soon destroyed without proper documentation. This is what happened in 1892-93 when a series of such tombs were discovered in St Francis Square. They consisted of a number of low-roofed interconnected chambers entered from a common shaft. The finds, including articles of glass and coins, suggest a third-century AD re-use, but the cinerary urns and a number of painted terracotta coffins suggest an earlier date (possibly Punic) for the original construction of the tombs. The same happened as recently as 1997 when excavation work took place in the courtyard of the Gozo Seminary and revealed several rock-cut tombs which yielded human and animal bones, broken glass, Punic and Roman pottery sherds, bronze fragments, and coins. But another tomb had been reported 'at the back of the Bishop's Seminary' in 1909, in the course of digging for the foundations of a new house. The finds included bronze objects, a gold earring, and 38 bronze coins ranging in date from the first to the third century AD. In the same street (Vajrinġa Street) a large glass bottle containing cremated human remains had been found before 1899.

The only tomb that survives in the Rabat area seems to be that discovered in 1960 in the grounds of the Gozo Lyceum Complex. It consisted of a shaft and two burial chambers. Even here, however, part of the roof of one of the two chambers was destroyed to make room for the foundations of the new building.

An unusual burial was discovered in Vajringa Street, Rabat, Gozo, in 1899. It consisted of a very large glass bottle containing cremated human remains. Probably second century AD or later.

A group of painted terracotta coffins were recovered from a series of roofed burial chambers that were discovered accidentally in 1892-93 in St Francis Square, Rabat, Gozo. Although the associated coins pointed to a third-century AD date for the last use of the tombs, the coffins seem to date to the Punic period.

Tas-Silġ Sanctuary

None of the three areas excavated by the University of Malta on the raised platform of the south side of Tas-Silġ have revealed stratigraphic levels belonging to Roman Imperial or later phases, giving the false impression that life stood still in this area outside the sanctuary since the first century BC. Short of suggesting that the upper archaeological strata corresponding to these last twenty centuries have been scraped off mechanically before 1996, I confess my inability to find a proper explanation for this phenomenon. The only Roman (and late Roman) horizons so far have started to emerge in a small trench around a square well located beneath the raised platform. It is hoped that this trench will shed light also on this phase.

In a recent update of the resumed investigations by the Italian Mission,

An aerial view of the excavated structures of the Tas-Silġ sanctuary. Roman pottery turned up in most of the areas except the three trenches excavated in 1996-2004 by the University of Malta on the south side (top right corner).

published in the *Malta Archaeological Review*, this phase has been identified as Horizon 7 ('Imperial Roman') in a series of twelve horizons. It is a real pity that the description of these horizons in this update does not take us beyond Horizon 6, leaving us in unsatisfied expectation. The impression one gets from this and previous reports is that in the Imperial age the sanctuary went into hibernation which lasted about four centuries. This, however, does not correspond to the importance given to it by the second-century geographer Ptolemy who lists it as one of the five most important landmarks of the archipelago.

Statuary

We have a much richer array of sculpture belonging to this phase, most of them with a secure local provenance. By far the most important of these is the cycle of portrait statues of Emperor Claudius and members of his family found within the grounds of the Roman house at Rabat in 1881 (see box). The group must have included more statues but three of them have survived in a sufficiently good state to be identifiable.

The key portrait for the identification of the whole set is the larger-than-life-size head of Claudius, an extremely warm portrait, which is considered to be one of the finest in the iconography of that emperor. The honey-coloured patina of the Parian marble enhances this effect and imparts effectively the intended message of the benign ruler. Calculations of the measurements of this head and those of a togate statue, also larger than life-size, found in the grounds of the same town house in 1922, have proved beyond reasonable doubt that the two pieces belonged together. The beauty of this portrait-statue must have been further enhanced by the warm colour of the Pentelic marble of which it was made.

Re-joined head and statue. Although found in the 1881 archaeological investigation of the Roman domus, investigations have revealed that the portrait head of Claudius belonged to the larger-than-life-size togate statue that was brought to light in 1922 in a close-by room. The respective dimensions fit each other well.

A similar combination is that of a marble head of a pretty young lady carved in one piece with the upper torso and the lower half of female draped statue. The combination is confirmed by comparison with similar statues of the same personage (or other contemporary ladies) discovered in other parts of the Roman empire. The design and flow of the drapery are convincingly similar. The facial features and hairstyle of the young lady are identical to those of Antonia the Younger, mother of Claudius, depicted on various coins issued under Claudius. But her youthful features, especially when compared to those of the middle-aged emperor, identify her more probably as a daughter of Claudius, such as Claudia Antonia, rather than his mother.

Four Roman draped portrait statues from the Roman domus, Rabat. The first two are male togate statues. The third and fourth are female. The third one was originally with veiled head, and belonged to the Pudicitia type. The fourth was originally joined to the bust of the young Julio-Claudian princess from the same excavations.

A third statue, portraying a young boy dressed in toga, is also very intriguing. Unfortunately, the head is missing, but the extremely fine quality of the carving, which compares very well with that of the other two statues of the group, suggests that it represents another member of Claudius' family. The only candidate one can think of for this personage is the young Nero, who in AD 50 was adopted by Claudius at the age of twelve when Claudius married Nero's mother Agrippina the Younger. Nero succeeded Claudius as emperor when the latter died in AD 54.

Veiled head of a bearded divinity. Variously identified as Pluto, Jupiter, or Asklepios, its facial features are more like those of Hercules. Found in 1924 in Temi Zammit's excavations near the Roman domus; it went missing in the early 1980s.

Until we start recognizing people from their feet, there is no way of identifying the men portrayed by three other togate statues in the same house, of which only the feet, at most a *scrinium* attached to a small part of the toga, survived at the moment of their discovery. We are much luckier with the draped female statue from Gozo, even though it is headless. It was already known to the French traveller Houel who in 1787 depicted it in a niche outside the old gate of the Gozo Citadel (see p. 204). Both Houel and Caruana (a century later) intuitively suggested that it must have been a portrait statue of an *augusta*. The inscription in honour of Julia Augusta as Ceres mentioned above, with its hollow upper surface intended for the insertion of a statue of the right size, added further evidence for an identification with that lady, the wife of the first Emperor Augustus. This identification is confirmed by the style of the sculpture, typical of the Julio-Claudian age, and by comparison with other statues of the same *augusta*, portrayed as Ceres, in several other museum collections abroad.

Another togate statue, probably also of the Julio-Claudian age, was rescued in two halves from a trench in Mdina in the eighteenth century. The torso of a statuette of a nude Aphrodite was found during trench cutting connected with drainage works in Rabat and Mdina in 1904-05. In 1924, then, during the continuation of his excavations inside and near the *domus* mentioned above, Temi Zammit came across a small marble head, only 10 cms high, identifying it with 'Pluto'. Broken off at the neck from the original statuette, it represented a veiled bearded god. The features can be compared to those of Herakles, Serapis, Asklepios, and even Jupiter, but none of the representations of these occur with a similar veiled head.

Among the sculptural pieces whose provenance has still not been identified one may mention an archaizing female draped statue (unfortunately headless), which probably dates to the age of Emperor Hadrian, a portrait of inferior quality of Emperor Antoninus Pius, and a striking third-century AD portrait of a young man with features resembling those of the Severan emperors. A statuette of the Egyptian god Bes, which

A headless, larger-than-life female statue of white marble represents a draped goddess of unknown identity. The 'Isis knot' under her breast and the 'Lybian' style of the surviving hair braids point to Isis. None of the known statues of the latter, however, wear the complex necklace hanging on her breast.

I inspected in a private collection in Rabat way back in 1970, probably belongs to this phase. Certain technical features, such as the incision of the iris and pupil in the eyes and the generous use of the running drill, suggest a second-century date.

A local sculptural production may be gleaned in some pieces of sculpture in local soft stone. The most remarkable one is the head of a satyr from Gozo, the product of a (by now) deeply Hellenized local workshop working in a local medium. Its provenance is, unfortunately, unknown. The telamon-satyr

A marble statuette of the Egyptian god Bes (30 cm high) in a private collection in Rabat. Claimed by the owner to be of Maltese provenance.

The bust of a satyr with arms folded on either side of the head to support an architectural element. Found during the 1910 excavations of the villa at Ramla Bay.

discovered during the 1910 excavations of the Ramla Bay villa seems to belong to the same vein. Unfortunately, we can only base our judgement on photographs since the sculpture went missing soon after its discovery.

Two smaller-than-life-size statues representing Amazons were probably intended as domestic or garden ornaments since they mirror each other in stance and attributes. As to their provenance, in a letter addressed to Thomas Ashby, Temi Zammit reveals that 'one was found a little far from the Roman Villa, whilst cutting the road for the Museum Station; the other one was, to my mind, found in the Villa itself'.

Three examples from a hoard of bronze coins found during construction works inside St George's basilica, in Rabat, Gozo. The coins covered a period in the third century (AD 259-273) during which the empire was facing a series crisis, including an economic one.

Coins

With the cessation of local coin minting at the end of the Republic, all coins in circulation in Malta in the Imperial phase were those in current use in this part of the empire, such as Sicily.

From the third century, however, one detects a tendency for a preference for coins minted in the eastern provinces.

A hoard of 4,000 bronze coins (dated to AD 259-273) was found in 1937 close to a shallow terracotta cistern while laying the foundations of the western aisle of St George basilica in Rabat, Gozo. Another coin hoard discovered in Rabat in 1961 is dated to the years AD 352-360 and, therefore, belongs to Late Antiquity.

THE AMAZONS

Two small female torsos in Globigerina limestone. They represent Amazons in opposite poses: probably garden ornaments. From the Roman domus surroundings.

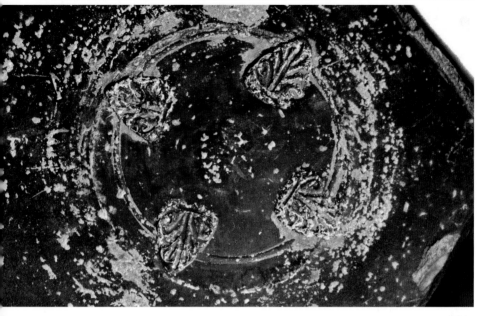

Pottery

Pottery of this phase is characterized by fabrics and shapes that have been classed by Claudia Sagona under her phase VI ('Romano-Punic') and, in part, under phase V ('Romanization'), of her chronology of 'Punic Malta'. The most outstanding pottery types are the imported fine table wares, like the Italian red-slipped ware, formerly referred to as 'Samian' or 'Pseudo-Samian' ware, now more commonly known as *terra sigillata*. These replaced their predecessors, the black-glazed Campanian and related Italian wares, and were in turn replaced by North African Red Slip ware (ARS). Pottery of this type comes mostly from excavations of domestic sites, like the 1881 Rabat town house and the surrounding ones excavated in 1920-23, as well as the country villas, including the

Top: The decorated base of black-glazed Campanian ware.

Opposite page: A selection of pottery shapes prevalent in this period. One immediately notices that most of the shapes are new, being typical of the pottery in use in other parts of the empire.
(After Sagona 2002)

Żejtun one. Single items occur also in tombs and serve as reliable dating objects.

At the villa of Ta' Kaċċatura an Italian *terra sigillata* cup was discovered by Ashby with the inscription L.RASINPIS *in planta pedis*. I strongly suspect that the 'local imitation of Samian ware, occasionally decorated with stamped designs and, in one instance, with a human figure in relief' mentioned by Ashby were really African Red Slip ware.

Coarse ware is found in great quantities in both types of archaeological

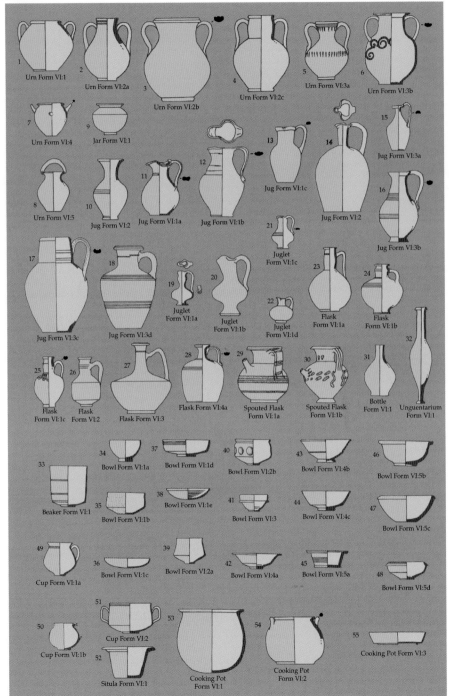

1 Urn Form VI:1

2 Urn Form VI:2a

3 Urn Form VI:2b

4 Urn Form VI:2c

5 Urn Form VI:3a

6 Urn Form VI:3b

7 Urn Form VI:4

9 Jar Form VI:1

13 Jug Form VI:1c

14 Jug Form VI:2

15 Jug Form VI:3a

16 Jug Form VI:3b

8 Urn Form VI:5

10 Jug Form VI:2

11 Jug Form VI:1a

12 Jug Form VI:1b

21 Juglet Form VI:1c

17 Jug Form VI:3c

18 Jug Form VI:3d

19 Juglet Form VI:1a

20 Juglet Form VI:1b

22 Juglet Form VI:1d

23 Flask Form VI:1a

24 Flask Form VI:1b

25 Flask Form VI:1c

26 Flask Form VI:2

27 Flask Form VI:3

28 Flask Form VI:4a

29 Spouted Flask Form VI:1a

30 Spouted Flask Form VI:1b

31 Bottle Form VI:1

32 Unguentarium Form VI:1

33 Beaker Form VI:1

34 Bowl Form VI:1a

35 Bowl Form VI:1b

36 Bowl Form VI:1c

37 Bowl Form VI:1d

38 Bowl Form VI:1e

39 Bowl Form VI:2a

40 Bowl Form VI:2b

41 Bowl Form VI:3

42 Bowl Form VI:4a

43 Bowl Form VI:4b

44 Bowl Form VI:4c

45 Bowl Form VI:5a

46 Bowl Form VI:5b

47 Bowl Form VI:5c

48 Bowl Form VI:5d

49 Cup Form VI:1a

50 Cup Form VI:1b

51 Cup Form VI:2

52 Situla Form VI:1

53 Cooking Pot Form VI:1

54 Cooking Pot Form VI:2

55 Cooking Pot Form VI:3

A small selection of examples of tableware. The top-left specimen is probably a small African Red Slip bowl and the bottom-right one is an imported thin-walled bowl with vertical walls. The other three specimens are local imitations, subjected to different firing atmospheres, of typical imported Roman cups.

contexts. In underground tombs they tend to survive whole or in reconstructable fragments. Imported amphorae, used for transport of fish sauces, oil, and wine, are recognizable mostly by their shapes and, like the fine ware mentioned above, are very informative on the commercial links of the Maltese population at this time. They have finally started to be given their deserved importance and specialized studies, in particular one on the rich repertoire yielded by the Tas-Silġ excavations.

A type of imported cooking ware which so far seems to have been identified in only one excavation is Pantelleria ware. It is characterized both by its fabric, rich in volcanic elements, and by its shapes. It was found in some quantities in the 1983-84 excavation on Museum Esplanade. I only know about them because I spent some time sorting and studying the pottery from those excavations in the following years.

With respect to local pottery production what we archaeologists miss most is the discovery of such production sites, for example, a pottery kiln. The only known incidents of such finds go back to the eighteenth century. One consisted of a 'large brick and pottery manufacturing site' found in Gozo in 1728. All the pottery from that site is reported to have been sold to the Museum of Lyons where it was still kept in 1899. Attempts to locate these finds in that Museum have largely failed. The second one was discovered on Jesuits' Hill, Marsa in 1768 and was said to be in use from Roman

Imperial to Byzantine times. Unfortunately, there are no records of any samples of pottery surviving from this important discovery.

Political Status and Social Structure

For the political status of Sicilian cities in the first century of the empire we depend on a list of the cities of Sicily and its neighbouring islands drawn by the elder Pliny before he died during the eruption of Vesuvius in AD 79 (*NH* III, 8, 92). Although he mentions Melita, Pliny does not say anything about its juridical status. We, therefore, have only negative evidence to go by. In the list Malta does not figure among the *coloniae*, nor among the towns with a considerable number of Roman citizens (*oppida civium Romanorum*) - while Lipari does - nor among the cities of Latin status (*Latinae condicionis*). By elimination it must have belonged to the group of the remaining tributary states (*stipendiarii*).

The post-Augustan Greek inscription, describing a certain Roman knight L. Castricius Prudens as *protos* and patron of the Maltese and as a former *archon* and priest of the god Augustus, seems to confirm this. These titles are not those of a Romanized community (*CIL*, X, p. 773) and would indicate that Melita was still a peregrine city during the reign of Tiberius. The title of *protos* (chief man) appears to be a predominantly honorary title, but it did carry enough prestige to involve a high degree of influence in internal decision-making. The same title was enjoyed by Publius, the chief man of Malta, who in AD 60 gave shelter and hospitality to St Paul after the latter's shipwreck on the island. This is not at all surprising since the date of this event is close enough to that of the inscription. Much more surprising is the fact that the same title, this time in Latin (*primus omnium*), occurs as late as the second century AD in a Latin inscription (*CIL, X, 7495*, line 1). If anything, this inscription confirms that it was an honorary title because by then Malta had a municipal status.

It is true that Malta is described as *municipium* in two Latin inscriptions, one of which has the words *[munic]ipi Mel.* (*CIL, X, 7495*, line 1) and the other, *i[tem patro]nus municip[ii] Me[litensium]* (*CIL, X, 8318,* lines 2-3). It is equally true that Gozo too honoured two such patrons of its *municipium* who were closely related to each other, one being a *flamen divi Adriani*. But all these inscriptions are reliably dated to the second century AD and both islands, or either of them, might have been granted their municipal status before then. We have the *terminus ante quem* but not the *terminus post quem*.

Bottom & opposite page: This inscription on a marble slab, now housed in the Mdina Cathedral Museum, is reported to have been discovered in 1868 in the Mdina area.

It commemorates a certain Claudius Iustus, patron of the municipium. A 3rd-century AD date is suggested by the lack of mention of the tribe to which this citizen belonged.

CLAVDIVS IVSTVS II VIR ET PATRO
NVS MVNICIPI MELITENSIVM
MARMOREVM CVM SIMVLACRO
ET OMNI SVO ORNATV PROB HONOREM
DECVRIONATVS   AV
SECVNDVM POLLICITATIONEM SVAM
EXSTRVXIT CONSECRAVITQVE   IN
QVOD OPVS AMPLIVS QVAM PROMISERAT
EROGAVIT

CLAUDIUS JUSTUS, TRIUMVIR AND PATRON OF THE
MALTESE MUNICIPIUM, BUILT AND CONSECRATED,
AS HE HAD PROMISED, A MARBLE TEMPLE WITH ITS
STATUE AND ALL ITS PROPER ORNAMENT AND IN
THE EXECUTION OF THIS WORK SPENT MORE THAN
HE HAD PROMISED.

It should be kept in mind that the population of Malta and Gozo, as opposed to individuals, probably became full Roman citizens only with the *constitutio antoniniana* decreed by Emperor Caracalla in AD 212, which extended Roman citizenship to all free-born inhabitants of the Roman empire.

Internal social differentiation was obviously the order of the day, as in a typical Roman society. The three references to a 'chief man' (*protos/primus*) of the island clearly point to a very influential person, wealthy enough in one case to qualify for a Roman knighthood (even though of a freedman status), in another case to own land near the spot of St Paul's shipwreck, and in the third case to finance the construction of a whole temple in marble. The *protos/primus* probably yielded some civilian power, even though limited to internal affairs and subject to the jurisdiction of the provincial governor. The first of these three, Lucius Castricius Prudens, had, as a matter of fact, been an executive magistrate (an *archon*).

The figure of the *patronus* conjures up a lively picture of the relation between the patron and his clients which permeated Roman society and which is depicted on several monuments in relief in the metropolis. Here this relation is raised on a higher, I would say, institutionalized level: it is the whole communities of Gozo and Malta who honour their generous benefactors and erect monuments in their honour by public subscription.

Social differentiation at times expressed itself in the holding of religious priesthoods. Lucius Castricius Prudens was at some stage a priest for the deified Augustus (*amphipoleusas theo Augusto*). The Lutatia mentioned in the Gozitan inscription dedicated to Iulia Augusta must have been a lady of character and consequence since she affirmed herself as the protagonist in the act of raising a statue and a commemorative inscription to the divine imperial lady. She had her own role in Gozitan society, that of a priestess (*sacerdos*) of the empress Iulia. Her husband played second fiddle to her, even if he was a high priest (*flamen*). Although she associates her husband and children with herself in the consecration of the statue, she finances the monument out of her pocket (*sua pecunia*). More

A 2nd-century AD inscription engraved on a marble slab now exhibited in the Gozo Archaeological Museum. It commemorates the setting-up of a monument in honour of Caius Vallius Postumus.

than a century later, even Caius Vallius Postumus is a priest (*flamen*) of the deified emperor Hadrian.

Compared to other urban centres in both Sicily and in neighbouring Libya, the local ethnic component in Malta is conspicuous by its absence. In Sicily the local Greek component remains quite prominent in the literary and epigraphic documentation of the Imperial age. In Tripolitania it is the Punic component which frequently surfaces, sometimes in the person of distinguished personalities with clearly Punic names who erect public monuments and have themselves portrayed in publicly-displayed marble statues (such as

Iddibal Caphada Aemilius and Annobal Rufus in Leptis Magna). It seems as if the Punic social component in Malta never quite made it to assert itself in high positions; at least not strongly enough to leave its mark in the epigraphic or archaeological records.

Even burial contexts and mortuary assemblages dating to imperial times fail to provide a clear ethnic (or cultural, for that matter) distinction between the new arrivals originating from Italy or other parts of the empire, and Romanized locals, and between them and conservative Punic locals. Only on one occasion are we informed, by an inscription in Greek, about the eastern Mediterranean origin of the commemorated dead person, the comic actor and lyre-player Hermolaos who hailed from Pergamon, and who could be, for all we know, an itinerant artist whose young life was cut short while performing on Malta.

Beside a class of merchants suggested by commercial activity in the harbours, a class of landed gentry is suggested by the country villas, especially the purely residential ones, like the Ramla Bay villa and, of course, by the oft-mentioned town house of Rabat. While the rustic villas were likely to be owned as a productive investment, the residential ones were probably owned for prestige and comfort. Suffice it to note that the Ramla Bay villa was situated in one of the most exclusive, paradisiacal locations of the island and was equipped with an artificially-heated bathing suite.

An old photograph of the 1910 excavations of the villa at Ramla Bay in Gozo. One can clearly see the large room whose floor was decorated with frames of marble of different colours.

The Roman town house probably had the same type of heated baths, but their existence can only be inferred from the varying levels of the artificially-cut rock surface. While it was constructed in the Republican phase, it was in Emperor Claudius' reign that it was furnished with a set of fine, and highly expensive, marble statues. These seem to suggest that the owner was not only wealthy but had close connections with the emperor or held a very high official posting. Claudius seems to have had a much closer rapport with Malta than the absence of the mention of such link in the sources tends to suggest. Another marble

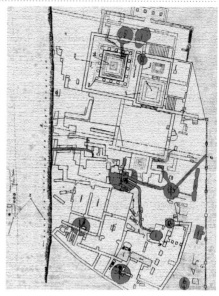

The site of the Roman domus *and adjacent houses is riddled with cisterns intended to collect the rain water from the roofs and courtyards.*

A detail from an illustration from Houel's Voyage Pittoresque, *showing another portrait of Claudius. It appears that Houel bought this portrait, which eventually ended up in the Louvre Museum, Paris.*

portrait of his (now in the Musée du Louvre in Paris) was present in Malta when it was purchased by Jean Houel, the French traveller who depicted it in one of the illustrations of his book published in 1787. This connection with Claudius could have been some privilege conferred on its inhabitants during his reign, or a brief stay on the island during which he was hosted by the chief man of the island. What is clear is that the owner of the house, who could possibly be the *primus* himself, went out of his way to adorn his house with the finest specimens of portrait statuary of the reigning emperor and other close members of his family.

Although the general impression of Malta is that of a backwater, a is that, when Caracalla assassinated his younger brother, soon after their father's death, and ordered his *damnatio memoriae*, the Gozitans made it a point to comply and erased all references to Geta in that inscription. Later still, at the beginning of the fourth century AD, the Gozitans made sure to honour by two separate inscriptions the two reigning Augusti, Constantius Chlorus and Galerius, the two senior members of the imperial tetrarchy (or rule of four) that had been introduced by Emperor Diocletian. But that episode takes us into the final chapter of our ancient history.

Ancient portrait of Emperor Hadrian inserted into a modern statue now preserved in the Boboli Gardens, Florence, Italy.

Two coins with the portraits of young Geta (AD 209-212) (top): Odessos in Thrace; and Geta as Caesar (AD 198-209) (bottom): Eumeneia in Phrigia.

remote, quiet, and reasonably prosperous corner of the empire, the islands were certainly not completely detached from the political vicissitudes of the imperial court. In this respect Gozo manifests a distinctly prominent role. Caius Vallius Postumus, the patron of that *municipium*, personally conducted a delegation on behalf of his city to the court of Emperor Hadrian. Later, the Gozitans put up a monument to Geta, the younger of the two sons and designated co-heirs of Septimius Severus, as documented by the respective inscription mentioned above. It is more than likely that they set up a similar monument to his elder brother Caracalla, but the relative inscription has not reached us. What is certain

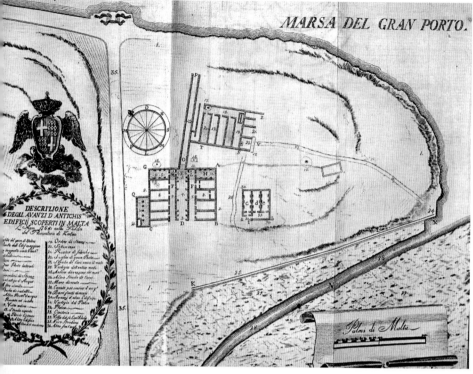

MARSA DEL GRAN PORTO.

Economy and Commerce

From Pliny the Elder we also learn that the system of taxation had been changed by the early or mid-Augustan period. Most of the cities of Sicily were now classified as *stipendiarii* (*NH*, III, 8,91). This means that now the major tax paid by the Sicilian *civitates*, including Malta, was by a fixed payment (*stipendium*) instead of the variable tithe (*decuma*) of the Republican period.

During the two centuries of *pax Romana* (first-second centuries AD) the islands must have enjoyed a certain degree of prosperity, in part resulting from their position in the centre of the maritime trade routes and in part from certain agricultural and industrial activities.

Map showing the Ta' Cejlu promontory (near the Marsa Power Station) where in 1768 extensive remains of buildings were discovered. The buildings consisted of stores and cisterns. A narrow canal for the passage of boats cuts through this interred part of the harbour.

This prosperity made it possible for a class of people to emerge who were wealthy enough to import luxury items, including statuary in expensive marbles, from Italy and other overseas sources and to finance the erection or the restoration of prestigious and costly public buildings, including temples. The restoration of the temple of Proserpina by Chrestion and the construction of the marble temple of Apollo by the 'chief man' (*primus*) of Malta are telling examples.

From Pliny (*NH*, III, 8 92) we also get to know the distances that separated Gaulos and Melita from Camarina (87 miles) and Lilybaeum (113 miles). This last piece of information relative to distances from Malta is repeated verbatim by the fourth-century AD writer Martianus Capella, possibly implying that these were regular routes between Malta and these two Sicilian coastal towns both in the first and in the fourth centuries AD - though Camarina should be considered more of an anchorage since the town itself long been almost totally abandoned in the Republican age. These references, and the mention in the *Acts* of an Alexandrian ship wintering in Malta, tend to suggest that the Maltese harbours were sufficiently well equipped for handling maritime commerce. This is confirmed by physical harbour remains occasionally surfacing in the Grand Harbour area.

The most extensive ones were those discovered in 1768 and described by Ciantar in his *Malta Illustrata* and by Marchese Barbaro in his *Degli Avanzi d'Alcuni Antichissimi Edificii Scoperti in Malta*. They consisted of a complex of rectangular buildings with corridors and rows of rooms and stores. A quay wall made up of large blocks extended to the south. One of the rooms contained 260 complete amphorae of which 24 had Greek inscriptions. The Greek inscriptions suggest imported commodities, but the possibility that they were in storage for eventual transhipment should not be excluded.

Other remains, consisting of several lengths of heavy masonry came accidentally to light in 1959 in Racecourse Street, Marsa and were taken by the Museum Department authorities to represent 'the remains of massive warehouses of a period when the area of the Marsa racecourse was still under the waters of Grand Harbour'. There

Some of the tombs discovered in 1961 on that part of Jesuits' Hill which is now occupied by the Electricity Generating Station. This find is not recorded in the Museum Annual Report *of 1961. Similar finds have been recorded on several occasions in this area. The remnants of two such tombs can still be seen on the vertical rock face flanking the road leading from Il-Menqa to the Electricity Generating Station.*

are also officially unconfirmed rumours of finds of similar harbour installations, including stone mooring-rings deep in the alluvial deposits inland from Salina Bay.

This harbour activity also implies the existence of a class of merchants involved in shipping. They would have handled the commercial activities passing through the harbours, both imports and exports, as well as any conceivable transhipment.

As in previous periods, agriculture must have been based both on cereal and cash-crop cultivation, as

Aerial view of Salina Bay. Given the number of Roman anchor stocks retrieved from off Qawra Point, this must have been a very busy harbour in Roman times. It seems that a good part of the ancient harbour has silted up over the centuries and in antiquity it extended for several hundred metres inland, an area now covered by fields.

well as on animal husbandry. Substantial amounts of olive oil must have been produced by the olive-pressing installations accompanying the rustic villas described above. The wide distribution of so many rustic villas (at least 23) on such a limited territory suggests, in the first place, an intensive diffusion of the cultivation of the olive-tree and, probably, of the vine; in the second place, that such cultivation was an important source of income or import substitution for these commodities.

The harvesting and pressing of both olives and grapes was, however, seasonal in nature. Agricultural activity must have been supplemented by wheat cultivation, as suggested by the representation of an ear of wheat on locally struck coins of the Republican phase, though for its wheat requirements

Five of a number of loom weights in stone that were uncovered during Temi Zammit's excavations in the houses adjacent to the Roman domus in the 1920s. One weight has the Greek letter Π engraved on it.

Malta is likely to have depended on supplies from Sicily, as it did in Medieval times. We are not sure what the material for the famous Maltese draperies was. It seems likely to have been linen, but wool is another possibilty. Since flax is known to have been cultivated in late Medieval Malta, it is likely to have been grown also in antiquity. We can only assume that such draperies continued to be produced in this phase because we do not find any mention of them in the literary sources from the first century onwards.

Unfortunately we do not have enough data to form an idea of the field systems and land-use patterns obtainable in this period. The Maltese terrain was not suitable for the regular parcelling of land on the orthogonal (*centuriatio*) principle which characterizes Roman territories with extensive plains, such as the hinterland of proconsular Africa and Italy. For the same reason centuriation is also absent in neighbouring Sicily.

Industry

Textile industry is attested to by the occurrence of loom weights and spindle whorls in the excavation of various sites. Weaving was probably a home-based industry. That there was a concentration of weaving establishments, including home-based ones, in town is quite natural to expect and was hinted at by Cicero's statement on Verres mentioned in the previous chapter.

Rows of Roman amphorae from one of the Xlendi shipwrecks. Most of the amphorae were intended for wine transport and belong to foreign imports (known as Dressel 1 and Lamboglia 2 types). The egg-shaped amphora with a short neck and round handles belongs to Type 1 of the two types of amphorae recently identified as being of local Maltese production, represented here by the amphora to the extreme right of the middle row.

The recent identification by Dott. Brunella Bruno of two locally-produced types of amphorae has introduced new elements in the organization of trade and the economy of Roman Malta. The first type of amphora is datable to the second-first century BC and is characterized by not only the shape but also the fabric, which are both of local derivation. The second type, datable to the first-second century AD, is characterized by a fabric whose constituent elements are partly of foreign derivation (quartz and volcanic material). These amphorae are thought to be either of foreign manufacture intended solely for the Maltese market – since they allegedly occur only in Malta – or manufactured locally with imported temper mixed to local clay. Whatever the origin, Type 2 has purely local imitations.

The first type, found in the stratification of Tas-Silġ and San Pawl Milqi, suggests that the local production of amphorae was intended for transport, and possibly export, of some locally-produced commodity, most probably oil. Its presence in Shipwreck A at Xlendi, whose main cargo consisted of wine amphorae of Dressel 1 and Lamboglia 2 types, in my view makes it more likely of foreign origin. By definition a shipwreck implies a foreign ship, or a local one returning from elsewhere with foreign commodities, although

Right: Two types of amphorae that have been recently identified as locally produced. Left: Type 1 (produced in the 2nd-1st century BC) is egg-shaped, possibly derived from the previous Punico-Maltese ovoid and neckless amphora. Right: Type 2 (produced in the 1st-2nd century AD) is squat, with body tapering out downwards (After Bruno 2004).

the even earlier (fourth-third century BC) Punic shipwreck consists of ovoid and neckless amphorae generally held to be of local, Maltese production. The shape of Type 1 is said to be inspired by two different foreign traditions: an Adriatic one (Lamboglia 2 and the 'Brindisina') and a North African one (e.g. Tripolitanian I). It replaces the traditional Punic one. This implies that, with the Roman conquest, Malta is exposed, certainly more directly and intensively, to other markets, such as the south Italian wine market whose by-product, its means of transport, is adopted for local production.

The second type, documented only in the National Museum stores, creates an even more complicated scenario, or two possible scenarios.

The first one is that the amphorae were produced outside Malta, in an area not yet identified, which is characterized by a volcanic/ quartzite geology and which produced the transportable commodity exclusively for the Maltese market. This scenario is already somewhat far-fetched, given the extremely limited Maltese market. The second scenario implies the traffic of specific sands for addition as temper to the local clays for the production of amphorae in different localities in Malta. Although not impossible – especially if the foreign elements could be explained as grog (crushed pottery) rather than sand – such a trade mechanism appears to be unrealistic at the time for which it is proposed.

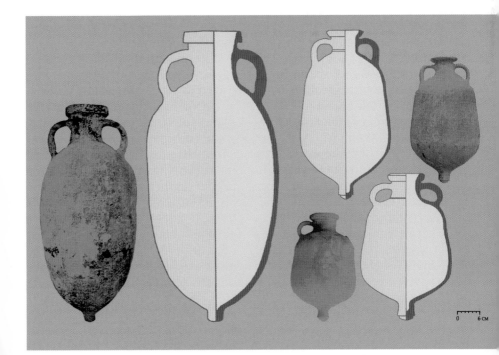

This aerial view of part of the south-eastern coast of Malta shows the great number of promontories, albeit not very long, projecting out into the sea. Delimara Point is the most prominent one in this area.

Settlement & Urban Organization

Well into the empire, in the second century AD, the geographer Claudius Ptolemaeus (*Geogr.*, 4. 3. 13) was still assigning a city to each island giving also the geographical co-ordinates of their position which, although not precise by modern standards, were not too far off the mark. Although some editions of Ptolemy add the word *polis* to another landmark in Malta, thus suggesting the existence of another urban centre (*Chersonesos Polis*), there is no archaeological or other reason to believe that this was the case, and most editions of Ptolemy's *Geography* refer solely to *chersonesos*, a promontory or peninsula. The term vaguely recalls the *topon dithalasson* of St Paul's shipwreck. Gozo does not have such prominent headlands; similarly the

south coast of Malta, except for Delimara Point. We are left with Qawra Point on the north coast and, with a little stretching of the imagination, the Valletta peninsula. In terms of settlement, Valletta has never produced any ancient remains, while Qawra Point has only quarries followed by late Roman tombs on the opposite side of Salina Bay. In terms of maritime fixtures for navigational purposes, Qawra and Delimara Points project much more prominently out into the open sea, while Valletta does separate two outstanding deep harbours.

There is no doubt that the two towns mentioned by Ptolemy continued to play an important political and economic role in the life of the two islands during the empire. They were the centres of the political administration. The protagonists in internal politics must have had their residences there. Some of them were immortalized by inscriptions which, in most cases, accompanied statues or other monuments raised in their honour. It should be assumed that most economic transactions were undertaken there.

Although an early imperial inscription (*CIL*, X, 7494) groups the two islands together under the procuratorship of Chrestion, the freedman of Augustus, several second century inscriptions (*CIL, X, 7501-8*) refer to Gaulos as a separate *municipium* with its own decurions. Another inscription, dated to the second century AD (*CIL, X, 7495*), carries the first reference to municipal status for Melite. Such inscriptions were normally commissioned to celebrate the erection of monuments, most often statues, in honour of important local citizens or imperial personages. It is not difficult, therefore, to imagine a series of such statues adorning public buildings and squares in the ancient Roman towns of Melite and Gaulos. It is most unfortunate that both the statues and the buildings they embellished have disappeared. The only surviving traces of these buildings, besides the inscriptions themselves, are several richly-decorated, marble architectural fragments preserved in the national collections.

Melite

The location and extension of the town of Melite in Roman imperial times are well known. Its remains lie buried under the old city of Mdina, the present fortifications of which, dated to the seventeenth-eighteenth century, probably cover the Roman as well as the Medieval ones. It also extended, however, beyond the fortifications of Mdina and covered a sizable portion of present Rabat. Its defensive walls must have reinforced the natural declivity of three sides of the plateau, while to the south-west they had required the addition of a wide ditch, only a section of which is still visible today, behind the church of St Paul. The concentration of tombs beyond this ditch, forming

Plan of Mdina and part of Rabat, Malta. The yellow line shows the boundaries and extent of the Roman city of Melite.

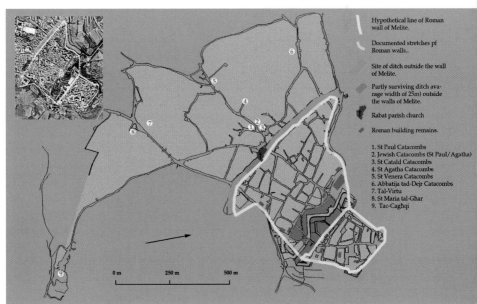

Hypothetical line of Roman wall of Melite.

Documented stretches pf Roman walls..

Site of ditch outside the wall of Melite.

Partly surviving ditch average width of 25m) outside the walls of Melite.

Rabat parish church

Roman building remains.

1. St Paul Catacombs
2. Jewish Catacombs (St Paul/Agatha)
3. St Catald Catacombs
4. St Agatha Catacombs
5. St Venera Catacombs
6. Abbatija tad-Dejr Catacombs
7. Tal-Virtu
8. St Maria tal-Għar
9. Tac-Caghqi

0 m   250 m   500 m

extensive necropoleis, further confirms the limits of the town in this direction.

Stone remains of the old Roman walls could still be seen in the seventeenth century on the city side of the ditch. Similar remains were observed in the late nineteenth century at the north-west end. None of these survive, and the more recently discovered traces are not sufficiently evident. In 1960 traces of masonry were revealed during excavations beneath the rear courtyard of Vilhena Palace inside Mdina, and a stretch of a similar structure was brought to light in 1963 during reinforcement works on the knights' fortifications on the slope behind the palace. These looked massive enough for defensive purposes, while a square structure, the foundations of which were brought to light in 1970 close to the Ta' Saura Hospital near Saqqajja, has also been tentatively identified as an ancient defensive structure. Similarly, a small stretch of wall consisting of massive ashlar blocks uncovered in 1988 some hundred metres to the east of it, could possibly be part of the Roman city fortification.

On the urban design and street network of Melite we know very little. The reticent and incomplete manner, by which accidental discoveries of ancient structures have been recorded throughout the years, does not permit us even to verify whether the present urban layout follows the ancient one. The only two instances of excavations that have revealed streets flanked by domestic

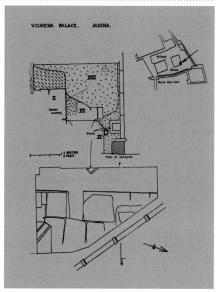

Drawing of the wall of large ashlar masonry discovered in 1960 beneath the floor of the rear courtyard of Vilhena Palace in Mdina.

buildings (the 1920s excavations of the area annexed to the outstanding Rabat *domus* described below, and the 1983-84 ones in the square in front of the Domus Romana) strongly suggest that the street plan of Melite did not follow a premeditated, rational design, such as the Hippodamian, or the Roman gridiron, one. The city must have grown organically, following the natural contours of the terrain.

Urban domestic architecture is represented by what could be considered the richest archaeological find of the Roman period in Malta, the *domus* discovered in Rabat, outside the walls of Mdina, in 1881. Although its elegant architecture and polychrome mosaics date its

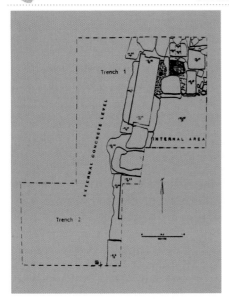

Plan of the remains excavated by the University of California Los Angeles in 1983-84. One can see the short stretch of road flanked by buildings on both sides.

original construction to the early first century BC, it must have continued to be, for more than a century later, a stately house belonging to a rich Roman, or Romanized Maltese, patron. The reason for this is because sometime in the reign of the emperor Claudius it was further furnished by a set of very fine portrait statues of members of the imperial family. The house is not likely to have survived beyond the Julio-Claudian age (AD 68) because otherwise they would have been replaced by others of later dynasties, like the Flavian or Antonine ones.

The archaeological remains of the Roman period recovered from this house and from other sites in Rabat and its surroundings, are on exhibit in the Domus Romana built over part of the ruins of the same *domus.*

CARUANS'S PLAN

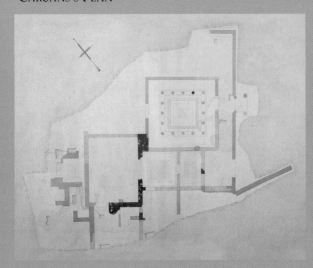

Plan of the remains of the Roman domus *discovered by A.A. Caruana in 1881. Caruana had already discovered the best part of the* domus *consisting of rooms gravitating around the peristyled courtyard. According to this plan the house had a monumental entrance, with a projecting portico, on the south-eastern side. The wall projecting at a tangent in an easterly direction from the southern corner of the house is difficult to explain.*

Gaulos

The main town of Gozo which, like that of Malta, stood almost in the centre of the island, occupied only part of the hill on which it was sited, with an acropolis planted on a much higher promontory at its north extremity. Also for the city of Gaulos scanty information comes to us from eighteenth-century writers who noted the existence of several architectural fragments. The limits of the ancient town are not known with any precision but we reproduce here a plausible reconstruction of its topography. It is hard to tell whether the present street layout reflects in any way that of the Roman town, as has been suggested.

The only significant archaeological investigation ever to be undertaken on the site of the city was in 1961 when a drain trench was cut the whole length of It-Tokk, the main square of the present town. The section of the trench, some 52m long, indicated occupation from the Bronze Age to late Roman times. During the construction of the oratory of the basilica of St George in 1976-77 foundation remains of a Roman building were discovered consisting of several ashlar blocks of large dimensions. One of these now stands outside the side door of the basilica. The other physical remains discovered over the last two centuries inside the hypothetical boundaries of the town have already been listed above.

Inscriptions and a series of architectural fragments - cornices, capitals, shafts, and bases of columns - noted by eighteenth-century writers in the streets of Rabat and the *Castello*, suggest that the town of Gaulos was prosperous enough to possess public and religious buildings adorned with marble architectural decoration. Remains of such buildings have been encountered on a number of occasions but they were covered over again, sometimes without a record being kept. Monumental remains were discovered in the seventeenth century while laying the foundations of the Gozo cathedral in the *Castello*; they were tentatively assigned to a temple of Juno. The *Castello* must have thus constituted the upper city, or citadel, while a section of today's Rabat formed the lower city.

The boundaries of the town seem to be fixed by the steep contours of the *Castello* on the north side and on the other three sides by the incidence of tombs, which were normally placed just outside the town, and the occasional discovery of ancient masonry that might be taken to be sections of the town wall. Traces of massive walling, in fact, are reported to have been encountered during building works in Main Gate Street. Unfortunately, these remains had to be covered over again. According to one view the Roman town walls could have stretched from the vicinity of the east demi-bastion of the seventeenth-century fortifications, down to the main crossroads of Republic Street and from there along Main Gate Street to St Francis Square, turning sharply west along Vajrinġa Street and then north again along St Mary Street to join the *Castello* again near St Martin demi-bastion.

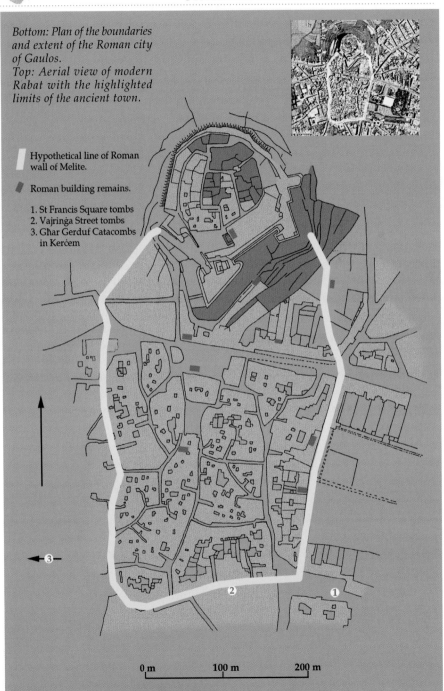

Bottom: Plan of the boundaries
and extent of the Roman city
of Gaulos.
Top: Aerial view of modern
Rabat with the highlighted
limits of the ancient town.

Hypothetical line of Roman
wall of Melite.

Roman building remains.

1. St Francis Square tombs
2. Vajringa Street tombs
3. Għar Gerduf Catacombs
   in Kerċem

0 m   100 m   200 m

Villas

Out in the countryside, the villas that had been constructed during the Republic continued to thrive in the empire, now receiving their definitive shape, the one that is generally unearthed during excavations. By the end of the empire most of them were abandoned without being occupied in later times. The only exception seems to be that of San Pawl Milqi which, having been fortified by a massive boundary wall and restored after a strong fire which took place at the beginning of the imperial age - or in the third century AD, as suggested by recent investiga-

Aerial view of a section of the Roman villa inside the grounds of the Zejtun government school excavated in the 1960s and 1970s. Clearly visible in the top-right corner are a circular stone vat and the stone anchor of an olive press.

tions - seems to have resisted against the increasing threats of incursions from overseas and survived well into the following period. The Żejtun villa, apart from an olive press bed, a *prelum* anchor, and stone vats, yielded a scatter of bronze coins, mostly of the third century AD. The 1915 excavations of the Ta' Kaċċatura villa produced a base of an Italian *terra sigillata* cup and several fragments of African Red Slip Ware, which date to the first three-to-four centuries AD, and a fragment of an inscription datable to the second half of the second century

In the imperial phase we can say that two distinct types of villas marked the Maltese landscape: the residential villas and the rustic ones. The former were intended solely for residential purposes, often furnished with the comforts of a heated bathing

A view of some of the rooms of the Roman baths at Għajn Tuffieħa. In the foreground is the calidarium *(the hot room) while in the background on the right is the latrine. What is odd with these baths is that the remains of a residential villa, to which the baths might have belonged, are nowhere in sight. The size of the baths qualifies them as private ones, but the presence of cubicles (small bedrooms) suggests a public purpose.*

system. The most intriguing one is the villa at Ramla Bay in Gozo; one might even call it a *villa marittima*, since it was situated right on the sandy beach of this stupendous bay. It had a series of nineteen rooms. Some were for habitation purposes, including a larger room with a floor decorated with successive borders of different-coloured stone and marble. In these rooms traces of wall painting (red and yellow patterns on a white background, probably imitation marble) were found, as well as small fragments of mosaic. But it also had a sequence of heated rooms for the passage from heated to cold baths, in the usual Roman bathing style. The cold bath was octagonal in shape and lined with thin grey marble slabs.

Substantially larger was the bathing suite at Għajn Tuffieħa in Malta. Its size and certain apparently collective facilities suggest a public bath rather than a private one attached to a villa. The remains of the latter are, in fact, nowhere in sight. What is odd is its location, miles away from town, but a mile or so from two beautiful beaches. It made use of a natural water spring underneath it. There are no hot springs in Malta. The heating here, and elsewhere, had to be provided artificially by special furnaces that forced hot air under the floors of the hot and tepid rooms and hot water wherever it was needed. The floors of the various spaces of the baths were decorated with mosaics of different geometric patterns. They date the whole establishment to the second century AD.

While on the subject of baths, mention must be made of a curious find made early in the eighteenth century (1729) on the shore of the Grand Harbour in Marsa, at the foot of the Capuchin bastion. The remains are described as 'baths' by Baron de Stadl who has left us a detailed record of them. Both the floors and the walls were decorated with mosaics representing 'fish, serpents, and dragons'. Sadly, the ancient relics were left to the mercy of children and vandals and eventually covered over.

The *villae rusticae*, the self-contained farming units, beside their own residential areas had complex production areas, equipped with sophisticated apparatus for the

Old photo of the excavations at Għajn Tuffieħa in 1929. Clearly visible are the surviving arches of bricks that supported the floor of the calidarium. The room was heated by hot air from the adjacent hypocaust.

pressing of olive oil. Although about twenty of these villas have been somehow documented, the Maltese landscape must have been marked by a scatter of several more of such buildings, some of which have been irredeemably lost. Each must have been accompanied by its estate which incorporated its own copse of olive trees. Presumably, these estates were run with the aid of a body of slaves but, so far, no traces of the presence of slave quarters have ever been identified.

One other thing that one seriously misses from these excavations is more specimens of fine sculpture like the ones found inside the Rabat townhouse. Mention of sculptural fragments are mentioned in the reports of the excavations of the residential villa at Ramla Bay which were conducted in 1910, but none of these survive.

Culture and Religion

During the early principate, the Maltese cultural scenario seems to have changed, possibly quite rapidly. In fact, by the time of Tiberius, the urban aristocracy seems to be completely Romanized. Latin must have become the official language, as it did in the rest of the western empire. Members of the community gradually acquired Latin names through enfranchisement. All the dignitaries mentioned in the texts (Publius) and in the inscriptions (Chrestion and L. Castricius) carry Latin, or Greek, names, although this does not rule out the possibility of a Punic extraction. There are, for example, no Punic names as there are in, say, Roman Tripolitania. This situation appears even more emphasized by the early second century AD (Vallius and Postumus inscriptions).

Portrait bust of Emperor Septimius Severus (reigned AD 193-211). Severus was born in Leptis Magna in Libya and, following a military career, he made it up to the highest political post in the empire. He regaled his mother city with impressive public works, including a forum and a basilica (court house).

Literary evidence, albeit limited to one single incidence, the one connected with St Paul's shipwreck, seems to suggest that Punic remained a spoken language in Malta, at least among the common folk, the ones who came to the immediate rescue of the shipwrecked. Again, this is not surprising. In Tripolitania, the future emperor Septimius Severus was fluent in Punic. Unlike Tripolitania, however, where neo-Punic inscriptions continue to be engraved, even on public monuments, often accompanying Latin ones, neither of the Maltese islands has produced such inscriptions belonging to the imperial age.

The inscriptions are very illuminating with regard to religious practices in the imperial age, especially in the Julio-Claudian period.

Luius Castricius was an officiating priest of divine Augustus, while Lutatia was a devout priestess of the divinized wife of the first emperor. Her husband too was a priest, a high priest to boot, but it is not clear whether he belonged to the same priesthood. Chrestion, on the other hand, restored the temple of a typical pagan female divinity, Proserpina. The other inscription that refers to another temple structure is that which describes in some detail the parts of the temple of Apollo; but it belongs to the second century AD. Slightly later is the Gozo inscription which qualifies Postumus as high priest (*flamen*) for the cult of the deified emperor Hadrian. Towards the end of the same century, the title of *mater castrorum* in the inscription in honour of Empress Julia Domna, wife of Septimius Severus, implies a certain degree of sacrality.

This epigraphic evidence shows unequivocally that the religion practised officially on both islands from the first down to the third century was the Roman pagan one, with a high dose of imperial worship. Of the practice of Christianity there is still no sign in the archaeological record. Not very surprising, as the same situation prevails in most of the Roman world, including Rome itself, even where there is undeniable literary evidence of Christian worship

Detail of a miniature cornice in soft local limestone. Found in Fiddien valley, together with three other fragments, it seems to have belonged to some miniaturized sacred shrine.

as early as the first-second century AD, as in Rome (Nero's accusations for the great fire) and in Bithynia (Pliny the Younger's letters). It is possible that some groups of Christians followed their new religion clandestinely, and without leaving any trace of their practice

Under the emperors, Maltese culture, especially sculpture, embraced the official stamp of imperial art. The surviving architectural fragments in marble betray a great affinity to Italian tastes and standards. So do the intriguing miniaturized cornices

Draped female statue from Gozo. Undoubtedly, it is the statue alluded to in the Ceres inscription, which served as a base for it. Even though headless, it fits perfectly with the iconography of the portrait statues of Julia Augusta represented as Ceres.

in Maltese stone from Fiddien valley. They are exquisitely carved. The Julio-Claudian set of portrait sculpture adorning the town house of Rabat, and the female draped statue from Gozo show no trace of provincial art. The only items that might be said to do so are the Satyr head from Gozo and the two Amazon torsos from Rabat, all in soft Malta stone.

A statuette of Bes in private possession goes to show that the ancient Egyptianizing component of Maltese culture and the worship of Egyptian divinities was still active in the advanced phase of the imperial age. By that time most cities of the Roman empire had sanctuaries dedicated to some Egyptian divinity or other, the more popular being Isis and Serapis.

UNDERWATER ARCHAEOLOGY

The Museums Department examining a deep-water wrecksite in 1993, with the help of the French Navy submarine Griffon.

An area which has not been given much attention in this volume is maritime archaeology, a field that used to be neglected for too long by the archaeological establishment but is whipping up greater and greater interest in young archaeologists. Several shipwrecks have been identified in Maltese waters over the years.

Shipwrecks are often suggested by the presence of Roman anchor stocks. One such anchor stock (below), discovered off Qawra Point, being over four metres in length, is an absolute record for its size.

Off the mouth of Xlendi Bay at least two shipwrecks have been recorded. Another one has been observed more recently in much deeper waters in the same region. Several other shipwreck sites are known around the Maltese archipelago, including cargoes that range from amphorae for the transport of wine and oil, to marble column drums for a monumental building and there are surely others awaiting to be discovered. Such heritage too needs systematic surveying and protection, which for obvious reasons is much more costly, in terms of time, money and human resources, than surveying on land.

Late Antiquity saw many profound changes in the Old World gravitating around the Mediterranean, all of which affected to various degrees life in the Maltese islands: the third century crisis of the empire, the barbarian invasions, the spread of Christianity, the division of the empire, the rise of Byzantium, the fall of the western Roman empire, and, finally, the Arab invasions.

CHAPTER 7

EPILOGUE

Early Christian and Byzantine Malta

The fourth-fifth centuries AD, in some respects even the third century, occupy a special place in the history of the Classical world, in particular of Roman civilization. They are generally referred to as Late Antiquity. It was caused by the deep political, economic, and spiritual crisis that affected all facets of Roman life and the Roman empire in the third century and ended with the deposition of the last Roman emperor of the west, Romulus Augustulus, by the Goths of Odoacer in AD 476. In between, Emperor Diocletian (AD 284-305) took enormous measures to instil order and military and economic stability in the empire. He was to a great extent successful, but not quite enough. Among other measures he introduced the rule of four (tetrarchy) by which the empire was substantially divided in two by a line following, more or less, the north-south

A typical rock-cut stibadium *(C-shaped banquet table) inside hypogeum no. 23 of the SS. Paul/ Agatha complex. On the wall at the back one can see two 'window' graves preceded by an arched recess. Between them, a set of tools (probably of a stone mason) has been engraved in relief.*

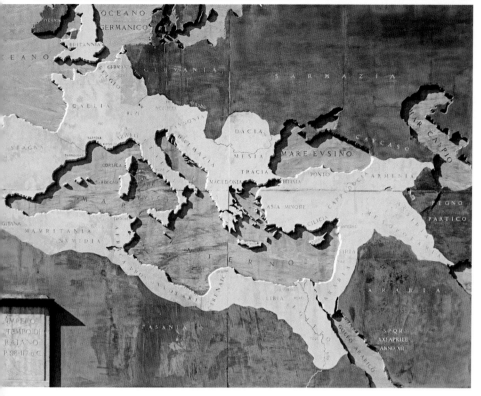

Adriatic axis, with each part ruled by a co-emperor (*Augustus*) assisted by a lieutenant (*Caesar*).

One of the third generation *Augusti*, Constantine I ('the Great'), further compounded the division of the empire by moving his seat of power to Byzantium, renaming the city Constantinople, thus giving rise to the Roman empire of the east, or the Byzantine empire. From that point onwards the Roman empire was effectively divided into two empires: the one in the west, the direct heir of Rome, was inexorably in decline with its capital shifting from one seat to another; the one in the east growing from strength to strength, reaching an apogee of territorial expansion

The extent of the Roman empire during the reign of Emperor Trajan (AD 98-117). One of the large-format maps affixed to the boundary wall of the Roman Forum on the Via dei Fori Imperiali in Rome.

with Emperor Justinian I and his able general Belisarius. It is in the reign of Justinian, in AD 535, that Malta was incorporated within the Byzantine empire, along with Sicily. It remained part of it until it was won over by the Muslim Arabs in AD 870. Before 535, however, Malta is likely to have experienced occupation first by the Vandals (probably *c*.445) and then by the Ostrogoths at an uncertain date (probably *c*.477)

This is, alas!, one of the darkest periods of Maltese history. It is documented by a few scraps of literary evidence, even fewer (almost negligible) shreds of epigraphic evidence. These will be dealt with extensively in the following volume of this series. My remit is to conclude the present volume by surveying only the archaeological heritage of the centuries that bring Antiquity to an end and herald in the Middle Ages. Compared to the scant textual evidence, Maltese archaeology is endowed with a substantial body of physical features which belong, however, almost totally to the religious world, namely, to underground funerary ritual. Religious worship above ground is attested to by just two buildings: the basilican church of Tas-Silġ and the shrine attached to the rock-cut cemetery complex of L-Abatija tad-Dejr in Rabat. The surviving specimens of material culture are practically limited to those associated with these two types of sites.

It is only recently that heavy masonry walls belonging to defence structures have been identified during essentially rescue operations in Mdina, one under the Xara Palace, and another in Villegaignon Street, near the eastern corner of the Carmelite church. They have been tentatively assigned to the Late Byzantine period, presumably on stratigraphic grounds. The implicit

uncertainty arises from the fact that these finds are still awaiting the publication of a proper excavation report and because the masonry in Villegaignon Street has been described as 'Dark Age' and 'possibly pertaining to a fortified structure of the eighth or ninth century AD'.

The construction of heavy fortification works in this area reflects the insecurity and the fear of attack at this point in time when the forces of Islam were exerting increasingly greater pressure on the islands and the northern shores of the Mediterranean. It is thought that this preoccupation with defence at these strategic points in Mdina implies the return of Mdina as a preferred and more secure area for habitation, possibly at the expense of the lower part of the town of Melite, now covered by Rabat. We need not push this

A section of the excavations undertaken under the floor of the Xara Palace Hotel, Mdina.

point so far, however, as to support the view frequently expressed in the past that the reduction of the inhabited town to the present Mdina happened in the Byzantine period rather than in the Arab one. The major argument against such a reduction at this point is the fact that so far no single burial place prior to the Islamic cemetery outside Greeks' Gate has ever been encountered within the western boundary of the town marked by the original 'Roman' ditch. This implies that,

Map of Malta and Gozo showing the distribution of Late Roman and Early Christian tombs and catacombs (after Buhagiar 1986, with additions and adjustments).
Each number may correspond to one single hypogeum (such as Torri Mamo) or to a cluster (such as Binġemma, Marsa, Ħal Pilatu, Taċ-Ċagħqi).

even in the worst scenario, people refused to bury their dead within those pre-established boundaries down to the very end of Antiquity.

Finds of Late Roman pottery of the fourth-fifth centuries AD have been remarkably scarce in the investigations conducted in Mdina since the 1990s. This seems to tie up with the next to total absence of any written records from the same period.

There are, however, two inscriptions from Gozo dating to the early fourth century AD, around 305-311, which cannot be left unmentioned. The first one was raised by the four men in charge of the 'republic' of Gozo in honour of Contantius I, known as Constantius Chlorus when he was co-emperor with Galerius (*CIL* X, 7504). It was engraved when F. Pollio and Rufus were the eponymous curators of

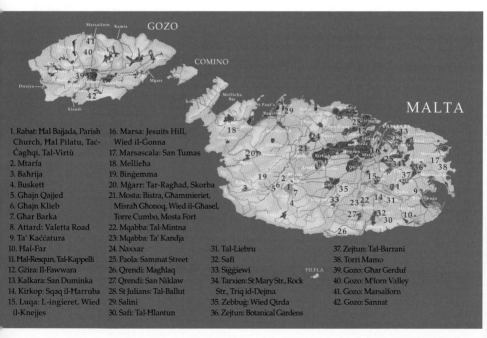

1. Rabat: Ħal Bajjada, Parish Church, Ħal Pilatu, Taċ-Ċagħqi, Tal-Virtù
2. Mtarfa
3. Baħrija
4. Buskett
5. Għajn Qajjed
6. Għajn Klieb
7. Għar Barka
8. Attard: Valetta Road
9. Ta' Kaċċatura
10. Ħal-Far
11. Ħal-Resqun, Tal-Kappelli
12. Gżira: Il-Fawwara
13. Kalkara: San Duminka
14. Kirkop: Sqaq il-Ħarruba
15. Luqa: L-ingieret, Wied il-Knejjes

16. Marsa: Jesuits Hill, Wied il-Gonna
17. Marsascala: San Tumas
18. Mellieha
19. Binġemma
20. Mġarr: Tar-Ragħad, Skorba
21. Mosta: Bistra, Għammieriet, Misraħ Għonoq, Wied il-Ghasel, Torre Cumbo, Mosta Fort
22. Mqabba: Tal-Mintna
23. Mqabba: Ta' Kandja
24. Naxxar
25. Paola: Sammat Street
26. Qrendi: Magħlaq
27. Qrendi: San Niklaw
28. St Julians: Tal-Ballut
29. Salini
30. Safi: Tal-Ħlantun

31. Tal-Liebru
32. Safi
33. Siġġiewi
34. Tarxien: St Mary Str., Rock Str., Triq id-Dejma
35. Zebbuġ: Wied Qirda
36. Zejtun: Botanical Gardens

37. Zejtun: Tal-Barrani
38. Torri Mamo
39. Gozo: Għar Gerduf
40. Gozo: M'forn Valley
41. Gozo: Marsalforn
42. Gozo: Sannat

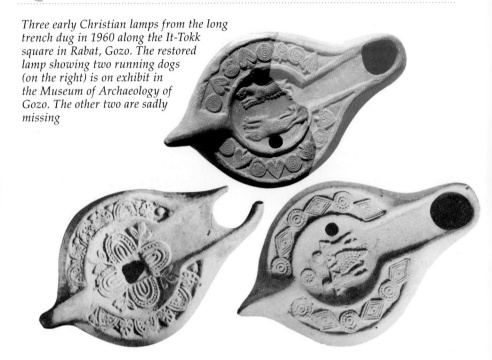

Three early Christian lamps from the long trench dug in 1960 along the It-Tokk square in Rabat, Gozo. The restored lamp showing two running dogs (on the right) is on exhibit in the Museum of Archaeology of Gozo. The other two are sadly missing

the 'republic' of Gozo. The second one was dedicated by the two men in charge of the same 'republic' in honour of Emperor Galerius during the curatorship of Lucius D... Pollio and Rufus (*CIL*, X, 7505). Unfortunately, the whereabouts of both inscriptions are unknown. The two inscriptions show, on the local level, the substitution of the term 'republic' for the previous 'municipium', implying a persistent autonomous local government for the Gozitan community, independent from that of Melita; on the external level, a close involvement in international politics, dominated as they were by the tetrarchic rule, of which Constantius and Galerius were the second generation of ruling *Augusti*. The adoption of the

term *respublica* is paralleled in an inscription from Palermo dated to AD 285 and dedicated to Emperor Diocletian (*CIL* X, 7282).

More abundant pottery, however, belonging to the first two centuries of the Byzantine period (sixth-seventh centuries) was encountered at various spots on the south side of Mdina, with a major concentration below Xara Palace. This, however, has been associated with 'habitation' rather than with fortifications. It is the eighth-ninth-century pottery that ties up with the Late Byzantine fortification works mentioned above.

Intrinsically tied with Late Antiquity and the Byzantine rule is the subject of early Christianity in Malta. In the previous chapter we have already dealt with the question of the claimed apostolic foundations of Christianity in these islands. I have highlighted the fact that no archaeological records exist to prove it and its presence through the first three centuries AD. At this stage it is of some relevance to recall that in neighbouring Sicily, with which Malta must have had frequent commercial and maritime contacts at this time, the first reliable written evidence for the presence of Christian communities goes back to the mid-third century. Archaeological evidence, however, dates even earlier since parts of the catacombs of St Lucia and St Maria di Gesù were already in use around AD 220-30. Although attempts have been made to push the date of the

> ⌀ D · N · M · GALERIO ⌀
>
> VALERIO · MAXIMIANO
>
> AVG
>
> *r* · P · GAVL · CVR · LV . . .
>
> D . . . *p*O *ll*ION*e* ET RVF . . .
>
> A . . . ANNII IIVIRR

Text of a missing Gozitan inscription as given by the Corpus Inscriptionum Latinarum *X, No. 7505. Dedicated to Emperor Marcus Galerius Valerius Maximianus, it is dated to the early 4th century AD (probably 305-11).*

Text of a missing Gozitan inscription as given by the Corpus Inscriptionum Latinarum *X, No. 7504. Dedicated to Emperor Caius Aurelius Valerius Costantius, it is dated to the early 4th century AD (probably 305-06).*

> ⌀ D · N · C · AVR · VALERIO ⌀
>
> CONSTANTIO · AVG
>
> R · P · GAVL · CVR
>
> F · POLLIONE . . RVFO
>
> NF . . . . . III VIRR
>
> ⌀ . . . . ⌀

Maltese catacombs back to the third century, and even beyond, the general view is that none of the Christian hypogea and catacombs predate the fourth century.

This is perhaps the opportune place to elaborate somewhat on this class of archaeological monument. It should be made clear that, although they are commonly referred to as catacombs, only a few of these underground structures really deserve that name. There are numerous small compounds, each consisting of a group of individual graves clustered together in one rock-cut, underground space. These are better known as hypogea. The number of graves in a single compound can range from as few as three to as many as a score, or more. These are arranged around a circular space or along a straight corridor. Within the same compound, which could be intended to serve for a family, a social group (such as, a guild) or a small community, one can find different types of graves, some more elaborate than others. In fact one can detect a whole scale of sophistication and investment. They range from a simple rectangular cut in the wall (*loculus*) or in the ground (*forma* or 'floor-grave'), both covered by slabs of stone or terracotta, to a burial chamber reached through a window carved on the side walls ('window grave'), to the most elaborate form consisting of a free-standing, rock-hewn sarcophagus surmounted by a four-arched canopy (or *baldacchino*).

Above: A passage inside the main Salina catacomb.
Below: An artist's impression of a canopied grave inside a typical Maltese early Christian catacomb.

Window grave

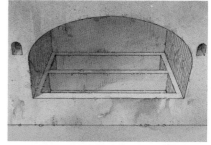

Arcosolium

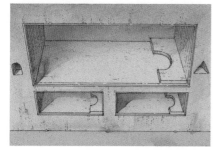

Loculi

Left: Saddle-backed canopied
Right: Canopied with burial troughs

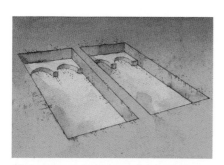

Floor-grave

Table-grave

Window opening to burial-chamber

Bench-grave

Occasionally, groups of graves are carved on the side walls of natural caves, like that of Għar Qasrana, near Mġarr. At other times, small hypogea are grouped together, sharing the same natural rock-face (like the necropolis of Binġemma) or the artificial face of an old quarry (like the Skorba and Salina groups).

On the other end of the spectrum are the two large complexes of St Paul's and St Agatha's catacombs at Rabat, this time correctly called so because their size and complexity come close enough to the even more extensive ones of neighbouring Syracuse and metropolitan Rome. The two Rabat complexes were clearly intended to serve a much larger community, the population of the whole town in fact, even though some individuals, families, leagues, and ethnic groups (like Jews) preferred to have their own small hypogea in the neighbourhood. Gozo continues to follow the same trend as before, having barely any subterranean structures with the characteristics that would place them in this period. The only collective burial place of this type is, in fact, the hypogeum of Għar Gerduf, near Rabat, and even here most of the characteristic features have been hacked

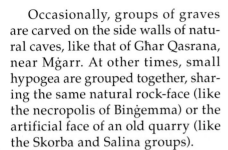

Different types of graves found inside the catacombs: window grave preceded by an arched recess; arcosolium (grave on the sill of an arched recess); loculus (rectangular recess in wall); canopied grave (vaulted roof with or without saddle-backed lids); floor grave; table grave (rectangular pits in raised rock tables); window grave without arched recess; bench grave.

away, rendering it very difficult to reconstruct the original layout and appearance.

Perhaps the most standard feature of all these graves, one that distinguishes them from all earlier rock-cut tombs, is the 'headrest'. This consisted of a slightly-raised pillow, a couple of centimetres high, with a shallow circular depression to receive the head of the corpse which was laid in a supine position. Another very frequent characteristic is the double-space in each grave, intended to receive two corpses side by side. One wonders whether this was part of early Christian ideology, allowing married couples to continue to lead their life in each other's company even in the next world. Research in contemporary literature for possible allusions to such a custom have so far proved fruitless.

Many of the hypogea are also furnished with a C-shaped *stibadium* (or *triclinium*), a small circular table surrounded by an inclined platform, the whole thing shaped in solid rock. It was clearly intended for some collective repast, referred to in contemporary literature as *refrigerium*. It must have been a very important part of funerary ritual because some hypogea have room for two or even more such arrangements. The larger catacombs had several, St Paul's having as many as eight. It is not known exactly when these meals were held, whether on the occasion of a burial or on its anniversary. Nor is the alleged connection with the celebration of the Eucharist very clear, if it existed at all. We know, however, that there came a time when these *refrigeria* started to get out of hand and were abolished by the Church authorities; we do, in fact, find features in some places that suggest their suppression.

Although contemporary with the catacombs, these rock-cut, C-shaped tables (whether we call them *mensae, triclinia*, or *stibadia*, or even *agape* tables) had predecessors in pagan funerary ritual way back in the Hellenistic age, and even beyond. Similar arrangements are encountered in the Hellenistic underground cemetery of Kom el Shogafa in Alexandria. *Triclinia*, laid out on three

Partly- mutilated rock-cut stibadium *in one of the catacombs at Tal-Mintna, near Mqabba. Notice the drain hole on the fore side of the central table and an arched 'window' grave on the side wall.*

sides of a square, occur in many of the collective tombs of Hellenistic Petra, in Jordan. Virtually identical *stibadia*, with a semicircular arrangement of the sloping bench for reclining diners around a table, are documented at Sidret el-Balik near Sabratha in Libya. It is known that these tables were used by members of an important family from Sabratha to dine near the tomb of an ancestor. One of these *stibadia* pre-dates even the Hellenistic age because its frescoed walls collapsed during an earthquake in 365 BC.

It should be noted that unequivocal Christian symbolism and iconography, as distinct from Jewish ones, occur somewhat rarely in these underground grave complexes. It is, therefore, quite possible that not all the hypogea were Christian though the two large catacombs outside

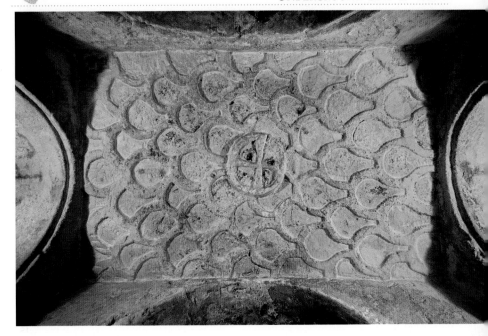

The ceiling of a canopied grave inside hypogeum I of the l-Abbatija tad-Dejr catacomb complex. It is decorated with a pattern of pelta shapes in imitation of a transenna *(chancel) carved in relief. In the centre is a roundel containing a mirror image of a* chi-rho *monogram.*

Melite and some others dispersed in the countryside (such as those of Salina and Ħal Resqun) manifest enough Christian diagnostic markers to qualify for that denomination. In a couple of cases, such as the family hypogeum near St Thomas' tower in Marsascala, they even have overtly Christian inscriptions. The St Thomas Bay inscription addresses the deceased: 'in the name of the Lord Jesus Christ rise and walk' as well as the Lord ('Lord, save me').

A later inscription on marble, found near the Grotto of St Paul in Rabat, marked the tomb of a certain venerable Domestikos, proudly declared to be both a medical doctor and a Christian. He was aged 55 when he departed. The date of the inscription is uncertain. Incorrectly dated to AD 810 by Count Ciantar, it has been tentatively assigned by Joyce Reynolds to the sixth century. The medical profession is also documented by a slab decorated with an array of surgical instruments carved in relief on one of its faces. It is likely that the hypogeum in which it was found, in the area between the catacombs of St Agatha and St Paul, belonged to a guild of surgeons. Other reliefs showing tinsmiths' tools, farming implements, and stone workers' tools, suggest that the hypogea in which they were found belonged to similar respective guilds.

A Jewish Community

A significant component of the population living in Melite in this period was a thriving Hellenized Jewish community. Similar communities are documented in neighbouring Sicily, particularly in Syracuse. The one of Melite is documented by a number of hypogea situated right amidst the numerous other early Christian ones, recognizable as such from graffiti representing the menorah and by inscriptions in Greek. In front of one of the underground tombs now forming part of the St Agatha complex, such an engraved seven-branched candlestick is accompanied by the words *'topos Dionysias he ke Eirenes'* ('the tomb of Dionysia also known as Irene'). The second name is more probably a ritualistic name, inferring the peaceful state of the dead Dionysia. The same seems to

An engraving of a menorah, the seven-branched candle-stick, a widely used symbol in Jewish burial places. This particular one comes from the 'Jewish' tombs at St Paul/Agatha at Rabat.

be the meaning of the name Eulogia in another inscription from a hypogeum in the St Agatha complex. The latter inscription refers to a man (whose name has not survived) who was a 'gerousiarch, lover of the commandments, and Eulogia the elder, his wife'. Clearly this lady held a position of respect (*presbytera*) among the Jewish community while her husband was a leader of the congregation.

While the use of the Punic language survived well into the fourth century AD in North Africa (see above, p.8) and Greek remained in regular use, along with Latin, in Sicily, the only faint evidence of survival of the Punic language and culture in this late period in Malta is the neo-Punic inscription found inside one of the Tac-Ċagħqi hypogea. There is the possibility, however, that this tomb was originally a Punic one, and I feel that this evidence is not sufficiently clear and reliable to make a strong case for such a late survival of the language.

The frequent occurrence of Greek in the unofficial inscriptions of this period is a clear indication that the population of Malta had a lot in common with that of nearby Sicily which remained predominantly Greek-speaking throughout Roman rule. Apart from the inscription of Domestikos mentioned above, another Greek inscription, reported in the seventeenth century to have been found in a cave with hewn graves in Marsa, refers to a cemetery (or, simply, a burial place) 'bought from Zosimetis and Anicetos'. It is tentatively dated to the fifth century AD.

Latin, however, apart from being the official language, as expressed in the few surviving official inscriptions, was currently spoken also among the townsfolk, as suggested by a number of funerary inscriptions from the Rabat area. Two such inscriptions give the name of the deceased (one of them is Desiderius), their age, and the date of their departure. Latin also managed to penetrate among the countryfolk, where one tends to find more resistance to Romanization. Proof of this is the Latin inscription incised on the wall of the small hypogeum at St Thomas Bay, already mentioned.

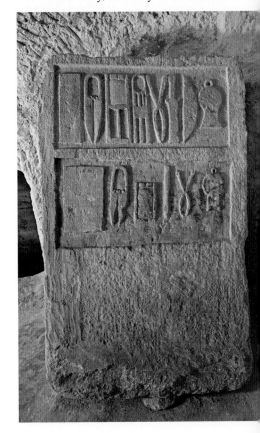

A displaced stone plug door, with surgical instruments carved in relief. Several of the smaller hypogea, both Christian and Jewish, had plug doors to seal their entrances.

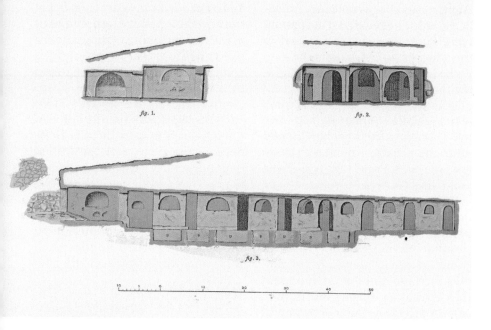

L-Abatija tad-Dejr

Close to one of the necropoleis of Rabat, a medium-sized cemeterial complex developed, consisting of a substantial number of graves, mostly of the *baldacchino* type, which is not, however, large enough to be called a catacomb. In fact, it is made up of four separate hypogea linked together and clustered together around a rectangular open space. One of the hypogea contains a canopied grave with an elaborately-carved ceiling with a cross monogram in the centre.

At some stage, one area inside this rock-cut complex was enlarged to fit a small chapel which was eventually (i.e. in Late-Medieval times) adorned with a fresco painting of the Crucifixion and the Annunciation. Outside, however, in the rock-cut

A cross- section of a group of canopied and window tombs at L-Abbatija tad-Dejr, Rabat (After Caruana 1889).

rectangular space between the hypogea, a religious building seems to have been erected, having an obvious association with the cemetery. Very little of it had survived when it was investigated by Temi Zammit in 1926-27 and in 1933. Only the scant ruins of a colonnaded building were discovered, along with a fragment of a polychrome floor mosaic. The site was subjected to repeated acts of vandalism which also destroyed the mosaic fragment; but some old photographs of the lost structural features and mosaic survive in the archive of the National Museum of

Archaeology. The cemeterial complex is dated to the fourth-fifth century, but it has not been possible to date the adjacent building.

It is difficult to decide whether a similar rectangular space adjacent to a group of hypogea at Salina had a similar function or was merely the result of previous, or indeed later, quarrying. The rectangular space inside the St Paul's catacomb was, on the other hand, obviously a chapel. In this case it is the date of this structure which cannot be established with any certainty. There are certain oddities, such as the imprint of an arch in the ceiling, which suggest a post-antique arrangement; but the rock-cut and plastered pillar, in the shape of four engaged fluted columns, that supports the corner closest to the entrance stairs of the catacomb, seems to be an ancient feature.

Tas-Silġ

Sometime in the fifth century AD - the excavators placed it in the fourth century - the paved courtyard of the previous pagan sanctuary was roofed over and converted into a church with a three-aisled, basilican plan and an apse on the east side. A stone choir enclosure was also installed in the centre of the church. A few pieces of marble carvings associated with it were discovered during the excavations.

A baptismal font was inserted right in the middle of the prehistoric temple - by now presumably razed down to foundation level - behind the eastern apse. It con-

The baptismal font behind the early Christian church at Tas-Silġ. The floor slab was vandalized during the long period the site was left virtually abandoned.

sisted of a cross-shaped basin sunk in the ground with three steps; the bottom slab had a drain hole. Around it, the floor was decorated with an *opus sectile* pavement of white marble and black stone. During the recent investigations inside and around the baptistry a small coin cluster was discovered under the broken bottom slab of the baptismal basin. It consisted of 275 bronze and silver coins, covering the reigns of several Byzantine emperors, and one gold coin, a tremis of Constantine IV, (AD 668-685) issued from the mint of Syracuse between AD 670 and 674.

A gold coin, a tremis, of the Byzantine emperor Constantine IV, found under the floor slab of the baptismal font at Tas-Silġ. The only gold coin of a number of coins that had dropped through the drain hole of the font.

The architectural remains of the Roman villa of San Pawl Milqi surviving below the present church. It is thought that this room still continued being used after the destruction of the villa.

San Pawl Milqi

According to the excavators, the Roman villa at San Pawl Milqi, in spite of a strong fire to which it was subjected sometime in the third century, continued to be in use in this period. Activities now were centred around one particular room of the imperial-age villa which was paved in stone and equipped with a water cistern. It is now situated beneath the present church building. According to a hypothesis advanced by the director of the 1960s excavations, Cagiano de Azevedo, not only was the imperial villa the country residence of the 'prince' of the island who, according to the *Acts of the Apostles* (XXVIII,1-10) gave hospitality to St Paul on the

A block of local Globigerina limestone, found during the excavations of San Pawl Milqi, which carries a graffito of a sailing ship on one side and a crude bearded male figure on another.

occasion of his shipwreck there in AD 60, but from around the fourth century the above-mentioned room gradually assumed a religious cult function, probably associated with the Pauline tradition. An architectural fragment was recovered inside the room, which was engraved with a very rough image of a ship and another one of a male bearded figure. This was readily interpreted as a direct reference to that event, the figure presumed to be a crude portrait of St Paul. Furthermore, the name PAULOS in scratched Greek characters was read on the external face of one of the wall blocks of the same room. The cistern, together with a stone block intended to support jars, was, according to the same hypothesis, associated with a baptismal rite.

THE LEGEND OF SAN PAWL MILQI

The site of San Pawl Milqi is traditionally closely attached to the Pauline cult in Malta. According to the Acts of the Apostles, St Paul was given shelter immediately after his shipwreck on Malta in the country estate of Publius, the 'chief man' (protos) of the island. There, Paul healed the father of Publius from a form of dysentery. After which the Maltese brought more of their sick relatives for Paul to heal. Since the shipwreck is generally thought to have taken place against some projecting reef on the north-west coast of Malta,

in the neighbourhood of St Paul's Bay, most Maltese believe that St Paul, together with some of his shipwrecked friends, were

given hospitality precisely in this villa, on the remains of which successive churches were built; hence the place-name.

That the site was occupied for some activity in this period is confirmed by the find of a North African red-slip lamp decorated with a cross on its discus and by other ceramic finds which are currently being intensively studied. According to a study of the pottery, which is about to be published, the continued use of the room under the church reached its peak in the seventh-ninth centuries. The existence of early churches, whose foundations have been identified by the excavators in the same area, has been seriously questioned by two other scholars.

Three early Christian lamps from Malta. Very often such lamps carried easily recognizable symbols on their upper surface (discus). *The lamp in the centre carries the chi-rho monogram standing for the first two letters of the word* Christos.

Material culture

Together with the rest of the Middle Ages this period has been one of the least studied and investigated by Maltese archaeology. Material culture is, consequently, very little represented. After the 1960s excavations of Tas-Silġ and San Pawl Milqi, which have revealed stratified horizons belonging to this period, the first systematic excavation of a Medieval site was that conducted at Ħal Millieri in 1977. It too yielded some Byzantine material, but of a residual nature, not associated with any structure. In general terms, it is only since the early 1990s that the respective levels in archaeological excavations, especially those undertaken inside Mdina and Rabat, have started to be given the attention they deserve. It is also since then that

Top: A small African Red Slip ware with curved wall and barbotine leaf and dot decoration.
Bottom: Part of a wide and flat plate of African Red Slip ware with rouletted decoration.

the respective pottery has started to be properly and systematically studied and understood. Before that, the pottery that was most easily identifiable was the late African Red Slip ware, most prominently, the lamps decorated with Christian symbolic motifs, the 'Palaeochristian lamps'. The great majority of these are Tunisian (Hayes Type 2A), but the occasional Tripolitanian ones are not missing. Several such lamps have been recorded in the past. One of three such lamps, found in a tomb in Strada Giardino Botanico in Żejtun in 1912 was immortalized by the national poet Dun Karm in his poem 'Il-Musbieħ tal-Mużew'. Fragments of a score of richly decorated lamps were yielded by Hypogeum 5 of the St Agatha catacombs. A substantial number of such lamps, or fragments thereof, were discovered during the cleaning operations of a small hypogeum at Tar-Ragħad near Mġarr.

African Red Slip cooking and table ware, which started to be imported from Tunisia from the very start of its production in the first century AD, continued to be imported right down to the seventh century, as can be seen from its distribution maps reproduced by John Hayes in his classic work on *Late Roman Pottery*.

Obverse of a gold solidus of emperor Phocas (AD 602-610)

Obverse of a gold solidus of emperor Heraclius (AD 610-641)

Obverse of an Arabic gold coin (AD 901)

Hoards of gold coins were accidentally discovered on various occasions in Malta. From their description they appear to have been Byzantine or Arabic coins. They were sadly melted down for their gold content, but some individual coins seem to have survived in the collection of the National Museum of Archaeology.

Coins

A bronze coin hoard dated to the years AD 352-360 was discovered in Rabat in 1961. These coins were struck in Rome and in eastern mints thus showing an increasing administrative gravitation of the Maltese islands on the eastern Roman empire, since bronze coins tend to be used locally for small change rather than for overseas trade.

Coins of the Byzantine period, especially gold ones, are best represented by finds of hoards that have been recorded as far back as the fifteenth century. A hoard of 248 Byzantine gold coins was, in fact, discovered *c.*1460 somewhere in the surroundings of Naxxar. They were found by five little children whose fathers lived in that village. One-hundred-and-two coins weighed as much as a *carlino* and 145 were *dila stampa pichula tunda*. A more substantial treasure, consisting of 1,300 gold coins referred to as *moneta di sancta Helena* or *dila impronta di sancta Helena*, was accidentally discovered in 1525 by the sons of another man from Naxxar. The biggest treasure of all, weighing some 14.5 rotolos (almost 12 kg), was found in 1698 in the square in front of the cathedral at Mdina. These were also described as *moneta e medaglie di Sant'Elena* but they seem to have been from Muslim rather than Byzantine mints.

Unfortunately, all these hoards were discovered before the advent of scientific archaeology and their contents were invariably melted down, so that no further details, such as of date and mint, can be extracted from them. Nevertheless, the very record of their find sheds important light on the period to which they belonged; they reveal a different picture from that of a mere backwater, a remote place of exile for political offenders suggested by the sources and by the scarcity of archaeological remains.

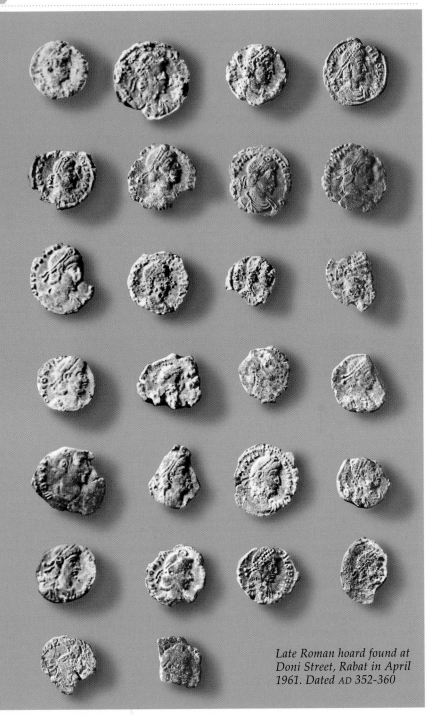

Late Roman hoard found at Doni Street, Rabat in April 1961. Dated AD 352-360

Conclusion

The period considered in this chapter is, as we have seen, the least documented one, both in terms of textual evidence and of archaeological documentation. For this, perhaps more than for other periods of Malta's history, we cannot afford to lose any more of the islands' unique heritage and its professional documentation. Now, in contrast with the past, Malta is equipped with a surfeit of professionally-trained archaeologists who can be profitably employed to look after the archaeological heritage of their own country, providing that they are given the necessary resources to do so. An increasing awareness and appreciation of the nation's cultural heritage is generating an escalating popular demand for its better protection and management. It is now up to the political executive to create the right environment for the development, preservation, and enjoyment of this rich national resource.

One other thing Maltese archaeology cannot afford is the creation of more myths than the many that already bedevil Maltese historiography. We cannot afford the waste of time, energy, and resources consumed in the endeavour to demystify them. Experience has shown that it could take as little as a momentary whim on the part of someone 'of authority' to create a myth. It could take generations of serious scholarship to demystify that myth. One such myth, that of a Greek colonization of the island, was introduced into Maltese historiography centuries ago and, in spite of scholarly and strongly-argued rebuttals, it is still finding support in current published literature.

As for proper documentation, there are a number of important excavated sites that are still awaiting publication. It is good to make public first impressions of such finds, to keep the general public's interest alive, even though certain generalizations from limited data may be premature and ultimately misleading, and should better be avoided. But it is of the utmost importance to publish, at the earliest possible time, the scientific reports of finds, supported by drawings, photographs, and stratigraphic evidence. Besides providing an 'objective' record of the evidence in its own right, such reports provide the opportunity of verifying the excavator's interpretation of the finds.

Current excavations conducted by the University of Malta at Tas-Silġ. Maltese students taking measurements and drawing plans inside Area A. This area has turned out to be the most complex of the three areas under investigation. It revealed unexpected structures, including partly preserved walls of huge, finely worked ashlar blocks. These seem to have belonged to a massive structure built in the Hellenistic phase in order to raise the level of the sloping ground to that of the surviving foundations on the upper field.

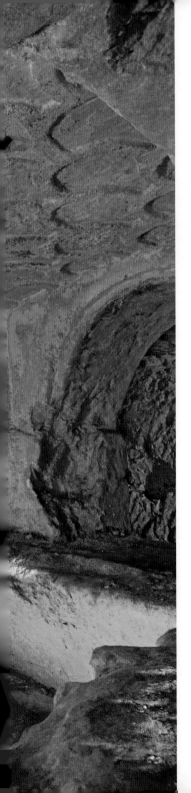

*The great majority of the archaeological
sites belonging to the periods considered
in this volume are no longer accessible.
Many of the tombs, for example, have
either been destroyed or covered over by
modern buildings. In view of this and
of the unwieldy number of such sites,
this chapter will limit itself to the more
significant and accessible ones.*

CHAPTER 8

THE SITES

Only three of the following sites are officially
open to visitors in an organized fashion with
ticket entry: the Roman Domus (now officially
denominated as Domvs Romana); St Paul's catacombs, and St Agatha's catacombs. Of these, the
Domus Romana and St Agatha's Catacombs have
their respective museums attached to them; in
the former case, the museum covers part of the
site itself.

Some of the other sites (like Tas-Silġ, SS.
Paul/Agatha catacombs, the Roman baths at
Għajn Tuffieħa, and San Pawl Milqi) can be visited only with special permission from Heritage
Malta. For the rest, a certain amount of pot-
luck is required. Some are on private property
and permission to visit can be obtained on the
spot if the owner or tenant is present. Minor
sites, such as single tombs, are so many that it
is well-nigh impossible to provide instructions
for their access within the framework of the
present volume.

*A view through a row of canopied graves at
l-Abbatija tad-Dejr, Rabat. None of these canopied
graves has a saddle-backed lid. They only have a
rectangular trough with places, and head-rests,
for two persons. The ceiling of the grave in the
foreground is decorated with a design in relief.*

GOZO

Ghasri
Żebbuġ
Gharb
San Lawrenz
VICTORIA
Xagħra
St Luċija
Kerċem Fontana
Nadur
Qala
Munxar
Xewkija
GOZO
AIRPORT
Ghajnsielem
Sannat
MĠARR
HARBOUR

COM

FERRY

CIRKEWWA
HARBOUR

Mell

Manikat

Ghajn Tuffieha

Mgar

Bahrija

1. Tas-Silġ Sanctuary
2. Għajn Klieb Necropolis
3. Għajn Qajjet Punic tombs
4. Mtarfa Punic tombs
5. Qallilija Punic tombs
6. Għar Barka Punic Tomb
7. Buskett Punic tombs
8. Tal-Virtù Punic tomb
9. Ta' Ċieda Round Tower
10. Ta' Wilġa Round Tower
11. Ta' Ġawhar Round Tower
12. Tat-Torrijiet Round Tower
13. Tal-Baqqari Round Tower
14. Żurrieq Punic 'Tower'
15. San Pawl Milqi Villa
16. Ta' Kaċċatura Villa
17. Żejtun (school grounds) Villa
18. Tad-Dawl Villa
19. Rabat Domus
20. Għajn Tuffieha Roman Baths
21. Ras ir-Raħeb site
22. St Paul's Catacombs
23. St Agatha's Catacombs
24. Abbatija tad-Dejr Catacombs
25. Salina Catacombs
26. St Thomas Catacomb
27. Binġemma Catacombs
28. Xarolla Catacombs
29. Tal-Mintna Catacombs
30. Tal-Bistra Catacombs
31. Ħal-Resqun Catacomb
32. Il-Magħlaq Catacomb
33. Sacred Heart School Catacomb
34. Mellieħa underwater wreck

Gozo:
35. Ras il-Wardija Sanctuary
36. Ramla Bay Villa
37. Tal-Gruwa (Xewkija/Mġarr ix-Xini) Roman remains
38. Kerċem 'Phoenician House'
39. Għar Gerduf, Kerċem
40. Tax-Xini, Taċ-Ċkejken, and Tal-Milied Punic Tombs, Żebbuġ
41. Xlendi underwater wreck
42. Comino burial

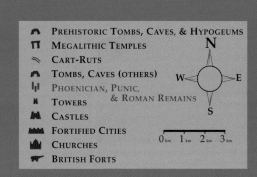

- **PREHISTORIC TOMBS, CAVES, & HYPOGEUMS**
- **MEGALITHIC TEMPLES**
- **CART-RUTS**
- **TOMBS, CAVES (OTHERS)**
- **PHOENICIAN, PUNIC, & ROMAN REMAINS**
- **TOWERS**
- **CASTLES**
- **FORTIFIED CITIES**
- **CHURCHES**
- **BRITISH FORTS**

N
W E
S

0 km 1 km 2 km 3 km

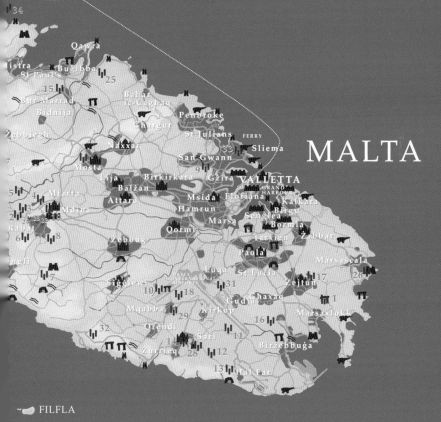

O

FERRY

34

Qawra

istra Bugibba
St Paul's
15 25

Bur Marrad Bahar
ic-Caghaq
Bidnija
Penbroke
Zebbiegh Ghargur
St Julians FERRY
Naxxar Sliema
San Gwann
Mosta 9
Lija Gzira
Mtarfa Birkirkara VALLETTA
Balzan GRAND HARBOUR
Attard Msida Floriana Kalkara
Mdina Hamrun Birgu
Rabat Marsa Senglea
Qormi Bormla
Zebbug Tarxien Zabbar
ingli Paola
7 Luqa Marsascala
Siggiew St Lucia 17 26
10 18 Zejtun
Mqabba Ghaxaq 1
29 Gudja
Qrendi Kirkop Marsaxlokk
32 16
Safi 11
Zurrieq 28 12 Birzebbuga
13 Hal Far

MALTA

FILFLA

TAS-SILĠ SANCTUARY
MARSAXLOKK

Covering virtually the whole top of a contained hill, the sanctuary of Tas-Silġ occupies a dominating position over Marsaxlokk harbour. The site takes its name from the nearby church of our Lady of the Snows (in Maltese 'Tas-Silġ'). Its position, away from the ancient city and in relation to a harbour which must have been a very busy one in antiquity, is highly significant. The close connection with the sea has been borne out by the finds made both during the major excavation campaigns by the Italian *Missione Archeologica* in the 1960s and those made from 1996 to 2004 by the University of Malta.

The story of the site starts in prehistory, with the construction of at least one temple typical of the Tarxien phase (3000-2500 BC). A scatter of megaliths

An old aerial photograph of the Tas-Silġ site before excavations were started in 1963. The terraced semi-circular projection over the lower field gives the site the appearance of a fortified hill.

over a great part of the hilltop suggests that this temple was accompanied by other structures. The hilltop was then occupied by the people of the following Bronze Age (2500-700 BC), but we still do not know for what purpose. The Phoenicians took over the site around 700 BC when they converted the prehistoric temple into their own

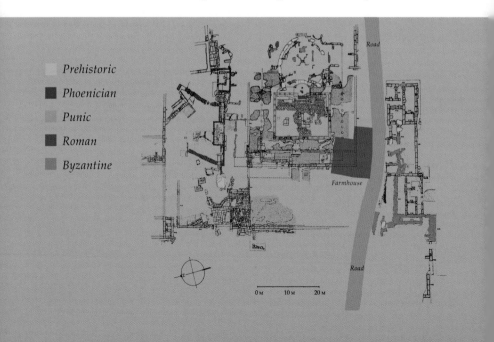

Prehistoric
Phoenician
Punic
Roman
Byzantine

Road
Farmhouse
Road

0 M   10 M   20 M

temple, by adding a forward extension of the curved façade which then folded inwards in a straight line to two symmetrical pilasters, each surmounted by a double cavetto cornice. The pilasters thus came to form the monumental entrance of the new temple. Between the pilasters a large rectangular stone slab was inserted into the hollowed-out rock surface, intended to support three small upright pillars (betyls), probably symbolizing the abode of the divinity.

The sanctuary grew in importance along the centuries. In the Hellenistic age (c.330-30 BC) it saw a sustained effort of monumentalization and embellishment involving the addition of an extensive rectangular portico that enclosed both the original Phoenician temple and a large courtyard in front of it. Further courts flanked by monumental altar enclosures were added on the north

A beautifully-moulded palmette in very hard stucco, from the University of Malta excavations at Tas-Silġ. It probably belonged to an architectural feature, like an Ionic capital.

Above: Aerial view of the site. On the south side (extreme right) are the three trenches opened by the Maltese expedition between 1996 and 2004.

Opposite: Plan of the excavations conducted by the Italian expedition in the 1960s.

Overview of the north side of Tas-Silġ from the north-west. The most striking feature is the opus signinum floor in the foreground. It is made up of crushed pottery with lines of white marble cubes placed at regular intervals.

side and more enclosed rectangular spaces were created on the south side. At both ends the topography of the hill required the use of heavy masonry walls to raise the level of the inclined sides of the hill. It seems that these structures were partially intended for defence purposes, and at the north-east end what looks like a defence tower has been identified.

In the last phase of its life, towards the fifth century AD, a church was built over the previous courtyard, with a basilican shape, that is, with a central nave separated from two lateral aisles by two rows of columns. A small baptismal font was constructed in the centre of what was originally the prehistoric temple.

The excavation of Tas-Silġ, beside a palimpsest of structures and archaeological strata belonging to different periods, brought to light a rich repertory of architectural, sculptural, and cultic finds (like the small metallic, 3.8 cm high, representation of Horus, left), together with an immense quantity of pottery and organic remains of sacrificial rites. The architectural finds include various fragments of cavetto cornices and an Egyptianizing carved capital. Sculpture includes a worn female marble head. A smaller item is a gilt ivory 'Aeolian' capital with a hanging palmette. Pottery ranges from fragments of imported amphorae to whole, locally-made plates and saucers, as well as imported fine table ware, including some Attic painted ware, both of the Black figure and Red figure technique.

A bird's eye view of the north side of Tas-Silġ during the excavations of the 1960s. In the centre is the paved courtyard, laid as part of the Hellenistic building programme, which was eventually roofed over to produce the early Christian basilica.

Only parts of the surviving blocks of the facade of the prehistoric temple (beyond the courtyard to the right) appear to have been uncovered at this stage.

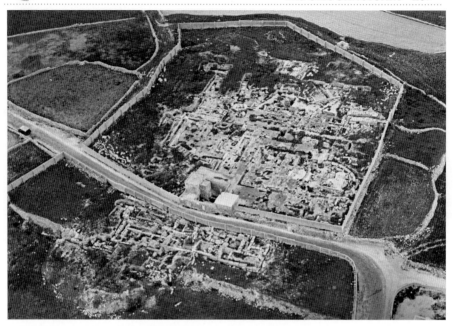

Aerial view of the Tas-Silġ site, dated 1974, that is, after the last Italian excavation campaign of 1970. It shows the extent of the site that had been excavated during

the yearly campaigns of 1963-1970. It also shows how intrusive the Żejtun-Delimara road is, separating the north side (top) from the south side (bottom).

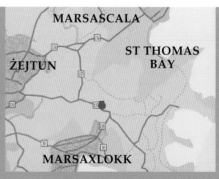

Photo of the west side taken from the roof of the then still intact modern farmhouse. Prominent is the large ritual basin hollowed out from a large prehistoric block. Some walls of large ashlar blocks are seen emerging from the ground.

The site is closed off with a boundary wall. Entrance by appointment can be obtained by calling the head office of Heritage Malta, Valletta, or e-mail info@heritagemalta.org. Go towards Marsaxlokk on Triq Marsaxlokk, then go left on Triq Axtart, up Triq Bir Rikka, and continue on Triq Tas-Silġ. The site is on the first road on the left.

A large architectural fragment (65x45x48 cm) carved on Globigerina Limestone.

A small bone plaque in the shape of an open lotus flower (3.8x3.5 cm)

Fragments of incense burners in Globigerina limestone. Left: an original fragment (8 cm diam.). Right: two reconstructions integrating original fragments.

The left ear (6.7x3 cm), in ivory, of what must have been a life-size statue.

An artist's impression of the sanctuary of Tas-Silġ as it must have appeared during the late Punic and Roman times. Only the foundations of the prehistoric temple behind the large peristyle are shown, since it is not known to what extent the temple, which had been incorporated within the Phoenician temple, was still standing at this point in time.

GĦAJN KLIEB NECROPOLIS
RABAT

A concentration of rock-cut tombs, mostly of the Phoenician-Punic period is found in the Għajn Klieb area, a spur of the Upper Coralline escarpment of which the ancient town of Melite formed the most conspicuous promontory. The spur overlooks Fiddien valley and is less than one kilometre west of Mdina. It is also on a slightly lower altitude than the Mdina-Rabat plateau.

In the area, numerous rock-cut tombs were reported and explored on various occasions since the nineteenth century, the more recent one (as yet unexplored) in 2001. As many as sixteen such tombs (A-K and M-S on the opposite map) were plotted in a survey conducted by Dr Nicholas Vella in 1999. On that same occasion six more tombs (in field V) were noted but not plotted.

The first recorded discovery took place in October 1890 when a large tomb was found in a good condition and 'not yet spoiled of its contents', as recorded by Dr A.A. Caruana, then director of the Public Library. Caruana was accompanied by a certain Lady Smyth who was either the owner of the field or the discoverer of the tomb. She subsequently donated the discovered artifacts to the Museum of the Public Library. We know, however, that one of three sections of a gilt-silver armlet (*armilla*) retrieved from the tomb ended up in the Ashmolean Museum of Oxford. The other two are still in the state collection. Each section is decorated in repoussé relief showing two winged griffins rampant flanking what has been described as a stylized palmette,

Photograph taken while tomb B was being excavated in 1926. Temi Zammit is seen taking notes on his field notebooks inside the shaft of the tomb.

The interior of tomb Z as it survives today. On the left wall, facing the entrance, one can still see 17 of the 45 holes or niches whose purpose is still unknown.

the whole scene being surmounted by a winged solar disc. The armlet has been dated to the eighth-seventh century BC, thus providing one of the earliest dates for a Phoenician tomb.

The most important of the group of tombs is the one (marked Z in the same map) inside which Temi Zammit discovered a remarkable Egyptian gold amulet in 1906. This tomb was re-located in 2000 on the side of the Rabat-Baħrija road with its chamber underneath the secondary road. It had forty-five square niches cut into the wall of the chamber whose meaning has not yet been understood. The amulet (top right) represents the Egyptian gods Horus (falcon-headed) and Anubis (jackal-headed) standing back to back on a common base with their heads joined together by means of a small ring. The date for this amulet has been set around the seventh-sixth century, again providing another early date for the tomb. More tombs were investigated by Zammit in 1925, 1926, and 1933. One of the tombs surveyed in 1926 still contained lamps of the Phoenician-Punic type as well as one Roman lamp of the first century AD, thus testifying to its re-use in Roman times.

A site plan of the Għajn Klieb area after the survey conducted by Dr Nicholas Vella in 2002.

Tombs   Buildings

Pottery Cluster   Clump of Trees

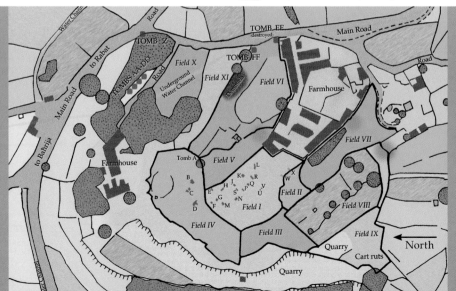

INSID

PHOENICIAN ROCK TOMB,

AT "GHAIN CLIEB" WITHIN THE LIMITS OF "RABAT", MALTA.

Surveyed by Prof: T. Zammit, M.D.

in October 1906.

"SKAK TA GHAIN CLIEB."

LONGITUDINAL SECTON.

SCALE ⅛

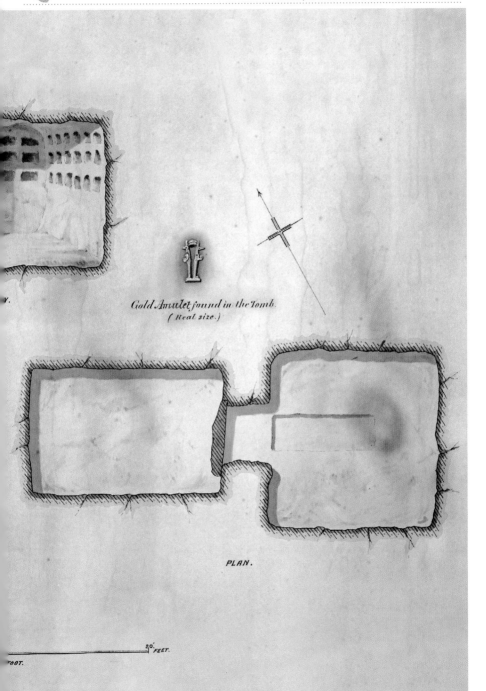

Gold Amulet found in the Tomb.
(Real size.)

PLAN.

20. FEET.

FOOT.

ROUND TOWERS
VARIOUS LOCATIONS

The 'Round Towers' of Malta are somewhat peculiar: they are isolated cylindrical structures, built of large ashlar masonry with the standard dimensions one normally associates with buildings of the Punic or Roman period. They appear to be without doors at the ground level. Six of these towers exist in Malta; none are known in Gozo. Four of them (Ta' Gawhar, Tal-Baqqari, Tat-Torrijiet, and Ta' Wilġa) are clustered together in the Żurrieq, Safi, Gudja area in the south of Malta, practically within view of each other. Two others, situated in other parts of Malta, are somewhat doubtful. Only one third of the outer circular wall survives of that of Ta' Ċieda in San Ġwann, but it has a cistern next to it, as the Ta' Gawhar

one has. So little of the Tas-Santi one survives that one cannot really be sure it is round, let alone a tower. Finally, a seventh one, claimed to be the 'scanty remains of a round tower obviously guarding the western approaches of the Roman capital' at Għajn Klieb (Trump 1990: 123), has turned out to be a circular threshing floor, confirmed by the toponym of the area, 'Il-Qiegħa ta' Għajn Klieb'.

Known as 'Roman Towers', these stuctures have little that dates them to that period. Nor do they have any close parallels outside Malta. Although the finds inside the Ta' Gawhar tower have dated its destruction to the third century AD, the pottery extends back to the Punic period. If their purpose was for

One of the best preserved of the round towers is that at Ta' Wilġa, to the north-west of Mqabba, on the west side of the secondary road from Qormi to Siggiewi. It was excavated by Thomas Ashby in 1910. Its external walls were preserved to a height of seven courses on the north-east side. The earliest pottery sherds he found were of the Punic period.

The Ta' Ċieda tower, now engulfed by modern houses in San Ġwann is exceptionally placed close to the north coast of Malta. Only a small segment of its external wall is preserved. It was partially explored by David Trump in 1960 who also noted an ancient cistern close by.

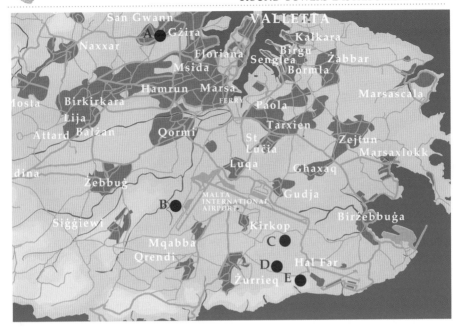

Map of eastern Malta showing the location of the surviving round towers. At San Ġwann is the Ta' Ċieda tower (A), at Mqabba, the Ta' Wilġa tower (B), at Kirkop, the Ta' Ġawhar tower (C), at Zurrieq, the Tat-Torrijiet (D)[meaning 'of the Towers'] and close to Ħal-Far the Tal-Baqqari tower (E).

Another round tower is that of Tat-Torrijiet, to the east of Żurrieq, on the north side of the road that leads from Żurrieq (Ix-Xarolla windmill) to Ħal Far. It is preserved up to four courses and its interior is filled up with modern quarry debitage. It has never been excavated.

On the same road from Zurrieq to Ħal Far, but closer to the latter, is another round tower. It lies behind a field wall near the ruins of the church of Tal-Baqqari. One has to peep over the field wall to a have a glimpse of the scanty remains of this tower.

Top: Part of a carbonized piece of bread brought to light during the excavations of the Ta' Ġawhar tower. No efforts have yet been made to carbon-date it.

Left: A small (19cm high) copper bucket with a slightly smaller one inserted in it. From the Ta' Gawhar tower. The buckets might have been set aside for melting down.

defense, there was very little reason for them to be built in the Roman period when the Mediterranean was controlled by the Romans; whereas they would make more sense if they were built when the central Mediterranean was being contested between the latter and the Carthaginians, say, in the third century BC. If, on the other hand their purpose was to guard farming estates, as has been suggested recently, they could have been built any time within the Punic and Roman dominations.

A heavy two-sided iron axe found during the 1960 excavations of the Ta' Ġawhar tower. The Maltese soil is far from ideal for the preservation of iron objects. This must be considered an exceptional find.

A gold earring from the same excavation. Gold is rarely found in such excavations and this find must be the result of an accidental loss or a tragic event. A Maltese coin of around 35 BC with the legend of Arruntanus Balbus was also found, together with another coin of Emperor Claudius II Gothicus (third century AD).

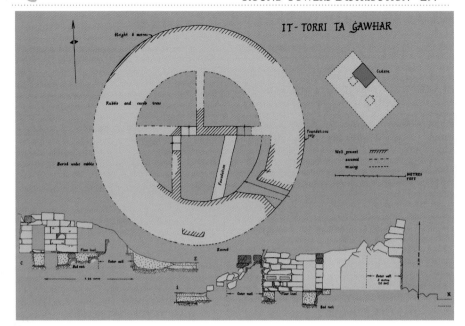

Plan and sections of the round tower of Ta' Ġawhar after the excavations there by David Trump. Note the thickness of the external walls in places surviving up to a height of seven courses.

Note also the internal walls creating separate rooms, and the rectangular water cistern outside the tower, with the roof supported on thick stone beams in turn resting on two vertical pilasters

One side of the surviving inner wall of the tower.

The surviving outer wall. A tree growing inside the tower is threatening the stability of the wall.

VILLA AT SAN PAWL MILQI
ST PAUL'S BAY

By far the most extensive remains of a typical Roman villa are those of San Pawl Milqi. These were brought to light by the *Missione Italiana* of the University of Rome between 1963 and 1968. The site is located halfway up the hill overlooking the fertile plain of Burmarrad and Salina Bay.

The excavations brought to light the remains of a large Roman villa that was occupied for at least six centuries, from the second century BC to the fourth century AD. The remains show signs of several reconstructions and additions which modified the general layout of the building. Most of the walls are built in a refined technique known as *opus quadratum*, in which perfectly rectangular blocks (parallelepipeds) are arranged in horizontal courses.

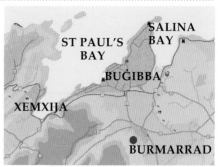

The site is closed off with a boundary wall. Entrance by appointment can be obtained by calling the head office of Heritage Malta, Valletta, or e-mail **info@heritagemalta.org**. Go towards Burmarrad (from Mosta) on Triq Burmarrad, then go left on Triq San Pawl Milqi. The site is at the end of the road on the left, next to the chapel.

Some of the walls are built with Coralline Limestone blocks.

The villa incorporated a sizable agricultural unit consisting of several stone instruments related to olive pressing. The presence of living quarters with fine wall paintings shows that the building was not only used for agricultural purposes. The

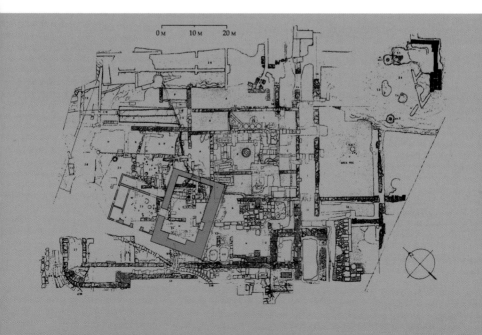

wall paintings seem to have been limited to imitations of different coloured marbles; no traces of figurative paintings were found.

When the perimeter was excavated, a semi-circular wall was brought to light on the south-west (?) corner, apparently intended to reinforce one of the corners of the villa. It looks very much like a bastion. Although the date of this structure was not stated specifically, in their original report the excavators referred to the insecurity of the times in this part of the Mediterranean immediately before the third punic war (149-146 BC) and in the following century, owing to the presence of pirates. They further pointed out the strategic position of the villa, dominating the then navigable port of Salina Bay. Since the resumption of work by the *Missione* in 1997, it seems that this tower-like structure, paralleled by a similar (but squarish) one on the south-east corner, is being attributed to a much later date, namely, the troubled years of the third century AD.

A section of the villa complex, that which eventually was incorporated under the seventeenth-century church, appears to have remained in use for a long time after. This prolonged use is most probably to be attributed to the presence of a water cistern. Whether its continued use had anything to do with the Pauline tradition or Christian ritual cannot be deduced from archaeological evidence and is a matter of hypothetical conjecture. Neither is much credibility now being given to a stone block forming part of a wall very close to the cistern which in the 1960s was thought to be inscribed with the word PAULUS in Greek characters.

A view of the original courtyard which at a second stage accommodated the apparatus for the pressing of olive oil.

The space underneath the present church, with a cistern in the centre, which appears to have continued in use for centuries.

Left: Plan of the remains of the villa at San Pawl Milqi, with the superimposed plan of the church building.

VILLA AT TA' KAĊĊATURA
BIRŻEBBUĠA

On a slightly smaller scale than those of the San Pawl Milqi villa are the remains of a villa situated on the lip of a ridge bound by two valleys flowing into the Birzebbugia side of Marsaxlokk harbour, Wied Ħas-Saptan and Wied Dalam. The site lies opposite the prehistoric cave of Għar Dalam.

The site might have been partially cleared as far back as the eighteenth century but the main part was properly excavated in 1915 by Thomas Ashby assisted by Temi Zammit.

The villa seems to have been constructed in the early Roman period (second century BC), but remains of earlier structures reveal a building technique known as *opus africanum* (with pillar stones framing spaces of lighter material) that one normally associates with Phoenician and Punic

The site can be reached either from a passage across the valley from the Għar Dalam Museum or via Birżebbuġa. Coming from Valletta pass through Triq Birżebbuġa, at the roundabout by the harbour go up Triq Żarenu Dalli and back again to Triq Birżebbuġa reaching the road, Triq id-Dar ta' Pultu, into the valley Wied Żembaq. Where the road along the valley becomes narrower, walk along the rubble wall until the wall surrounding the big cistern becomes visible on the top of the hill behind the carob trees.

buildings, such as at Carthage and Motya. The rest of the building was constructed of Globigerina Limestone, in regularly-cut rectangular blocks laid horizontally. The position of dowel holes on some blocks suggested that these had been moved

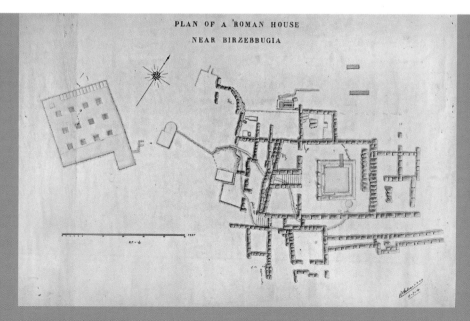

PLAN OF A ROMAN HOUSE
NEAR BIRZEBBUGIA

VILLA AT TA' KAĊĊATURA 301

from their original position. The central element of the building was a small square peristyled courtyard surrounded by rooms and a corridor. The peristyle was supported on twelve fluted Coralline Limestone columns of the Doric order.

It appears that this residential part of the villa had an upper floor because Ashby found traces of a staircase. Fragments of painted plaster and coloured marble showed that some rooms were decorated with marble veneering and painted walls. A fragment of grey marble inscribed with the letters PII could belong to an inscription mentioning one of the Antonine emperors who reigned in the second half of the second century AD.

Remains of presses, rock-cut vats, troughs, and channels, suggesting agricultural activity connected with olive pressing, were located mainly on the western side of the site.

Two water cisterns, both rectangular in shape, are of particular interest. The one underneath the courtyard was roofed with rough stones set in mortar forming a low arch. Oddly, the internal surface of the roof was lined with white plaster still showing the impressions of cane shuttering. This framework was originally supported by seven wooden beams since the holes for these are still visible. The other cistern, located about twelve metres further uphill to the southwest of the villa, is even more impressive. It was entirely cut in the rock and its interior was accessible by a flight of sixteen rock-cut steps. It was roofed with four rows of huge flat slabs supported by stone cross beams which, in turn, rested on the solid rock walls and on twelve gigantic square pillars each consisting of two or three blocks.

Left: Plan of the villa at Ta' Kaċċatura excavated by Thomas Ashby in 1915. Note the flight of steps leading up to a higher level from the small peristyle.

Above left: An aerial photograph of the remains a few years after they were excavated. The large cistern is, surprisingly, on a higher level than the villa building.

Above right: A section of the remains as they appear today. The Għar Dalam Museum is the building on the top-centre-left of the photo.

Overleaf: The huge water-cistern at Ta' Kaċċatura. The slabs covering the roof are supported by the 12 huge stone pillars.

VILLA INSIDE SCHOOL GROUNDS
ŻEJTUN

As far back as 1960, while clearing the ground for a new village school on the south side of the west end of Luqa Briffa Street in Żejtun, the first traces of 'Roman masonry' were brought to light, but these were considered to be 'slight'. Archaeological excavations were taken up in 1964 when a large cistern with water channels leading to it was uncovered, together with a stone paved area. In 1972 investigations were continued by Tancred Gouder, revealing various parts of the complex stone apparatus used in Roman times for the production of olive oil. A second cistern was discovered, this time cylindrical in shape, as well as two rock-cut 'silo-pits' containing Borġ in-Nadur pottery. A preliminary plan was drawn by the then director of the Museums Department, Francis S. Mallia. Short excavation campaigns were conducted up to 1976, mostly coinciding with visits to Malta by foreign students who were entrusted with the actual digging. Plans are on hand for the resumption of full-scale scientific excavations.

The remains belong to a typical Roman rustic villa combining a residential area with an area for the pressing of olive oil. The residential area comprises at least three rooms with floors paved with lozenge-shaped terracotta tiles of different colours. Some traces of ancient painting were noted in 1976 on the surviving stumps of the walls of these rooms. At one spot the painted plaster was not supported by any stone blocks behind it, making me

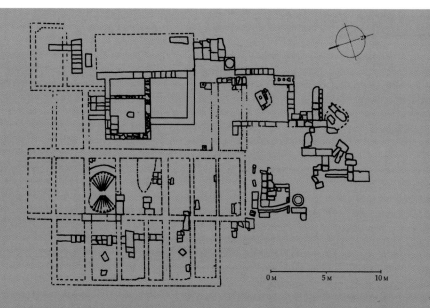

0 M   5 M   10 M

suspect that the elevation of the wall above the foundation was of mud brick which had crumbled into powder by the time it was brought to light. If my observation was correct, this would be the first time that such a construction technique has been met in a Roman context in Malta. It would also serve as a warning that we are not always to expect stone walling in Roman constructions and that we should keep our eyes wide open for flimsier techniques such this one.

Immediately to the north of the residential area stood the industrial area, some of whose components are still visible, namely: a large stone block used as counterweight for the pressing wooden beam; a section of the press bed; and a stone vat, probably one of several originally used for settling oil. The water from the cylindrical cistern close by could well have been used in the same process.

The smaller cylindrical cistern was excavated and is still visible. The larger cistern whose roof was supported on three arches contained an accumulation of debris which could not be investigated 'because of evident danger to life and limb.'

In 1963 five rock-cut tombs with 'Punic type pottery and a third-century AD lamp' were discovered in a field 'immediately to the east of the new village school MR5825 6875'. This location falls on the east edge of the present grounds of the same school, on the west side of Degabriele Street. More similar finds are reported to have been discovered, but never officially documented, under the houses along the east side of the same street. No doubt, these tombs were connected with the villa.

Left: *Plan of the remains of the villa. Above left: An aerial view of the same. A couple of rooms, paved with lozenge-shaped terracotta tiles, can still be made out, in spite of the vegetation overgrowth. To the north of these rooms are the olive press bed, a vat, and the stone anchor block for holding the capstan.*

The remains are still enclosed within the grounds of the Carlo Diacono Junior Lyceum in Żejtun. They can be visited by special permission from the head of the school. The school is close to the medieval church of St Gregory and can be reached either from Triq San Girgor via Triq San Piju X or from the Żejtun by-pass (Triq President Anton Buttigieg) through Triq Arcipriet Degabriele.

VILLA TAD-DAWL
ĦAL KIRKOP

One of the gravest known losses to the Maltese archaeological heritage is the remains of a rural villa discovered and explored by Dr A.A. Caruana in 1888. All that survives of this agricultural complex is the excellently preserved olive mill (*trapetum*) on exhibit at the National Museum of Archaeology. We probably can count ourselves lucky that the three-page report written by Caruana, the only record of this find, was accompanied by an excellent plan of the site signed by Caruana himself, dated 21 April 1888.

The villa, which Caruana believed to be of Greek origin, lay to the west of Ħal Kirkop, between Luqa and Imqabba, some eight kilometres to the south of Valletta. Today, the area of Tad-Dawl, immediately to the east of the airstrip, is riddled with soft stone quarries. Since no mention of these remains is found in post-1888 literature, it is more likely that they were gobbled up by the quarries than by the airstrip.

The building seems to have had almost exactly the same orientation and layout of the villa at Ta' Kaċċatura; but only the industrial wing of the building was uncovered. The residential area probably extended to the north-east of this. It is interesting that Caruana was in a position to identify some rooms as 'stables or sheep-pens' (P, P, P) and other rooms as 'stores for olives' (Q, Q).

Like the other villas, the one at Tad-Dawl was constructed of large blocks of limestone.

Very unusual are the large round stone slabs (eight feet in diameter) that sealed two doorways (L and O) by being rolled down in specially-

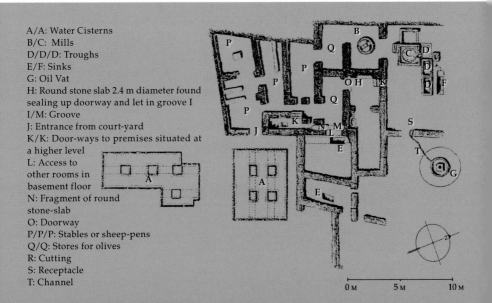

A/A: Water Cisterns
B/C: Mills
D/D/D: Troughs
E/F: Sinks
G: Oil Vat
H: Round stone slab 2.4 m diameter found sealing up doorway and let in groove I
I/M: Groove
J: Entrance from court-yard
K/K: Door-ways to premises situated at a higher level
L: Access to other rooms in basement floor
N: Fragment of round stone-slab
O: Doorway
P/P/P: Stables or sheep-pens
Q/Q: Stores for olives
R: Cutting
S: Receptacle
T: Channel

0 M   5 M   10 M

cut grooves. Similar devices were used to seal tombs in the Levant. The legend of the plan suggests that doorway L led to 'other rooms in basement floor.' Besides the olive-crusher mentioned above, the plan shows the presence of a system of vats and troughs for the decantation of the pressed oil (D, D, D).

On its south side, the villa was also equipped with two rock-cut cisterns, one L-shaped, the other square-shaped (A). The roofing technique of both cisterns is identical to that of the cistern of the villa at Ta' Kaċċatura. In each cistern four square pillars supported horizontal thick stone beams over a span of 1.5m over which in turn lay the horizontal roof of thick stone slabs about 1.7m in length.

Top: Aerial photo showing the area where the 'villa' used to be situated. The area is now riddled with Globerigina Limestone quarries.

Opposite page: Plan of the remains of the villa at Tad-Dawl, near Ħal Kirkop.

Below: The olive crusher from the Tad-Dawl villa reconstructed from the original stone parts.

THE RABAT DOMUS
RABAT

The remains of this Roman house were accidentally discovered in 1881 while trees were being planted on the glacis of the Mdina fortifications, just outside Greeks' Gate. Dr A.A. Caruana was entrusted with a full-scale uncovering of the remains, about which he published a short report of a few pages accompanied by a plan and one photo showing the various retrieved pieces of sculpture. A section of the remains was later roofed over and turned into a museum.

The various rooms of the house gravitated around a richly-decorated peristyle courtyard. The elevation of the latter was in the elegant Hellenistic version of the Doric order with columns and entablature in Globigerina Limestone, covered with polychrome painted plaster.

The floors of both the courtyard and the surrounding rooms were covered with mosaics of the highest artistic quality. Lively geometric patterns, some with intriguing optical illusions, framed small figurative pictures formed with coloured *tesserae* of minute size. These mosaics date the architecture firmly within the fifty years spanning the last quarter of the second century and the first quarter of the first century BC.

Among the debris of the collapsed building Caruana found various fragments of statuary that, together with the torso of a colossal togate statue discovered by Zammit forty years later, have now been found to constitute a cycle of imperial portrait statues. Two of these portrayed Claudius and his daughter, Claudia

Top: The larger-than-life-size statue of Claudius's portrait statue being lifted from its find-spot in 1920.

Left: Part of the original Doric architrave and part of an original column integrated within the reconstructed peristyle.

View from above of the well- preserved mosaic floor of the peristyled courtyard. A sequence of frames of different widths and colours (red, white, black, red, white) enclose a pictorial frame with a trompe l'oeil *effect, which in turn encloses further frames around the central* emblema.

A section of the fine mosaic floor of the large room next to the 'triclinium'. It is in opus vermiculatum *and shows an intricate overlapping lyre pattern known also as 'guilloche' motif. The motif is used for a strip on one side of the floor, rather than a whole, four-sided frame.*

A section of the floor from the same room. On the left is part of the main motif with illusionistic cascading cubes and on the right is part of the frame with a trompe l'oeil *meander motif. In the centre is some patchwork with hexagonal terracotta tiles.*

Antonia (left). A third statue, showing a togate boy, may have portrayed his adopted son, the future emperor Nero. This statuary cycle suggests that by about AD 50 the house had assumed some official role.

In 1889 the road leading to the railway station was cut through the unexcavated parts of the house to the east, destroying important structures without any records being kept. Excavations in the area were resumed by Temi Zammit in 1922, starting with the eastern side of the new road. This showed that the knights-period glacis was built over the ruins of Roman buildings, using some of their building material. Inside an L-shaped water cistern, apart from fragments of fine Italian *terra sigillata*, a strange male bearded head in Globigerina Limestone was found. The Oriental style and features of the head date it to a pre-Roman period. Zammit's exploration extended to the remains of other domestic structures further to the north and west of Caruana's stately house. Most of these were of grossly inferior workmanship and belonged to other houses flanking a narrow ancient street. One of the rooms had its floor resting on vertically placed amphorae; no doubt, for damp-proofing purposes.

View of the reconstructed peristyle. Beyond it is the new museum set-up. On the far left is a marble well-head covering an underground cistern originally intended to collect the rain water from the courtyard.

The large room adjacent to the 'triclinium' and the peristyle, with the illusionistic opus scutulatum (cascading cubes) framed by a meander motif. On the left is the re-joined portrait statue of Claudius.

A selection of ceramic containers in terra sigillata *of different origin, some from northern Italy, others from North Africa.*

The top item is a 'pilgrim's flask'. Below it on the left is a feeding bottle (askos).

A view of the remains of houses, beyond the Roman domus, excavated by Zammit in the 1920s. In the distance are the Gheriexem valley and Mtarfa heights.

The Roman Domvs Museum is within walking distance of Mdina. From the walled city's main gate, walk through Howard Gardens. The classical building housing the museum is visible on the opposite side of the gardens. By car, drive up to Mdina but instead of turning towards the main gate of Mdina, drive on to the parking in front of the museum on Museum Esplanade. For opening hours see www.heritagemalta.org.

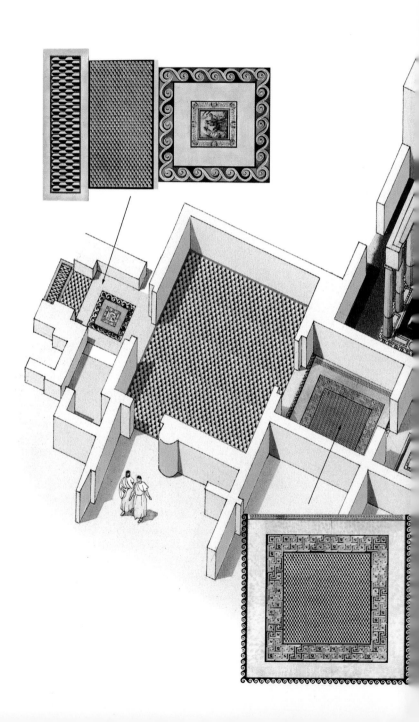

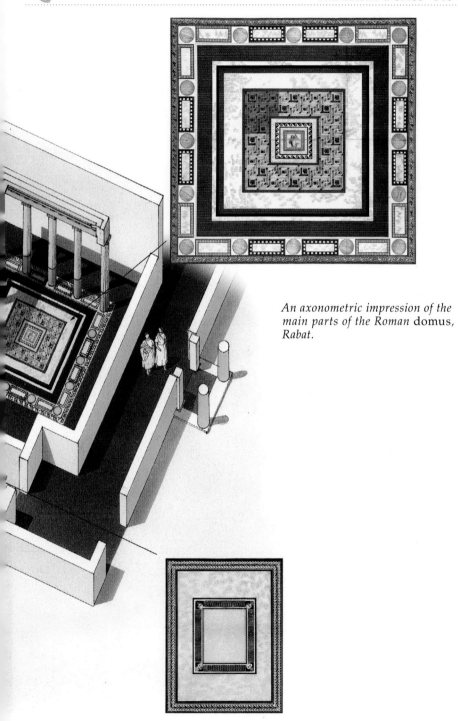

An axonometric impression of the main parts of the Roman domus, *Rabat.*

Other remains

Road to Railway Station

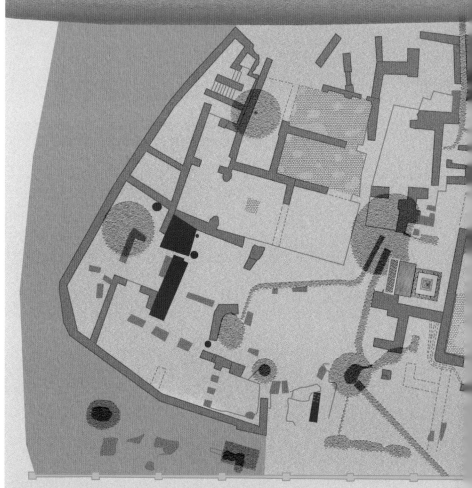

This plan integrates plans and information from both the 1881 and the 1920s excavations of the Roman domus and adjacent buildings. It highlights the great number of cisterns and canals hewn in the natural bedrock discovered under and in close proximity to the domus. The plan also shows the ancient walls, parts of walls, and single stone blocks that were found in situ, mosaic floors, as well as the modern walls built over and around the remains.The Railway Station Road, cut in the bedrock between the Roman remains and Mdina, has destroyed a good part of the archaeological deposits.

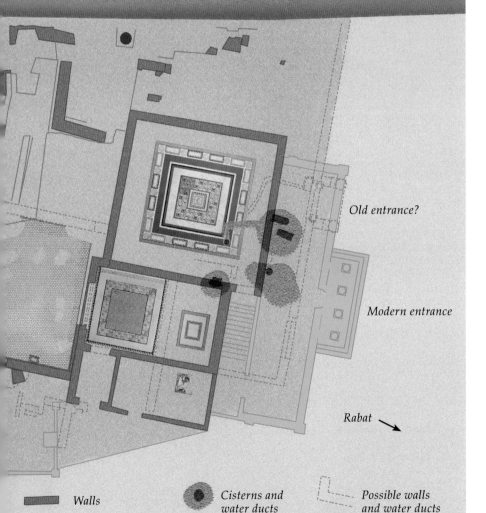

Mdina

Road to Railway Station

Old entrance?

Modern entrance

Rabat

Walls

Modern buildings

Cisterns and
water ducts

Remains of mosaic
flooring

Possible walls
and water ducts

Pits

Silver signet ring found on the hand of a skeleton buried in the Islamic cemetery located on top of the Domus remains

Coins minted in Malta during the Roman period

Many Kufic inscriptions were discovered during excavations of the Islamic cemetery

A draped marble statue representing Isis or Ashtart

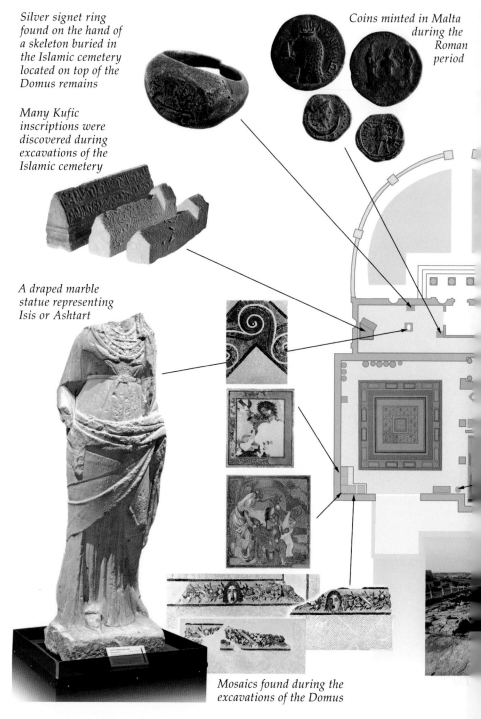

Mosaics found during the excavations of the Domus

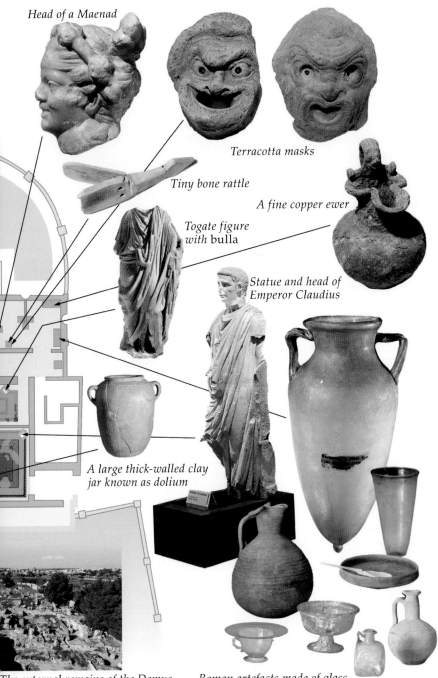

Head of a Maenad

Terracotta masks

Tiny bone rattle

A fine copper ewer

Togate figure with bulla

Statue and head of Emperor Claudius

A large thick-walled clay jar known as dolium

The external remains of the Domus

Roman artefacts made of glass, clay, and bone

ROMAN BATHS AT GĦAJN TUFFIEĦA
MĠARR

Extensive structures, clearly connected with bathing, were discovered in 1929 at Għajn Tuffieħa (the 'Apple Spring') beneath the edge of the Upper Coralline escarpment of western Malta, this time on the side facing the sea, a kilometre or so from two enchanting sandy bays. The choice of the site must have determined by the presence of an abundant spring of fresh water. The building incorporated an artificial heating system involving a furnace which supplied hot water as well as hot air that heated the adjacent rooms. For this purpose the floor of the room which incorporated the furnace was suspended on rows of low arches of fired bricks. Sadly, all these arches have since then disappeared.

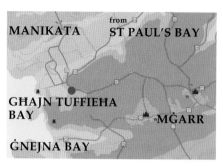

The site is closed off with a boundary wall. Entrance by appointment can be obtained by calling the head office of Heritage Malta, Valletta, or e-mail **info@heritagemalta.org**. Before entering Mġarr turn on the road to the right towards the Għajn Tuffieħa and Golden Sands bays. Before reaching the coast, take notice not to miss the sign of the site on the left. Otherwise the site can be reached from St Paul's Bay. Follow the signs to Għajn Tuffieħa Bay until you see the sign to Mġarr. Go up this road and the sign to the site is soon visible on the right of the road.

The heated rooms were arranged in such a way as to provide for the bathing ritual practised by the Romans in the large public thermal

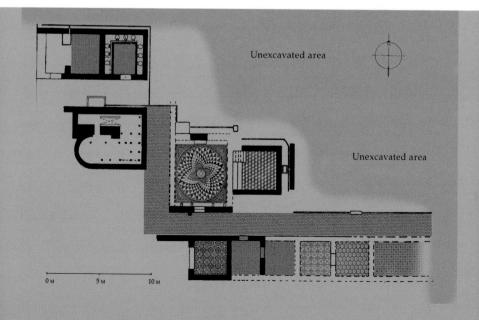

Unexcavated area

Unexcavated area

0 M   5 M   10 M

baths in their large cities, involving the passage from a hot, steaming room (*calidarium*) to a moderately warm room (*tepidarium*) and finishing into a cold bath (*frigidarium*). But the size of the Għajn Tuffieħa complex is too small and is situated too far away from town for such a purpose. It is more befitting for a private residential villa, like those found both in neighbouring Sicily and Libya. The problem is that so far no adjacent structures of such a villa have come to light; so we are left to guess whether this was a private set-up attached to a typical Roman villa, or a public one addressed to a limited clientele on the road between the town and the sea.

Besides an outdoor swimming pool, and a communal latrine that could accommodate eleven persons at any one time, the complex had a series of small rooms of the right size to serve as bedrooms (*cubicula*). This arrangement makes it more likely to be a small public bathing establishment (a *balneum*) situated in an idyllic Mediterranean landscape some distance from town. Judging from the mosaics that decorated the floors of the bathing rooms, the swimming pool and several of the *cubicula*, it very probably catered for members of the better-off echelons of Maltese society of the second half of the first century and the first half of the second century AD.

All the mosaics carry geometrical patterns, that of the cold-dip bath showing the illusion of cascading cubes, as in one of the side rooms of the Rabat domus. The 1929 excavation also brought to light some remains of painted wall plaster. This site is the only one so far in Malta to have yielded fragments of flat glass sheets, obviously used as window panes.

Above left: Aerial view of the site. The apodyterium *(changing room) and some cubicles, the ones that were paved with mosaic floors, have been roofed over for protection against the elements.*

Opposite page: Plan of the Roman baths at Għajn Tuffieħa.

Above right: The mosaic floor of one of the cubicles. In spite of the protective roof, the mosaic floors have suffered considerably since their discovery in 1929 and are in urgent need of conservation.

*An axonometric graphic
reconstruction of the Roman baths
at Għajn Tuffieħa with an integrated
picture of the mosaic floor of each
room where they occur.*

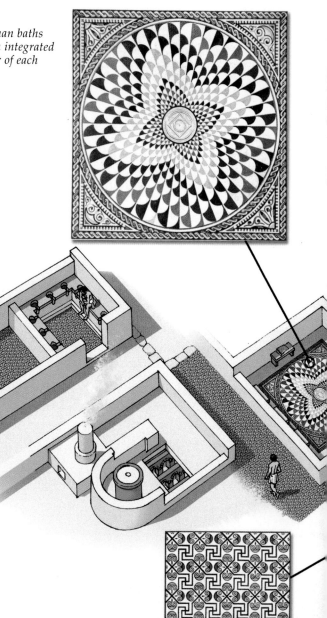

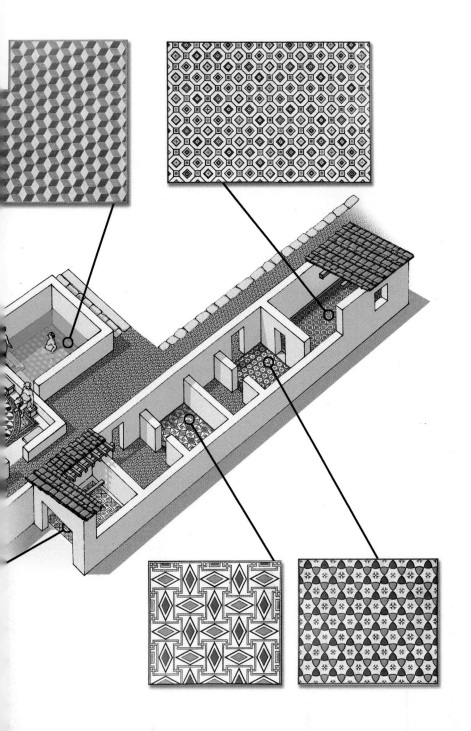

RAS IR-RAĦEB
BAĦRIJA

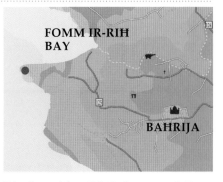

FOMM IR-RIĦ
BAY

BAĦRIJA

As the place-name suggests, Ras ir-Raħeb, known to Gian Francesco Abela as 'Gebel el Raħeb', is a promontory. It juts out conspicuously into the sea on the west coast of Malta and must have been a very important landmark for seafarers. But neither Abela, nor his contemporaries, including Antonio Bosio and Marc' Antonio Axiaq were aware of any antiquities on it. By Ras il-Knejjes, Abela and company surely meant the promontory further inland, on which the more conspicuous remains of a prehistoric temple stood (and still stand) which they identified with the temple of Juno mentioned by Cicero.

On approaching the site, the most conspicuous elements of the surviving ancient remains at Ras ir-Raħeb are two upright megaliths, beyond which

Take the road from Baħrija down towards Fomm ir-Riħ Bay. At one point the road forks out into two roads. Take the left road. From the parking-space walk along the footpath to the very end of the promontory. Some land is private land (usually marked with RTO) so walk with caution.

are the foundations of a building consisting of a courtyard surrounded by a wide corridor. The corridor was connected to a room immediately to its west by a doorway whose threshold still survives. At the north-east corner of the corridor is the head of a rectangular cistern. The courtyard is paved with a crushed pottery concrete floor

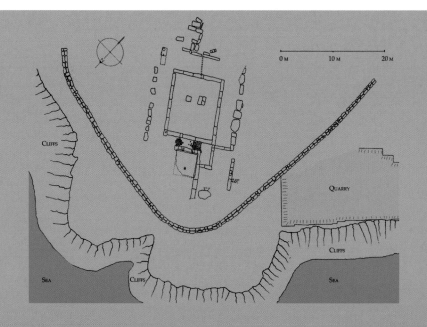

CLIFFS

0 M   10 M   20 M

QUARRY

CLIFFS

SEA   CLIFFS   SEA

(*cocciopesto*) with white marble cubes (*tesserae*) embedded in it, similar to the one at the Tas-Silġ sanctuary, while the room further to the west is paved with lozenge-shaped clay tiles.

These ancient remains were first mentioned in 1922 when Temi Zammit was called to examine the site by the owner of the land. Zammit already recognized that the two upright megaliths had been recycled from some prehistoric structure. The room with the clay tile floor had just been exposed. He also noted the cistern. The numerous sherds of 'household pottery' scattered in the area made him propose 'a numerous settlement'.

The site was further investigated in 1961-62 when it was hastily and awkwardly dug up by a team of officers from the Royal Navy. It is clear that all the diggers did was to trace and uncover walls, heaping up the excavated earth on both sides of the walls. Captain D. Scott, the leader of the team, gave an account of the 'dig' in a typewritten report addressed to the curator of archaeology at the Valletta Museum.

Among the finds, the most remarkable ones are: an ivory plaque with a crouching boar in low relief, whose pedigree has been traced in fifth-century Etruria; two clay satyr masks (probably handles); and several terracotta figurines, among which two of a nude male and one of a draped female holding a pyxis. Another figurine showed a male, probably Hercules, with a lion skin tied in a knot round his waist. Coins ranged from Sicilian Punic (Republican period) to a late Roman one of Constantius II (AD 337-361).

The purpose of the ancient building is still debated. Some have suggested a religious site, possibly the sanctuary of Hercules; others find evidence for a country house.

Above left: This aerial view of the site remains shows clearly the unorthodox method of excavation used in the 1961-62 operation. One can see the spoil heaps on either side of each exposed wall.
Opposite page: Plan of the remains of an ancient building at Ras ir-Raħeb, in relation to the promontory.

Above right: The promontory of Ras ir-Raħeb, with its sheer cliffs, as seen from further inland. Gozo is in the background.

ST PAUL'S CATACOMBS
RABAT

The most extensive early Christian underground cemetery in Malta that, with an approximate area of 2000m², comes closest to the real catacombs of Rome is St Paul's Catacombs, situated just outside the ditch of the ancient city of Melite. It appears to have taken shape after a number of minor hypogea, some of which being enlarged Punico-Roman tombs adapted to the current needs, were linked together and extended further both horizontally and, to a limited extent, vertically to cater for the burial needs of late-Roman and Byzantine Melite.

After being abandoned in the centuries of Arab domination, parts of them seem to have been revived in later medieval times when the area closest to the stepped entrance was converted into an underground rectangular church. Antiquarian interest in the catacombs, compounded by the augmenting Pauline tradition, was high in the seventeenth century when Gian Francesco Abela wrote the earliest account of them. It is noteworthy that Jean Quintin, a century earlier, had made no mention of the catacombs, even though he had given a full account of the Pauline tradition among the Maltese and made a more than passing reference to St Paul's Grotto in Rabat.

The original access was down 18 high, rock-cut steps, today covered by a flight of more manageable stone stairs. The walls on both sides are covered with lamp-holes and *loculi*, rectangular hollows for the burial of dead bodies. Their size suggests that most of them were for children. The steps lead to an open hall on the right, with a C-shaped *stibadium* at both ends, and another hall on the left, this one

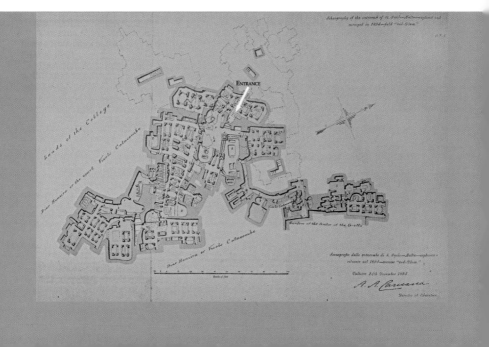

View of the 'atrium' of the catacomb complex of St Paul from behind the stibadium *that is visible in the foreground.*

The circular table of the stibadium *has a raised edge. The sloping floor around it was for people to recline on.*

Above left: View of the so-called 'chapel' inside the catacomb complex. At the back one can see a large arcosolium *grave, while on the opposite wall to the right, there is a small* loculus.
Opposite page: Plan of the catacomb complex of St Paul, Rabat, signed by A.A. Caruana.

A canopied grave with two separate troughs for burial laid transversally. Beyond it is another with four troughs laid lengthwise.

shaped like a rectangular church. The two halls are separated by a massive pilaster consisting of four pseudo-Doric columns fused together. Even the rectangular hall has graves of different types hewn out of the rock on its walls and floor.

Beyond these halls is a maze of corridors flanked by graves of all types most of them with places for two burials, side by side. The majority of graves here is of the canopied type without, however, any carved decoration.

The surface of the walls appears to have been plastered over in many places. In some spots the plaster was decorated with coloured lines. One or two canopied graves had at least one side covered with a figurative painting. Unfortunately, very scant fragments survive of either, the best-preserved one being a picture of a seated figure on the pilaster of one of the canopied graves. Above it is

the shape of a small anchor, an early Christian symbol, and above the latter the Greek word ΕΥΤΥΧΙΩΝ, the name of the seated figure, or ΕΥΤΥΧΙΩΗ, meaning 'good luck' or 'farewell' (photograph above).

Another view of the catacomb complex of St Paul, Rabat. One can see two small loculi on the wall to the left and several others on another wall in the distance, beyond the doorway.

Top: A system of corridors cross each other more or less at right angles, generally separated by arched doorways. On the right is another arcosolium.

Opposite page, left: View of part of the 'atrium' of the catacomb with a stibadium in the foreground and another one in the background

Internal view of one of the chambers of Catacomb 3 of the SS. Paul/Agatha complex of separate hypogea.

Opposite is a stone door with two rows of surgical instruments carved in relief.

The street directions to the catacombs are well marked. From the main square of Rabat, Misrah il-Parroċċa, take Triq Sant'Agata (with your back to the church, the road to the left). St Paul Catacombs are on the left of this road where there is a gap in the buildings. The main entrance is through the green metal gate. For opening hours see **www.heritagemalta.org**.

ST AGATHA'S CATACOMBS
RABAT

The second largest early Christian underground cemeterial complex is that of St Agatha, only a few metres away from that of St Paul in Rabat. It too, or parts of it, was visited in the knights' period and Gian Francesco Abela noted its large size and quantity of tombs.

Although it is extensive by Maltese standards, compared to those of Rome, Naples, and Syracuse, it hardly qualifies as a 'catacomb'; on plan it looks like a series of smaller hypogea linked together; but, as that denomination is in current use, we might as well stick to it. Access is through St Agatha's religious complex from St Agatha Street. A flight of 20 rock-cut steps leads one down to a rock-hewn church decorated with a series of fresco paintings, some datable from their style and iconography to the early sixteenth century, others clearly much earlier (late thirteenth to early fourteenth century), albeit more fragmentary. The underground church seems to have been formed by cutting away a section of the pre-existing cemetery for one can still identify vestiges of earlier rock-cut tombs both on the walls and on the ceiling.

Like its neighbours, the St Agatha catacombs contain the whole variety of types of graves, ranging from simple *loculi*, hewn on the walls and simple rectangular pits in the ground (*forma*), to elaborate canopied graves with saddle-backed rock-cut sarcophagi. Two hypogea with separate entrances (numbers

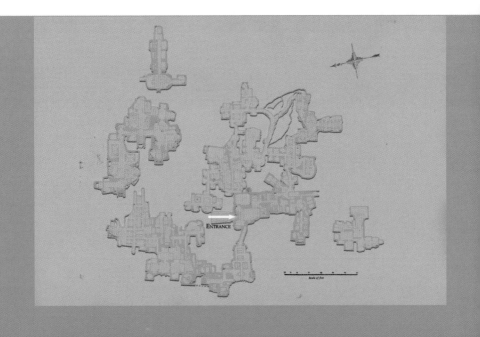

ENTRANCE

Scale of feet

One of the finest and best-preserved fresco painting in an early Christian catacomb inside the St Agatha complex. It is painted on the surface of an apsed niche on a wall facing a mutilated stibadium. It shows a scallop-shell fanning out over a chi-rho monogram flanked by two vases and two birds.

Above left: One of the sides of a canopied grave inside the same complex, with a fresco painting representing a bird rendered in a somewhat crude style and enclosed by a patterned border.
Opposite page: Plan of the catacomb complex of St Agatha.

Another grave within the same complex, which preserves a fresco showing a cross-shaped motif enclosed within a thick garland.

17 and 18 in Buhagiar's catalogue) have been identified as Jewish from fragmentary inscriptions and carvings of menorahs on their walls. As usual, a striking feature is the duality of most interment spaces suggested by the head depressions on the stone pillows. Almost all the individual hypogea are endowed with the characteristic C-shaped rock-cut table (*stibadium*). This element is, perhaps symptomatically, missing from Jewish hypogea.

The St Agatha catacombs also preserve some of the better preserved and more defined fresco paintings. A score of fragments of North African oil lamps, many with clear Christian symbolism, discovered during a survey that was conducted in 1955-58, together with fresco motifs and two Constantinian cross monograms, date the complex to the fourth century or later.

Between St Paul's catacomb complex and the St Agatha one is an open area with several individual hypogea, each one accessible through a small room built in the early twentieth century. They are marked by numbered marble tablets. Hypogea 12, 13, 14, and 17A seem to be Jewish, judging by the inscribed or painted symbolism. The others are more probably Christian. Most of them are accessible through a gate opposite St Paul's Catacombs. One of the Jewish hypogea still preserves the original stone swivel door, while others still have the holes for such a device behind the doorway.

St Agatha's complex: An arcosolium grave between two corridors.

St Agatha's complex: A canopied grave with two separate burial troughs.

Right: St Agatha's complex: A menorah on a stand engraved above the doorway to a corridor in catacomb no 13.

A canopied grave with one trough accommodating two skeletons with their heads resting on the rounded cavities in *the rock-cut pillow. Along the edge of the trough runs a rebate for the sealing slabs.*

The street directions to the catacombs are well marked. From the main square of Rabat, Misraħ il-Parroċċa, go into Triq Sant'Agata (with your back to the church, the road to the left). St Agatha's Catacombs are on the right of this road a few meters from the entrance of St Paul's Catacombs. A narrow ally to the right of the stone cross leads to the church and catacombs of St Agatha.

SALINA CATACOMBS
NAXXAR

A small group of early Christian hypogea are hewn out of the Lower Coralline limestone outcrop towards the inner end of the east side of Salina Bay, to one side of the church of the Annunciation. Their size and number suggest the presence of a sizeable late-Roman community in the area. This is not surprising, given that this bay was probably a busy harbour in Roman times, extending much further inland than it does at present. The large number of Roman anchor stocks recovered from the sea off Qawra Point probably belonged to ships that did not quite manage to enter harbour in rough weather.

The earliest mention of these hypogea goes back to 1772 when Gian Antonio Ciantar referred to the 1721 discovery of a gold coin of

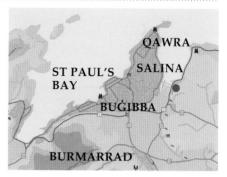

The main catacomb is closed off with a metal gate but the site is in open fields. Entrance by appointment can be obtained by calling the head office of Heritage Malta, Valletta, or e-mail info@heritagemalta.org. Coming from St Paul's Bay along the coast-road take the road to Naxxar just by the salt-pans. Immediately turn left and the site is reached by a path on the right behind the small chapel.

the Byzantine emperor Phocas and of several tombs still containing intact skeletons. The description of an arched tomb carved in the rock and containing one skeleton seems to fit the typology of these late-Roman and Byzantine burials.

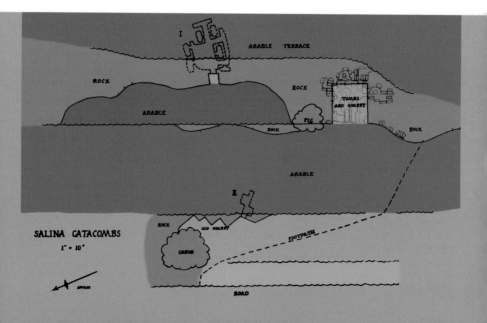

The five hypogea are of varying sizes but almost all their doorways are carved into the vertical face of a previous quarry. The impression is that the hypogea belonged to individual families, or guilds. Each of the two largest hypogea had at least one C-shaped *stibadium*.

One of these two hypogea has been partially mutilated by later quarrying activity, depriving it of part of its roof and destroying some of the graves. Even here, most of the grave pits have place for two individuals lying side by side. Judging from surviving evidence of mutilated graves on the sides, this hypogeum seems to have had a sort of rectangular atrium in front of it. It is a pity that no proper record was kept of the finds therein when it was excavated in 1937.

The second one is the most interesting hypogeum because it is adorned with several relief carvings. The most conspicuous ones are two sets of spirals flanking the two shorter ends of a canopied grave. The opening of one of these is further decorated by an elaborate arch resting on two short half-columns with spiral flutings. Two side pilasters of another canopied grave have a pseudo-Corinthian capital with three sets of volutes. Besides this scroll decoration, a crude animal is inscribed on the right wall inside the entrance and a Greek cross enclosed within a circle is carved on the right hand pilaster of a saddle-backed canopied grave. Even the entrance to the hypogeum is flanked by slender engaged half-columns with pseudo-Corinthian capitals and fluted shafts.

A rectangular rock-cut court surrounded by small hypogea.

Opposite page: Plan of the two major catacombs, and some of the minor tombs, at Salina.

Internal view of the main catacomb at Salina. Two canopied graves with saddle-backed lids. The grave on the left is decorated with scrolls in relief.

LATE ROMAN AND BYZANTINE HYPOGEA
VARIOUS LOCATIONS

Besides the catacombs and larger hypogea described above and in chapter 7, Malta is riddled by scores of smaller hypogea scattered widely in the countryside and, often enough, also in built-up areas. The latter were also open country in antiquity and have been covered by urban sprawl since then. These have been systematically described, drawn, and catalogued by Prof. Mario Buhagiar in a comprehensive corpus published in 1986. In this entry, only a small representative number of hypogea are very briefly described.

These hypogea range from single tombs, like the one whose entrance found itself on the side of the ditch surrounding Mamo tower, near St Thomas Bay, to larger and more complex (but still isolated) hypo-gea, like the one near St Thomas tower in Marsascala, to clusters of such hypogea, the most numerous and impressive one being the necropolis of Binġemma (top opposite page). The latter consists of more than 30 hypogea, only 27 of which are described by Buhagiar. They perforate the side of Dwejra hill where the Victoria Lines cross over a narrow gorge, overlooking the village of Mġarr. One cannot fail to see the similarity of their setting to that of the complexes of tombs and troglodytic habitations of Cava d'Ispica, and other *cave* near Modica in southeastern Sicily.

Most of the hypogea consist of a longish corridor leading from an entrance through a door to a

Left: Internal view of the catacomb at Marsascala, near St Thomas tower. The main corridor flanked by window tombs. The inscription is on the right wall.

Right: The inscription inside the catacomb near St Thomas tower, Marsascala.

rectangular room surrounded by tombs accessible through window openings. Once more most graves have been carved to provide room for two persons. The raised pillow contains two head rests. A few are not hypogea at all, but single graves with separate window entrances. One hypogeum still preserves a *stibadium* (C-shaped table), while in another only the apse-like space for a mutilated one survives.

Top: A stibadium *and a lamp-hole can still be made out inside this tomb of the Bingemma (Dwejra hill) necropolis.*

Left: A somewhat untypical entrance to another tomb of the Bingemma necropolis. The square entrance has an arched recess on top of it.

Another group of tombs that are worth visiting, even though heavily mutilated in parts, is the group adjacent to the Xarolla windmill, between Safi and Żurrieq, which have been exposed since Buhagiar's publication. A few graves have short columns flanking their entrances, with carvings on the capitals and shafts. The visit of this site can be combined with that of the windmill.

Not very far from these are the Tal-Mintna 'catacombs', near Mqabba. These can be visited on request or on certain occasions. These three hypogea have some special features like triangular lamp-holes, entrance niches decorated with beautiful conches sculpted like scallop-shells in relief, and short carved columns. One hypogeum has a *stibadium*. A similar decorated entrance niche occurs also in one of a group of hypogea at Il-Magħlaq, behind the Mnajdra pre-historic temples, on the opposite side of the road leading to Għar Lapsi.

A much larger cluster of as many as 43, joined together or with separate entrances is the group of Tal-Bistra, on the vertical face of a rocky terrace on both sides of the road from Rabat to Tarġa Gap, a few metres down from the Mount St Joseph complex. Extensive quarrying has eaten up parts of most hypogea and several tombs have ended up in private properties and put to unfitting uses. At the time of writing, only a few of the tombs can be visited, and with great difficulty. It is hoped that the site will be rehabilitated and opened to the public.

Small hypogea have occasionally turned up in private properties and in school grounds, like the ones inside the grounds of the Sacred Heart School, St Julians. These can only be visited by special arrangement.

View of the Xarolla windmill between Żurrieq and Ħal Safi, with the group of early Christian tombs in front of it. Some of the tombs have been damaged by quarrying. Others have preserved attractive sculptured features.

The Tal-Bistra catacombs. A small section of an otherwise extensive system of Early Christian tombs with their entrances perforated on a vertical quarry face. Parts of the system are in private property.

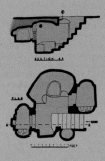

Plan and section of the Hal Resqun catacomb (above). Three views of different parts of the catacomb, with graphic reproductions of two engraved motifs. The catacomb has been sealed after its excavation. It lies in the middle of the roundabout next to the airport.

CART RUTS
VARIOUS LOCATIONS

Although this enigmatic imprint of human activity on the Maltese rocky landscape has already been extensively discussed in the volume dedicated to prehistory in this series, and has been attributed to the Bronze Age, I feel I should include a few paragraphs on the same subject because I am equally convinced that the cart ruts, at least most of them, are the product of the Classical Age. They might even be the most significant component of material culture, a technological one, that was common to all the cultures that were active in these islands from the eighth century BC to the ninth century AD. It is up to the reader to decide which is the more convincing of the multifarious attributions and interpretations, preferably after a personal investigation of the primary sources, the cart ruts themselves. Starting with the date of their creation, I find that the cart ruts are far too seldom found in the vicinity of the megalithic temples to even consider a related date. The Bronze Age date, one associated with Borġ in-Nadur settlements, has so far been the most favourite one. After Temi Zammit, both John Davies Evans and David Trump, the foremost prehistoric archaeologists to involve themselves deeply in Maltese field archaeology, have favoured the latter attribution; mostly on two counts. One, that many sets of cart ruts are found in close vicinity to such Bronze Age fortified settlements, some apparently even leading into them. Secondly, that they accept the *ante quem* argument proposed by Zammit, namely, that they precede some tombs that were apparently cut

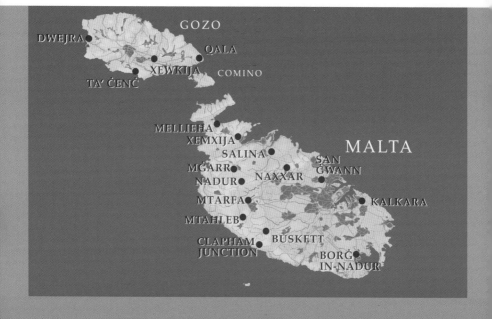

into such cart ruts at Mtarfa. Since these tombs were labelled Punic by Zammit, the ruts had, in their view, to belong to an earlier age.

I have already had the opportunity of exposing the weakness of the latter argument. Even if those specific tombs were Punic, the cart ruts they cut into could be older even by a few years, not necessarily by centuries. Besides, the Punic period in Malta lasted for a few centuries and the burial tradition of rock-cut tombs with vertical shaft and lateral chamber survived well into the Roman period.

My attribution to the Classical Age was forced on me by circumstantial evidence in Malta, reinforced by identical situations abroad. In my search for ancient quarries I used to find cart ruts virtually whenever I spotted quarries. I also found this same association with ancient quarries in several Classical sites abroad: in Syracuse, behind the *cavea* of the Greek theatre and elsewhere; in Agrigento, all along the edge of the ridge where the temple of Hercules and other temples stand; near the amphitheatre in Cagliari, and elsewhere in Sardinia. David Trump found them outside Marseilles, and former students of mine discovered more in Italy. Confronted by such a formidable body of evidence, I had no choice but to explain them as a means of controlled transportation of heavy building blocks from the quarry face to the made-up road. Incontrovertible evidence has now been discovered near the group of cart ruts outside Buskett (popularly known as 'Clapham Junction') that the type of cart ruts of that area are contemporary or later than the quarries of the Classical Age.

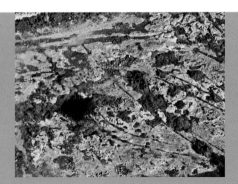

The group of cart-ruts at Mtarfa. One set is interrupted by an ancient tomb. (It is not certain whether this tomb is Punic or Roman).

Opposite page: Map of Malta and Gozo with the distribution of the main clusters of cart ruts.

One example of frequent associations of cart-ruts and ancient (Punic or Roman) quarries, outside Buskett on the way to Siġġiewi.

RAS IL-WARDIJA
ST LAWRENCE, GOZO

The site is located on the very edge of a promontory with precipitous cliffs falling directly into the sea some hundred metres down. Like Ras ir-Raħeb, it must have been a very visible landmark for ancient mariners.

The most prominent feature is a rectangular chamber, 5.80m long by 4.67m wide and 2.10m high, whose rugged ceiling suggests that it was originally a natural cave on the side of the hill, whose walls and floor were carved and smoothed into shape. What make this rock-cut feature more intriguing are five deep niches finely hewn into its three walls. Originally they were crowned by elaborately moulded cornices which have almost been eaten up by aeolic erosion. On the

Leaving Kerċem from behind the parish church take Triq Anton Calleja, then Triq Qasam San Pawl and to Triq ta' l-Ghadira. When reaching the parking space by the small pond of 'Sarraflu', take the path on the left which takes you to Wardija point. The site is on private land and if the owner is present ask for permission before entering the area.

back wall of the niche of the south wall there was once a deeply-incised figure that looked very much like a crucifix. Two more incised crosses on the wall space between niches are impossible to date, whereas some holes on the north and south walls may possibly be original lamp holes.

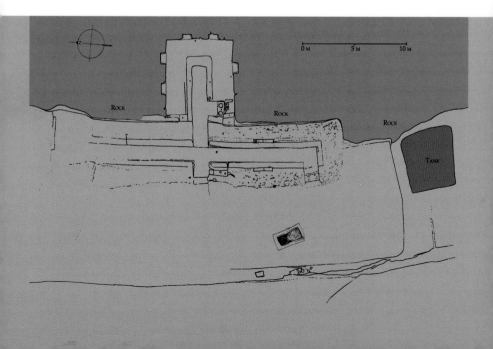

A 1m-wide shallow trench is cut in the middle of the floor on the axis of the chamber, in an east-west direction, joining with a transversal one on the outside. Inside, it branches off towards the south where it is interrupted by a smoothly-cut ledge carrying two conical holes, possibly for libations or other offerings. A similar feature is found at the south end of the transversal trench outside. The rock on either side of the latter is cut to form continuous 'benches' with raised ledges along the back.

On the terrace below the same trench, to the south, is a square-shaped water cistern, about 3m deep, with rock-cut steps leading down. The *Missione* archaeologists interpreted this as a sacred pool for ritual bathing. Another cistern, this time roughly bottle-shaped, is on the west side.

On the lowest terrace, close to the edge of the cliff was a quadrangular building of roughly-squared blocks, only two walls of which could be traced by the excavators. Traces of plaster suggested that the walls were plastered both on the outside and the inside, and possibly painted. The excavators suggested a hypaethral temple.

The pottery retrieved from the excavation of the site consisted of small sherds, mostly of modern items. The datable ancient ones ranged from the third century BC to the first two centuries AD. This and its apparently domestic nature make the interpretation of the whole complex even more problematic and we should be very cautious over certain highly conjectural suggestions. A sacred purpose is suggested by the location and by some features like the niches and the 'libation holes'; but suggesting 'sacred prostitution' is taking things beyond reasonable limits.

Opposite page: Plan of the rock-cut complex at Ras il-Wardija showing the rectangular cave-like chamber linked to the outside set-up by a system of surface trenches. On a lower level to the west is the small cistern, and a larger one to the south.

Above left: View of the shallow trench with the bench-like ledges in front of the rectangular chamber just after the excavation of the site in the 1960's. Above right: View of the rock-cut rectangular chamber from the south-west. Two of the internal niches are visible on its north wall.

THE RAMLA BAY VILLA
NADUR, GOZO

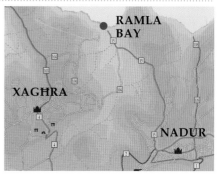

Although it is now protected under a cover of sand and, therefore, not visible, the Roman villa excavated by Temi Zammit in 1910-11 is so important a site as to deserve a separate entry.

Unfortunely nothing of the site is visible anymore since, after excavation, it was re-buried under the sands of the bay of Ramla. One can reach Ramla Bay either from Xaghra or from Nadur.

It is a villa of the purely residential type, a sea-side resort, provided with heated bathing system and adorned with marble floors and painted walls. The building must have extended over a considerably large area. Portions of it, like the main entrance, did not survive at the time of the excavation. As many as 19 rooms were discovered, six of them (1-6 in plan) probably intended to serve as living quarters. These were not connected by doorways to rooms 7-11 which seemed to be related to the bathing complex (rooms 13-19).

The latter consisted of an interconnected series of rooms and baths provided with a sophisticated heating system.

The heating was supplied by a furnace which transmitted hot air beneath the floors of rooms 14-18. The limestone concrete floors of these rooms were supported on low pillars

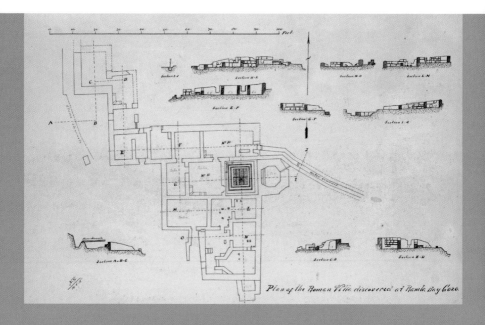

Plan of the Roman Villa discovered at Ramla Bay Gozo.

of stone or clay bricks. Some hollow flue-tiles were also discovered, that originally permitted the hot air to rise through the walls.

The Romans followed a prescribed itinerary in bathing. After undressing, they moved first into a warmed room (*tepidarium*) and then into the hot room (*calidarium*) where they sometimes took a warm bath. The process ended with a cold dip in the cold room (*frigidarium*) which, in the Ramla Bay complex, is represented by the octagonal room (1) on the east end. The warm and hot rooms could be any of those numbered 14-18, while it is likely that rooms 10, 11, and 13 were the dressing rooms (*apodyteria*).

The villa was decorated with marble veneering of different colours. The cold bath, for instance, was veneered with slabs of grey marble. But the most richly-deco-

rated room was the one between the hot rooms and the cold bath (13). Its floor consisted of successive rectangular bands of 'Gozo stone', grey, black, red, and grey marble framing a central square of eight slabs of fine breccia, perhaps Africano. The walls were covered with painted plaster in imitation coloured marble. Fragments of mosaics were found in room 1 but no designs were recovered. Several pieces of sculpture came to light, including one which must have been intended to support an architectural element in room 2. It represented a nude young satyr with pointed ears and head crowned with ivy. Sadly, this and the other sculptures have since been lost.

A photograph taken during the 1910 excavations. Clearly visible are the large room with marble-paved floor (right) and the cold bath (left).

Opposite page: Plan and various sections of the remains of the villa at Ramla Bay.

An old photograph taken during the excavations of 1910. It shows the large square room with a floor paved with several successive frames of differently-coloured marbles and local hard stone enclosing a central square of breccia slabs.

OTHER GOZO SITES
VARIOUS LOCATIONS

In comparison with its prehistoric legacy, Gozo's archaeological heritage of the period under consideration is not as rich as we would expect it to be. One reason for this state of affairs is that whenever archaeological discoveries were made during development, the remains were somehow destroyed or covered over without the authorities getting to know about them in time to save them for posterity. The following are some examples of destroyed or concealed archaeological finds.

According to the eighteenth-century Gozitan antiquarian Agius de Soldanis, as early as the seventeenth century, during the construction of the Gozo cathedral marble remains of a Roman temple were discovered, some of which were scattered in and outside the *castello*. In 1937, when the foundations of the basilica of St George were being laid, two ancient cisterns and a deposit of 4,000 Roman bronze coins (AD 259-73) were discovered. The coins were retrieved but no information regarding the cisterns is given in the *Museum Annual Report* of that year. Presumably they were destroyed or re-buried. Later on, during the construction of the oratory of the same basilica in 1976-77, foundation remains of a Roman building were discovered consisting of several blocks of the same dimensions as the one which today stands outside the side door of the basilica. In 1997, while mechanical excavation was taking place in the courtyard of the Gozo seminary, several tombs were encountered, none of which was saved for posterity.

A series of rock-cut tombs were discovered in 1892-93 in St Francis

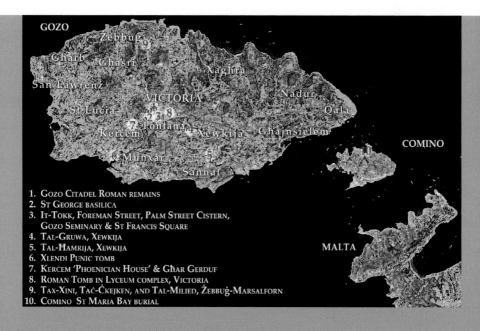

1. GOZO CITADEL ROMAN REMAINS
2. ST GEORGE BASILICA
3. IT-TOKK, FOREMAN STREET, PALM STREET CISTERN,
   GOZO SEMINARY & ST FRANCIS SQUARE
4. TAL-GRUWA, XEWKIJA
5. TAL-ĦAMRIJA, XEWKIJA
6. XLENDI PUNIC TOMB
7. KERĊEM 'PHOENICIAN HOUSE' & GĦAR GERDUF
8. ROMAN TOMB IN LYCEUM COMPLEX, VICTORIA
9. TAX-XINI, TAĊ-ĊKEJKEN, AND TAL-MILIED, ŻEBBUĠ-MARSALFORN
10. COMINO ST MARIA BAY BURIAL

Square, Rabat. They consisted of a number of low-roofed interconnected chambers entered from a common shaft. The finds included cinerary urns, cremated bones, articles of pottery and glass, coins, and a number of painted terracotta coffins, as well as a large, lidless sarcophagus constructed of pottery tiles. The coins suggest a third-century re-use, but the cinerary urns suggest an earlier, Punic origin.

The greater part of an olive pipper, now housed in the Gozo Archaeological Museum, was discovered in 1958-59 in a field wall c.700m south of Xewkija. No further details are given in the *Museum Annual Report* of that year. Vaguely, 700m south of Xewkija corresponds to a large tract of land, south of Wied ta' Mġarr ix-Xini water course, named 'Tal-Gruwa'. Some ancient features seem to survive in the area, awaiting investigation.

Another ancient olive crusher found in 1906 in the land 'Tal-Ħamrija', north of Xewkija, was for a time kept in the Gozo Library. Now it is placed beneath the inscription of Vallius by the old gate of the *Cittadella* (photo below).

With regard to tombs, an early Christian one was discovered in an unspecified locality in Ta' Sannat in 1929. It was discovered in a quarry and contained a heap of human bones and some pottery, including an early Christian lamp with two oil-holes and a dove between them. It carried a large B engraved at the back.

Another rock-cut tomb, probably Punic, and containing several burials, was discovered in 1965 during repair works on the highest part of St Simeon Street, Xlendi. The entrance, on the vertical rock surface facing the bay, led to a sub-rectangular chamber. A

Fifth-century BC terracotta head allegedly found in a cistern at Tar-Rokon, St Lawrence.

rock-cut trench covered by stone slabs occupied the whole width of the inner half of the chamber. It served as a coffin for the burials. No mention is made of other material in the *Report*.

Much more shocking is the story of the remains of a 'Phoenician house', consisting of several rooms with walls made of large stones that were discovered in 1907 in an unspecified locality at Ta' Kerċem.

The ruins, we are told, were cleared under the direction of Father E. Magri. After the site was excavated and recorded, the owner 'deliberately destroyed the remains'.

The following are other finds that have somehow managed to survive the destructive forces of both nature and humans.

Remains of a masonry wall built of large ashlar blocks of Globigerina Limestone (2m long by 0.75m wide) are preserved on the western clayey slope of the *Cittadella*, about 20m up from Foreman Street. Extensive parts of the wall have been destroyed over the years by building developments. At one point, a number of ashlar blocks were left exposed in a section. Here a trench was excavated by the Museums Department in 1996 and a number of similar blocks were uncovered. Abundant pottery deposits were also discovered.

A barrel-shaped cistern measuring around 4m in diameter and 4m in height was encountered under the courtyard of the Franciscan nunnery of Rabat during building works in

An old photograph taken in 1906-07, during the excavation of a building identified by its excavator as a 'Phoenician house' in Ta' Kerċem, Gozo. The archaeological remains were soon after destroyed by the owner of the field who was not happy with the compensation offered.

Part of an ancient wall discovered accidentally during some construction works on the street leading up to the Citadel discovered in 2003.

1993. It had already been cleaned of its contents and roofed over in concrete before I was given access to it. But the nuns had collected an interesting series of Roman pottery fragments which were eventually given to the Museums Department. The cistern is built of largish ashlar masonry and is still in use. It fills naturally from the surrounding water table. The cistern is indicative of the existence of an ancient building in the immediate vicinity.

A typical Roman tomb hewn in the Globigerina Limestone was broken into during the building of the present Lyceum Complex at Victoria in 1960. The tomb consisted of a rectangular shaft with two chambers. Parts of the tomb, including half of one of the chamber's ceiling, were destroyed to make room for the foundation walls of the modern building. At present the tomb is enclosed by

A Punic-period metal ring found in a rock-cut tomb in the limits of Rabat.

an iron gate and on investigation a few years back it was partly filled with rain water

Several rock-cut tombs survive on the steep hill that separates Marsal-forn from Żebbuġ, such as those in the fields known as Tax-Xini, Taċ-Ċkejken, and Tal-Milied. The Tax-Xini chamber tomb is hewn horizontally into the Globigerina Limestone facing north. The entrance of the chamber is partly blocked with ashlar blocks of stone forming a smaller rectangular doorway. The chamber is rectangular in form, but apsidal towards one of

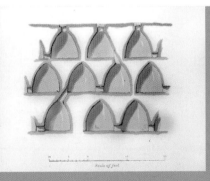

An illustration from A.A. Caruana's Ancient Pagan Tombs *(1898) showing a system of cavities (numbering close to 100) which Caruana identified as a 'columbarium'. They were found in 1859 on Telgha tal-Belt Street, just outside the fortifications of the Gozo citadel.*

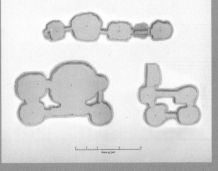

Three other illustrations, also from Caruana, of various tombs discovered in St Francis Square, Rabat, Gozo. One (top) contained cinerary urns, four small terracotta sarcophagi and other material. In another tomb a large sarcophagus, built of pottery tiles, contained a skeleton.

the sides. Two niches are present on the side facing the entrance. Between them is what remains of a small niche, probably a lamp hole. Marked as 'Phoenician & Punic Rock Tombs' on the 1965 Survey Sheet, at an area known as Tal-Milied, what survives is a rectangular chamber hewn out into the vertical face of a Globigerina Limestone ledge. Its south-facing entrance is partially closed by a rubble wall. At the back are two large recesses (c.0.60m deep) with their base raised a few centimetres above the ground of the chamber. A number of loopholes and a lamp-hole are also present on the walls.

At Għar Gerduf, in Ta' Kerċem we find the remains of the only surviving early Christian catacomb in Gozo. It is hewn into the Globigerina Limestone on the western slope of the Lunzjata Valley. It has suffered severe damage by extensive quarrying during the nineteenth century. As indicated by marks present on the ceiling and on the walls, originally the complex consisted of a long corridor which extended for about 14m in an east-west direction. It was flanked by a number of arcosolia hewn into the walls. These arcosolia varied in size: a couple contained one trough-tomb while others incorporated from three to five. At present four of these trough-tombs with head-rests can still be identified on the walls.

Yet other remains have been temporarily covered awaiting the appropriate opportunity for a proper excavation and presentation. Perhaps the best example is that of structures discovered between the ditch of the *Castello* and the La Stella Band Club. When the right conditions materialize, they will be properly investigated and preserved.

One example of the several combinations of rock-cut pans on either side of Wied ta' Mġarr ix-Xini, south of Xewkija. The age and real purpose of these pans are still unknown. They might have been used for linen retting or dyeing.

The heavily-mutilated catacomb of Għar Gerduf, near Ta' Kerċem. The original level of the floor was much higher. It has been cut down, probably by quarrying activity.

Left: *Of unknown provenance is the head of a satyr exhibited in the Museum of Archaeology of Gozo. Its material, local limestone, suggests a local artistic tradition.*

Top: *An unusual burial, consisting of a skeleton covered by two sliced halves of a Roman amphora, was discovered on the small island of Comino.*

An oscillum *reported to have been found in Gozo, now kept in the Museum of Archaeology of Gozo. An* oscillum *is a disc, normally of white marble, with relief decoration on both sides. This one depicts a*

typical Greek theatrical mask on one side, and a griffin with a ram's head under his left front paw on the other side. Oscilla can also be of other shapes and coloured marbles.

A fragmentary oscillum was reported by Ashby to have been among the objects discovered during the excavations of the Roman villa at Ramla Bay, but this one does not seem to fit with his description.

GLOSSARY

Abacus: square-shaped top part of a column capital.

Amphora: clay container with two handles for transportation of, mainly, liquids.

Amulet: normally a pendant, worn to ward off evil.

Anat: a prominent goddess in the pantheon of the Levant, but not in the west.

Aphrodite: the Greek goddess of love.

Aryballos: small globular or egg-shaped bottle for holding oil or perfume.

Ashlar: perfectly rectangular blocks of stone, known also as parallelepipeds.

Ashtart: Phoenician female goddess, equivalent to Greek Hera and Roman Juno.

Asklepios: Greek god of healing, equivalent to Roman Aesculapius.

Baal Hammon: the supreme god of the Phoenician pantheon.

Bes: a grotesque dwarf Egyptian god who protected pregnant women.

Betyl: vertical aniconical blocks of stone representing the abode of a divinity, or the divinity itself.

Bilychne: oil lamp having two wick nozzles.

Bronze Age: a period (*c*.2500-1200 BC) characterized by the introduction of bronze tools and weapons.

Bulla: metal disc worn by Roman children before coming of age.

Campanian ware: black-glossed fine table ware from Campania (region around Naples).

Canaan: coastal plain north of, and in part overlapping, ancient Israel.

Capital: top element of a column.

Catacomb: extensive underground cemetery, containing hundreds of graves.

Cavetto cornice: simple architectural cornice having an overhanging concavity separated from the rest of the vertical wall by a projecting semicircular band.

Censor: one of two Roman magistrates appointed every five years to collect and revise data on Roman citizens.

Civitas **(pl.** *civitates***):** a city, or an organized and structured community, and its territory

Domus: typical Roman town house

Emblema: central square mosaic picture, often prepared in transportable stone tray.

Eshmun: Phoenician god of healing, equivalent to the Greek Asklepios

Ex-voto: an object offered to the divinity in gratitude for a satisfied vow.

Faience: opaque glass paste used for small pendants and figurines, as well as miniature perfume containers.

Hellenistic: belonging to the culture dominant in the lands that had been conquered by Alexander the Great.

Hera: wife of Zeus, the supreme god of the Greek pantheon. Equivalent to the Phoenician Ashtart and the Roman Juno.

Hypogeum: small catacomb, underground complex containing several graves.

Juno: wife of Jupiter, the supreme god of the Roman pantheon. Equivalent to the Phoenician Ashtart and the Greek Hera.

Kotyle: a stemless drinking cup with small horizontal handles.

Lekythos: small, single-handled flask with narrow neck, for containing oil or perfume.

Loculus: rectangular cut in the wall, large enough to receive a human corpse.

Megarian bowl: drinking cup with figured decoration in relief, originating in Megara.

Molk: sacrifice of a child through burning.

Municipium: municipality, a town whose inhabitants had the rights and duties of Roman (or Latin) citizenship

Necropolis (pl. necropoleis): a conglomeration of burials (literally, 'city of the dead').

Opus: craft product, here referring to mosaic typology or building techniques.

Opus africanum: building technique with vertical pillar stones framing spaces of lighter stone material.

Opus scutulatum: Roman mosaic giving the illusion of cascading cubes formed of lozenge shaped tiles of three different colours.

Opus tesselatum: the most common type of Roman mosaic formed of small cubes of white and coloured hard stones and glass.

Opus vemiculatum: a finer type of Roman mosaic formed of minute cubes of coloured stones and glass to produce pictorial effects.

Palmette: a sylized floral design with leaves arranged like a palm shoot.

Parallelepipeds: perfectly rectangular blocks of stone; known also as ashlar blocks.

Peristyle: courtyard surrounded by a colonnaded corridor.

Polis **(pl. *poleis*):** Greek version of the Roman *civitas*.

Praetor: Roman magistrate in charge of the administration of justice.

Proconsul: Roman magistrate whose office is extended by one year to govern a province.

Propraetor: a magistrate acting as praetor in the provinces on behalf of Rome.

Proscription: the publication of lists of persons who were thus declared outlaws and had their property confiscated. Their killers were rewarded and their protectors punished.

Proxeny: an honour bestowed on a wealthy and influential man who looked after the interests of the members of a *civitas* in a foreign country.

Quaestor: Roman magistrate in charge of the administration of finances.

Rab: one of two magistrates governing Gozo in the late Punic period.

Red-slipped ware: early Phoenician pottery characterized by a distinctive red slip obtained by dipping the leather-hard clay pot in a liquid clay before firing.

Refrigerium: feast or meal held on the *stibadium* on the occasion of the death, or the anniversary of the death, of a member of the community.

Rhython: horn-shaped drinking vessel, sometimes terminating in an animal's head.

Sarcophagus: terracotta, stone, or rock-cut container for a human corpse.

Silo-pit: Bronze Age round pit in the ground, probably for storage of grain.

Skyphos: two-handled stemless drinking cup, deeper than a *kotyle*.

Stibadium: C-shaped rock-cut *triclinium* (dining table) found in many of the Maltese early Christian catacombs and hypogea.

Stipendiaria: civitas paying taxes but not enjoying citizen rights

Tanit: the Carthaginian (and, in general, western Phoenician) version of Ashtart.

Tas-Silg: the area between Zejtun and Delimara in which an ancient sanctuary was excavated in the 1960s.

Temenos: the physical boundary, normally a high wall, of a sanctuary.

Terra sigillata: red-glossed fine Roman table pottery.

Thymiateria: modelled stone supports for burning incense.

Triclinium: Roman dining room.

Villa: typical Roman country house

Other topics discussed in detail:
Cart-ruts: pages 338-339
Cisterns: page 107

RECOMMENDED READING:

Abela, G.F. *Della Descrittione di Malta, Isola del Mare Siciliano con le sue Antichità ed altre Notizie* (Malta, 1647).

Agius de Soldanis, G. *Il Gozo Antico-Moderno e Sacro-Profano, Isola Mediterranea Adiacente a Malta Africana*, NLM Bibliotheca Ms. No. 145 (1746).

Amadasi Guzzo, M.G. Divinità fenicie a Tas-Silg, Malta - i dati epigrafici, *Journal of Mediterranean Studies* 3.2 (1993): 205-214.

Ashby, T. Roman Malta, *Journal of Roman Studies* 5 (1915): 23-80.

Aubet, M. E. *The Phoenicians and the West: Politics, Colonies and Trade* (Cambridge, 1993).

Boisgelin (de), L. *Ancient and Modern Malta* (London, 1805).

Bonanno, A. & Frendo, A. (ed.) Excavations at Tas-Silg, Malta. A preliminary report on the 1996-1998 campaigns conducted by the Department of Classics and Archaeology of the University of Malta, *Mediterranean Archaeology* 13 (2000): 67-114.

Bruno, B. *L'Arcipelago Maltese in Età Romana e Bizantina: attività economiche e scambi al centro del Mediterraneo* (Bari, 2004)

Buhagiar, Mario, *Late Roman and Byzantine Catacombs and Related Burial Places in the Maltese Islands* (Oxford, 1986).

Busuttil, J. (several articles on various aspects of Roman Malta in *Journal of the Faculty of Arts* and *Melita Historica* between 1970 and 1976)

Cagiano de Azevedo, M. Le opere di epoca bizantina a Tas- Silg. Gli scavi in S. Paolo Milqi e Ras-il-Wardija', *Rend. Pont. Acc.* XXXVII (1964-5): 139-54.

Camilleri, V.J. *Saint Agatha* (Malta, 1984).

Caruana, A.A. *Recent discoveries at Notabile* (Malta, 1881).

Caruana, A.A., *Report on the Phoenician and Roman Antiquities in the Group of the Islands of Malta* (Malta, 1882).

Caruana, A.A. Remains of an ancient Greek building discovered in Malta in February 1888, *American Journal of Archaeology* IV, no.4 (1889): 453.

Ciasca, A. 1976-77. Il tempio fenicio di Tas-Silg. Una proposta di ricostruzione, *Kokalos* 22-23: I, 162-72.

Ciasca, A. Insediamenti e cultura dei Fenici a Malta, in Niemeyer, H.G. (ed.) *Phönizier im Westen* (Mainz, 1982): 133-154.

Coleiro, E. Maltese coins of the Roman period, *The Numismatic Chronicle* Se.VII,11 (1971): 67-91.

Cutajar, N. Recent discoveries and the archaeology of Mdina, *Treasures of Malta* VIII, 1 (2001): 79-85

Dommelen (van), P. Colonial constructs: colonialism and archaeology in the Mediterranean, *World Archaeology* 28, 3 (1997): 305-323.

Ennabli, A. Acholla, in Stilwell, R. (ed.). The Princeton Encyclopedia of Classical Sites (Princeton, 1976): 6-7.

Frendo, A.J. Some observations on the investigation of the Phoenicians/Canaanites in the ancient Mediterranean world, *Journal of Mediterranean Studies* 3.2 (1993): 169-174

Frendo, A.J. A new Punic inscription from Zejtun (Malta) and the goddess Anat-Astarte, *Palestine Exploration Quarterly* 131 (1999): 24-35

Gouder, T. *The Mosaic pavements in the Museum of Roman Antiquities at Rabat* (Malta, 1983).

Gouder, T.C. *Malta and the Phoenicians*, reprinted from the Lombard Bank (Malta) Ltd. - Annual Report 1991 (Malta, 1991).

Guzzo Amadasi, M.G. Le iscrizioni fenicie e puniche delle colonie in occidente' (Rome, 1967).

Heltzer, M. The inscription CIS, 1, 132 from Gozo and the political structure of the island in the Punic period, *Journal of Mediterranean Studies* 3.2 (1993): 198-204.

Hölbl, G. Ägyptisches Kulturgut auf Malta und Gozo (Vienna, 1989).

Houel, J., *Voyage Pittoresque des Iles de Sicile, de Malte, et de Lipari*, IV (Paris, 1787).

Krings, V. (ed.). *La Civilisation Phénicienne et Punique* (Leiden-New York, 1995).

Lipinski E. (ed.) *Dictionnaire de la Civilisation Phénicienne et Punique* (Turnhout, 1992)

Locatelli, D. The Roman villa at San Pawl Milqi: history and perspectives of an archaeological site, *Treasures of Malta* VII, 2 (2001): 73-77

L. I. Manfredi, Tipi monetali a Malta e Biblo, *Rivista degli Studi Orientali* 70, 3-4 (1996): 289-302.

Markoe, G. E. *Phoenicians* (London, 2000).

Mingazzini, P. Sulla natura e sullo scopo del santuario punico di Ras il-Wardija sull'isola di Gozo presso Malta, *Rivista di Studi Fenici* 4, 2 (1976): 159-166.

Missione Archeologica Italiana a Malta 1963-70 (Rome, 1964-73).

Moscati, S. Some reflections on Malta in the Phoenician world, *Journal of Mediterranean Studies* 3.2 (1993): 286-290.

Müller, H.-P. Ein phönizischer Totenpapyrus aus Malta, *Journal of Semitic Studies* 46, 2 (2001): 251-265

Quintinus, I. *Insulae Melitae descriptio ex commentariis rerum quotidianarum*, (Lyons, 1536).

Sagona C. *The Archaeology of Punic Malta*, (Leuven, 2002).

Said-Zammit, G. A. *Population, Land Use and Settlement on Punic Malta. A Contextual Analysis of Burial Evidence* (Oxford, 1997).

Vella, N. *et al.* Ghajn Klieb, Rabat (Malta), *Malta Archaeological Review* 4 (2000): 10-16.

Vella, N.C. The lie of the land: Ptolemy's temple of Hercules in Malta, *Ancient Near Eastern Studies* 39 (2002): 83-112

Wettinger, G. *Place-Names of the Maltese Islands ca. 1300-1800* (Malta, 2000)

Wilson, R. *Sicily under the Roman Empire* (Warminster, 1990).

Zammit, T. Excavations in Malta, *The Antiquaries Journal* 2 (1922): 131-4.

Zammit, T. Excavations at Rabat, Malta, *The Antiquaries Journal* 3 (1923): 219-225.

Zammit, T. Phoenician ring from Malta, *The Antiquaries Journal* 5 (1925): 266-7

ACKNOWLEDGMENTS:

Dr Frances Zammit Dimech,
Minister for Culture and Tourism,
Dr Louis Galea,
Minister of Education
Mr George Pullicino
Minister for Rural Affairs and the Environment
Dr Mario Tabone,
Chairman Heritage Malta
Mrs Antoinette Caruana,
CEO Heritage Malta
Mr Anthony Pace,
Superintendent of Cultural Heritage
Prof. Anthony Frendo,
University of Malta
Mrs Suzannah Depasquale
Curator National Museum of Archaeology
Mrs Sharon Sultana,
Collections and Site Executive Archaeology
Mr Reuben Grima
Curator World Heritage Sites
Ms Katya Stroud
Collections and Site Executive World Heritage Sites
Mr Pierre Bonello
Exhibitions and Events Executive
Mr Pierre Cassar
Manager - Public Programmes
Ms Rosella Schembri
Personal Assistant to the CEO
Mr Mario Coleiro
Coordinator Exhibitions and Maintenance
Mr Charles Borg,
Gallery Site Officer - Archaeology
Mr George Azzopardi
Collections and Site Executive - Gozo museums and sites
Mr Nathaniel Cutajar
Superintendence of Cultural Heritage
Dr Nicholas Vella
University of Malta
Dr Richard Reece
formerly University College London University
Dr Biagio Vella
formerly University of Malta
Mr Emmanuel Azzopardi
Ms Marie Louise Calleja

The 'Discover Road Map of Malta and Gozo' (maltamap.com) was used as reference to the site maps.

PHOTO CREDITS:

T: Top, C: Centre, B: Bottom
R: Right, L: Left

Anthony Bonanno: Pg.2-3; Pg.8BR; Pg.31T; Pg.43; Pg.126; Pg.176; Pg.197; Pg.226T; Pg.271

Midsea Books/Inklink: Pg.93; Pg.144; Pg.177; Pg.180; Pg.183; Pg.191; Pg.263B; Pg.264; Pg.288-289C; Pg.312-313C; Pg.320-321C

National Museum of Archaeology Library (Heritage Malta): Pg.8 CB; Pg.15; Pg.16, Pg.17, Pg.21; Pg.31B; Pg.32; Pg.27B; Pg.50; Pg.59BL; Pg.67; Pgs.70-71; Pg.77; Pg.83; Pg.86; Pg.89; Pg.104; Pg.106BL; Pg.110; Pg.117; Pg.121; Pg.139; Pg.141; Pg.148; Pg.150; Pg.151; Pg.154; Pg.155B; Pg.179; Pg.185; Pg.194; Pg.204; Pg.214; Pg.215; Pg.216; Pg.224; Pg.226B; Pg.235; Pg.236 T&B; Pg.238; Pg.239; Pg.246; Pg.247; Pg. 252; Pg.253; Pg.261 (B&W images); Pg.270; Pg.277; Pg.284T; Pg.286B; Pg.287T&BL; Pg.292-293; Pg.294BR; Pg.295BL; Pg.299BL; Pg.300B; Pg.301BL; Pg.308BR; Pg.312-313 (Mosaic Patterns); Pg.320-321 (Mosaic Patterns); Pg.323BL; Pg.324; Pg.327BL; Pg.328; Pg.334; Pg.337; Pg.341BL; Pg.342B; Pg.343; Pg.347 B L&R

The National Library: Pg.81BL; Pg.198; Pg.202

Gozo Library Archives: Pg.346BL

Superintendence of Cultural Heritage: Pg.255C; Pg.259

MEPA Orthophotos: Pg.59T; Pg.240; Pg.245; Pg.249; Pg.307T

Cathedral Museum Archives: Pg.42BR

NASA Website: Pg.18; Pg.26B, Pg.41; Pg.56; Pg.78; Pg.128; Pg.140; Pg.149; Pg.344

Architetto Giovanni Nuzzo: Pg.142

Ms Katya Stroud: Pg.161; Pg.217

Mr George Azzopardi: Pg.212

University of Malta Archives: Pg.290BL

Malta's Living Heritage Series is produced by
Midsea Books Ltd in collaboration with

 Heritage Malta

and with the support of

The Ministry of Finance

Malta's Living Heritage
Edited by Louis J. Scerri

MALTA. PHOENICIAN, PUNIC AND ROMAN
First Published in Malta in 2005

Midsea Books Ltd

ISBN 99932-7-034-2 Hardback
ISBN 99932-7-035-0 Paperback

Fuji FinePix digital cameras (FinePix 610, S2 & S3)
were used for the photography of this book.

Printed and bound by Studio Leonardo, Firenze, Italia.